Teaching and Learning Shakespeare through Theatre-Based Practice

RELATED TITLES

Creative Shakespeare: The Globe Education Guide to Practical Shakespeare
Fiona Banks
978-1-4081-5684-1

Essential Shakespeare: The Arden Guide to Text and Interpretation
Pamela Bickley and Jenny Stevens
978-1-4081-5873-9

How to Teach a Play: Essential Exercises for Popular Plays
Edited by Miriam Chirico and Kelly Younger
978-1-3500-1753-5

ShakesFear and How to Cure It: The Complete Handbook for Teaching Shakespeare
Ralph Alan Cohen
978-1-4742-2871-8

Shakespeare and Digital Pedagogy: Case Studies and Strategies
Edited by Diana E. Henderson and Kyle Sebastian Vitale
978-1-3501-0971-1

Teaching Shakespeare with Purpose: A Student-Centred Approach
Ayanna Thompson and Laura Turchi
978-1-4725-9961-2

The RSC Shakespeare Toolkit for Primary Teachers
Royal Shakespeare Company
978-1-4725-8518-9

Teaching and Learning Shakespeare through Theatre-Based Practice

Edited by
Tracy Irish and Jennifer Kitchen

THE ARDEN SHAKESPEARE
LONDON • NEW YORK • OXFORD • NEW DELHI • SYDNEY

THE ARDEN SHAKESPEARE
Bloomsbury Publishing Plc
50 Bedford Square, London, WC1B 3DP, UK
1385 Broadway, New York, NY 10018, USA
29 Earlsfort Terrace, Dublin 2, Ireland

BLOOMSBURY, THE ARDEN SHAKESPEARE and the Arden Shakespeare logo are trademarks of Bloomsbury Publishing Plc

First published in Great Britain 2024

Copyright © Tracy Irish, Jennifer Kitchen and contributors, 2024

Tracy Irish and Jennifer Kitchen have asserted their right under the Copyright, Designs and Patents Act, 1988, to be identified as editors of this work.

For legal purposes the Acknowledgements on p. xiii constitute an extension of this copyright page.

Cover image: King John, 2019, featuring Rosie Sheehy
© Steve Tanner/Royal Shakespeare Company

All rights reserved. No part of this publication may be reproduced or transmitted in any form or by any means, electronic or mechanical, including photocopying, recording, or any information storage or retrieval system, without prior permission in writing from the publishers.

Bloomsbury Publishing Plc does not have any control over, or responsibility for, any third-party websites referred to or in this book. All internet addresses given in this book were correct at the time of going to press. The author and publisher regret any inconvenience caused if addresses have changed or sites have ceased to exist, but can accept no responsibility for any such changes.

A catalogue record for this book is available from the British Library.

A catalog record for this book is available from the Library of Congress.

ISBN: HB: 978-1-3502-9205-5
PB: 978-1-3502-9204-8
ePDF: 978-1-3502-9206-2
eBook: 978-1-3502-9207-9

Typeset by Deanta Global Publishing Services, Chennai, India
Printed and bound in Great Britain

To find out more about our authors and books visit www.bloomsbury.com and sign up for our newsletters.

CONTENTS

List of Contributors viii
Foreword by James Stredder xi
Acknowledgements xiii
Note on the Text xiv

Introduction 1
    Why now? 1
    Active and theatre-based Shakespeare: Definitions and context 4
    Rhetorics of cultural value 7
    Summary 10

PART ONE Perspectives from multidisciplinary research 13

1   The pedagogy question 15
    Progressive principles 15
    Embodied cognition: Learning through doing 22
    Ensemble 28
    The effective teacher 32

2   The cultural value question 38
    Cultural literacy 39
    Cultural capital 42
    Cultural and intercultural democracy 44
    Shakespeare as an icon of literary heritage 49

3   The literature question 53
    Shakespeare the storyteller: Why do we need stories? 54
    Shakespeare the dramatist: Why do we need theatre? 58
    Shakespeare the poet: Why do we need poetry? 64

4 The language question 70

    The humanity of language 71

    How sixteenth-century poetry develops twenty-first-century language skills 76

    Shakespeare for oracy 83

PART TWO Perspectives from organizations and practitioners 87

5 Perspectives from organizations and practitioners: Introduction 89

    Approach 90

    Funding 91

    Online 92

    Common values and themes 93

6 Aims, scope and areas of focus 94

    Aims 94

    Scope 97

    Particular areas of focus and interest 100

7 On teaching, schools, and culture 105

    On teaching and schools 105

    On culture 109

8 Why Shakespeare? 114

    Challenging language 116

    Raising questions 120

    Impact 124

PART THREE Perspectives from the classroom 127

9 Perspectives from the classroom: Introduction 129

10 Dirty Shakespeare: Outdoor learning with primary pupils *by Mary Carey* 138

11 How relevant is Shakespeare in an international school context? *by Judith Berends O'Brien* 143

12 *Macbeth*, ماكبث, *Макбет:* Utilizing students' code-switching as a tool for engaging with Shakespeare at secondary level *by Kirsty Emmerson* 148

13 Salvaging the bard: A success story of theatre-based practice for neurodiverse learners *by Eleni Kmiec* 153

14 Transference and Integration: Using Shakespeare to teach composition *by Carol Parker* 159

15 Theatre-based pedagogy in a knowledge-rich curriculum: Perspectives from initial teacher training *by Karen McGivern* 164

16 Much ado about decolonized Shakespeare *by Nobulali Dangazele* 170

Epilogue 175

References 177
Index 195

NOTES ON EDITORS AND CONTRIBUTORS

Part One – Contributors

Tracy Irish (co-editor) is an experienced teacher, theatre practitioner and education researcher with a specialism in Shakespeare and communication. She has worked with a wide range of schools, theatre companies and cultural organisations in the UK and internationally, is an associate learning practitioner with the Royal Shakespeare Company and teaches regularly at the Shakespeare Institute, University of Birmingham. She has authored a range of resources and publications including the *RSC School Shakespeare editions* and *Shakespeare and Meisner*.

Jennifer Kitchen (co-editor) is a theatre education practitioner and researcher with a focus on theatre-based Shakespeare education and social justice. Jennifer has published and presented widely in these areas, and her monograph *Critical Pedagogy and Active Shakespeare* is out in 2023. Jennifer has also worked for many years as a theatre education practitioner with schools and theatres including Shakespeare's Globe. She currently holds an honorary research fellowship at The University of Warwick and teaches at The University of Glasgow.

James Stredder was formerly head of drama and theatre studies at the University of Wolverhampton, UK. He is the author of *The North Face of Shakespeare: Activities for Teaching the Plays* (2009).

Part Two – Interviewees

Evonne Bixter is the head of engagement at Shakespeare North Playhouse in Prescot, UK. Shakespeare North opened its new building with its replica Elizabethan theatre in 2022. It aims to 'bring people together to participate in a unique programme of performance, activities and conversations, inspired by Shakespeare and relevant to all of us' (Shakespeare North 2023).

Lucy Cuthbertson is the director of education (learning) at Shakespeare's Globe in London. The theatre is 'a world-renowned performing arts venue, cultural attraction and education centre located on the bank of the River Thames'. Its education programme offers a wide range of resources, workshops and projects at all levels (Globe 2023).

Francesca Ellis was at the time of interviewing the head of creative and programmes for Coram Shakespeare Schools Foundation (CSSF), leading in the creation of their programmes and workshop content. CSSF is a UK-based cultural education charity that seeks to instil 'curiosity and empathy, aspiration and self-esteem, literacy and teamwork' through the performance and practical exploration of Shakespeare (CSSF 2023).

Karl Falconer is a teacher and artistic director of Purple Door in Liverpool, UK. Purple Door is a theatre company with a focus on Shakespeare and community that aims to show 'how theatre can be more affordable, more relatable, and more useful to the people it's supposed to serve' (Purple Door 2023).

Emma Manton is an actor and theatre education practitioner. She is a globe education practitioner for Shakespeare's Globe and an associate learning practitioner for the RSC.

Chris Nayak is an actor and theatre education practitioner. He is a globe education practitioner for Shakespeare's Globe and an associate learning practitioner for the RSC.

Cassandra Nwokah is an actor and theatre education practitioner who has worked with New York companies: Theatre for a New Audience (TFANA), Classic Stage Company and Manhattan Youth.

Peggy O'Brien is the director of education at the Folger in Washington DC. The Folger Shakespeare Library is 'the world's largest Shakespeare collection, the ultimate resource for exploring Shakespeare and his world'. Its education methodology shows 'how the study of his work deepens knowledge and hones skills across key academic areas' (Folger 2023).

Jacqui O'Hanlon is the director of learning and national partnerships at the Royal Shakespeare Company (RSC) in Stratford-upon-Avon, UK. The RSC states its purpose as 'to ensure that Shakespeare is for everyone, unlocking the power of his plays and live performance, throughout the UK and across the world' (2023). Its education programme offers a wide range of resources, workshops and projects at all levels.

Darren Raymond is the artistic director of Intermission Youth in London. Intermission was set up in 2008 to 'transform disadvantaged young people living in deprivation and experiencing high levels of anti-social behaviour, family breakdown, dependency and criminality'. Though an ethos of care, and a playful approach to Shakespeare's language, Intermission supports young people to 'make positive choices and change the course of their lives' (Intermission 2023).

Part Three – Contributors

Judith Berends O'Brien is a secondary international schoolteacher of English and drama, who has taught in South Korea, Spain, England, Ireland, Norway and the Netherlands. She is interested in the magical power of a school Shakespeare festival.

Mary Carey is in her 18th year of being sole teacher of a small primary school in the Channel Islands. She believes creativity and the arts has a vital part to play in schools and makes use of the local environment, taking Shakespeare outside. Her favourite question is 'why?'.

Nobulali Dangazele is an actor, scholar and lead facilitator of ShakeXperience, an applied theatre company based in Johannesburg. She was awarded a PhD from the University of Warwick and is particularly interested in overlaps between the worlds of the arts, business and education.

Kirsty Emmerson is a secondary school English Teacher in North London. She holds an MA in Shakespeare and education, and has research interests in student perceptions of Shakespeare's value which she intends to pursue through PhD study.

Eleni Kmiec serves as the director of education for International Theatre & Dance Project: Greece and Theatre Chair for ICON – School for the Arts, USA. She holds an MA in Shakespeare and education and has taught in a special education school for eight years. Her interests are in creating greater accessibility for all students to study and enjoy Shakespeare as literature and drama.

Karen McGivern was a secondary school English teacher for eighteen years before moving into teacher education. She has recently completed a PhD exploring student and teacher perceptions of the value of Shakespeare and how the types of texts used in English teaching allow this value to be accessed.

Carol Parker is an associate professor of English and Literature Department chair at Pikes Peak State College in Colorado, United States. She recently earned her MA in Shakespeare and education at the Shakespeare Institute in Stratford-upon-Avon.

FOREWORD

James Stredder

The works of Shakespeare continue to thrive in the educational institutions of many different cultures throughout the world: in Wales and England, study of his work has been a compulsory part of the English Literature curriculum since 1989. The question of what approaches and methods we might use to teach Shakespeare remains fundamental. In answer to this question, Tracy Irish and Jennifer Kitchen's book examines 'theatre-based practice' in the classroom which, they propose, functions as a rehearsal room, where the plays are explored 'as scripts incomplete without the playful criticality' that theatre-based practice invites. They see this practice as effective not only in terms of delivering test and examination results but also in its deeper and wider educational context. A good example is their account of the potential of Shakespeare in the exploration of vital questions of social justice. They hold that it is important to recognize and utilize the worlds that children bring with them into the classroom and, rather than setting ideas of 'Shakespearian universality' above children, to provide opportunities to 'combine intellectual, social and emotional learning through embodying the text'. The book, however, is very far from dealing only with theatre-based practice. It seeks to incorporate the full range of teaching and learning processes. At one time, active approaches and close reading sometimes appeared to be in opposition: 'get on your feet' or 'sit and study', though this was always a false and conflictual separating out of valuable and potentially complimentary experiences.

In the four chapters of Part One, the authors seek to utilize a range of disciplines to establish the rationale for theatre-based practice. They survey and explore underlying questions of pedagogy, cultural value, literature and language. In these matters, the book is particularly timely and important in its determination to probe and test conceptual origins and connections. We are also reminded to pay careful attention to the location of students themselves, to what they bring to the text, when actively engaging with and embodying it. Part Two gives the floor to a range of theatre practitioners: 'joy's soul lies in the doing'. Whether working in famous institutions, the Coram Shakespeare Schools Foundation, the Folger Shakespeare Library, Shakespeare's Globe, the Royal Shakespeare Company or in less well-known organizations, the ten interviewees all offer fascinating perspectives on their own practice in differing social and theatrical contexts. The editing and presentation of short comments and observations is a brilliant technique: it's as though we are at a conference or a seminar, in which the contributions are particularly pertinent and well-focused.

In the final part of the book, contributors speak of their own classroom experience of teaching Shakespeare through theatre-based practice. The 'classroom' might actually be outdoors, at primary or at secondary level, in South Africa or West Bengal, the United States or the Channel Islands, London or in international schools all over the world. There are many examples of ingenious and intriguing theatre-based practice, with descriptions of wide-ranging learning benefits deriving from the varied practices and contexts. One contribution tellingly reminds us of the challenges faced by teachers, especially as they begin their teaching careers. They may encounter hostility to their chosen methods from traditional opinion and official educational policy; and, of course, whatever methods they use, teaching remains an art practised through the teaching relationship.

As we read the editors' Epilogue, we can look back on a refreshing opening-up and widening of thinking about the teaching of Shakespeare. Readers may feel, as did I, exhilarated by a sense of new and multiple connections, individual for each reader but sharing a common, rich environment. I feel that a similar experience awaits those fortunate enough to be taught Shakespeare through the 'theatre-based practices' explored in this book. It is also appropriate that Chapter 16, the final teacher contribution, is set in a global context. As the editors comment in Chapter 9: 'Shakespeare is a global resource reinterpreted daily across the world as young people encounter him through the lenses of their own cultures and languages'.

ACKNOWLEDGEMENTS

Most of all, we want to say a big thank you to all the young people, teachers and colleagues, whose practice, scholarship, conversation and provocation have informed and shaped this book. Some more specific thanks are due to some special people in our lives, not least all our contributors who gave so generously of their time and their thoughts. From both of us, thank you to our drama and education colleagues at the University of Warwick: Jonothan Neelands, Joe Winston, Rachel Dickinson and Rachel Turner-King. This book owes its genesis to us both being supervised by the inimitable Jonothan Neelands for our PhDs, and the influence and support of all four were essential on that journey. From Tracy: additional special thanks to James Stredder, Rachel Gartside, Aileen Gonsalves and Abigail Rokison-Woodall, among many other colleagues, for all those work-focused but also fun and joyous conversations along with your support and friendship over the years. From Jennifer: additional special thanks to Micheal Finneran and Mark Boylan for their support and mentorship; to UHI colleagues Steph Smart and Lorraine Hemmings; and to Warwick colleague Cheryl Cane for creative inspiration and encouragement.

We also both owe huge gratitude to our partners, Dom and Tamin, for all their support and to Jennifer's in-laws for sharing the responsibilities and joys of childcare. While we are affiliated to academic institutions through temporary teaching posts, and Jennifer has gratefully held an honorary research fellowship at the University of Warwick, we are both independent scholars who have carved out time in our lives to write this book because we are passionate about education in general and the educational value of Shakespeare study in particular. Both have been hugely important in our own lives as two women from low socio-economic backgrounds for whom education has brought opportunities our mothers and grandmothers never had. We recognize that privilege, and it has made us passionately believe that education should open doors for everyone.

NOTE ON THE TEXT

All quotations from Shakespeare's works refer to Arden Shakespeare Third Series editions. Series editors: Richard Proudfoot, Ann Thompson, David Scott Kastan, H. R. Woudhuysen.

Introduction

Why now?

Why a book about theatre-based practice for teaching Shakespeare now? What are we hoping to share with our fellow teachers, practitioners and scholars? What practices and what questions are we inviting you to explore? In order to answer this, we want to introduce this book partly with considerations of what Shakespeare needs from us, as teachers, to be accessible and relevant to young people; but more centrally to explore what do young people need, if anything, from Shakespeare? In this introductory chapter, we outline the contours of these key questions and debates that we will further shape and engage with in this book as a whole.

What are young people facing in their futures as we move towards the fourth decade of the twenty-first century? Despite the assurances of thinkers like Rosling (2018), Harari (2018) and Pinker (2018) that people's lives are generally getting better, they offer no guarantees. None of them doubt the threats from a growing environmental crisis, deepening the complex picture of how humanity survives together or not at all. Furthermore in more recent years, we have seen a shift towards increasing political extremism, instability and a global pandemic. Educationalists have long expounded on the need for a curriculum and pedagogical focus on 'twenty-first-century skills', but as we move further into the twenty-first century itself, our understanding of what these skills might be has moved beyond the initial call for a creative, digital-focused, knowledge-based economy and now points towards something much more complex and fundamental. The Organisation for Economic Co-operation and Development (OECD) calls for teachers across the globe to 'do more than transmit educational content' if they are to prepare students for the uncertainties of the future. This means cultivating 'students' ability to be creative, think critically, solve problems and make decisions' (Schleicher 2016: 3) in order to thrive in 'a world where trust will have to bridge differences and a world in which their lives will be affected by issues that transcend national boundaries' (Schleicher 2016: 16). A more recent OECD report looks specifically at the exponential progress of artificial intelligence (AI), proposing that shifts in education will need to happen to better equip young people in dealing with a world where AI levels of literacy and numeracy are generally higher than their own.

The report specifically suggests that 'Strengthening people's ability to evaluate and reflect on texts would not only give them an important advantage over machines. This skill would also enable them to cope with the information overload of the digital age and determine the accuracy and credibility of sources against the background of spreading fake news and misinformation' (OECD 2023: 120). Futurists surveyed for a recent BBC podcast support these findings and emphasize that schools should focus on developing complex and creative social skills in response to the rise of AI, the ability to critically analyse information and the resilience, empathy and innovation to deal with the 'massive systems change' caused by shifts in the global climate (Varaidzo 2019).

If this is what's needed, where does a 400-year-old playwright fit in? Despite technology expert Evgeny Morozov's suggestion that reading *A Midsummer Night's Dream* 'will do so much more to increase the intelligence in our world' than trying to compete with AI (2023), it is patently obvious that the study, performance and appreciation of the works of Shakespeare cannot *solve* any of the big issues looming in young people's lives, or instantly transform students into creative, critical, resilient problem solvers with pluralistic outlooks. But could Shakespeare be *part of* a pedagogy which is oriented towards these big, humanistic questions of the twenty-first century? Ayanna Thompson and Laura Turchi (2020) argue that young people themselves are hungry to engage in questions of social justice within their learning of Shakespeare and welcome structured opportunities to do so. Having spent much of our careers working with young people and teachers on the teaching and learning of Shakespeare, we agree. We believe that learning about and learning *through* the works of Shakespeare can offer opportunities, from primary levels upwards, to develop the complex and creative social skills; the critical thinking capacity; the collaborative resilience; and the appreciation of diverse cultural perspectives that young people need, not only to achieve fulfilling and productive lives for themselves but also to offer hope of achieving a sustainable and equitable future for humanity as a whole. Specifically, moreover, we believe it is *theatre-based* teaching and learning of Shakespeare that can best facilitate this. In essence, this means working with Shakespeare as a living artist who offers us texts that invite us to bring our own creativity, imagination and experiences into dialogue with him. Part One of this book sets out our arguments for that position. Parts Two and Three bring in the voices of other practitioners and teachers working with these aims.

Throughout this book, we view the question of why Shakespeare should be studied at school, as well as how he is taught, to be live questions for continuous pedagogical evaluation. Although the oft quoted '50 per cent of the world's school children study Shakespeare' is exaggerated (Irish 2015), he is the most widely prescribed author in school systems across the world: a fixture on the curricula of English-speaking countries and often found on other curricula either as part of learning about English language and culture or as classic literary works in translation (Irish 2012). Shakespeare is performed more widely than any other playwright, more often than not in languages that would be unfamiliar to him. References to the man and his work abound in many and varied forms of popular culture and as a brand, his name and image carry immense economic and cultural weight (Keenan and Shellard 2016). He is woven into the fabric of our global cultural heritage: owned, often passionately, by people from San Francisco to Soweto, Kolkata to Kyoto, Minsk to Montevideo. It seems then that there is a shared global perspective that *something* about Shakespeare makes him worth young people knowing, but what that something is, and how we get to know him, is not always easy to agree on.

Shakespeare's exceptionalism is often linked with the concept of a genius offering insights into the universal human condition 'not of an age but for all time'. Despite Ben Jonson's praise, however, Shakespeare was, unavoidably, of his time and place. Talent, hard work and opportunity propelled him to local success and the subsequent expansion of literacy and publishing, education, colonization and the whole warp and weft of history propelled him to the iconic status he now holds. It can be hard, therefore, to disentangle the extent to which his current global ubiquity is attributable to the richness of his work from the historically dominating influence of the English language and colonizing cultures. In the globally entangled world of the twenty-first century, Shakespeare can seem very much of his time in the most unwelcome ways. How then, in our teaching, can we best consciously explore and navigate these linguistic, cultural and social justice focused issues, for ourselves as teachers and with our students?

A useful guiding principle in this can be found in progressive and pragmatic pedagogue John Dewey's exploration of art as *experience* in education. On the first page of his influential text *Art as Experience*, Dewey writes: 'When an art product once attains classic status, it somehow becomes isolated from the human condition under which it was brought into being and from the human consequences it engenders in actual life-experience.' Dewey calls for a restoration of continuity between 'admired works of art and the experiences they symbolize' (1934: 1–2). As formal education grew globally across the nineteenth and twentieth centuries, Shakespeare, as experienced by many young people, found his plays fitting all too well this description of an art product elevated to the status of icon of literary heritage and abstracted museum piece. In the late twentieth century, renowned Shakespeare education agitator Rex Gibson felt the need to state firmly that 'Shakespeare is not a museum exhibit with a large 'Do Not Touch' label, but a living force inviting active, imaginative creation' (1998: xii). If a 400-year-old play is not to be merely an untouchable piece of literary heritage but also a site for critical and creative engagement, it needs to be regarded as living art speaking of the present as well as the past. In *Experience and Education*, Dewey observes the reductive value of education systems that provide transmission of information to learn about the past as an end in itself and calls for learning encounters that 'make acquaintance with the past *a means* of understanding the present' (1938: 78, italics original). It was this commitment to tearing down the red velvet ropes of Bardolotry, of retaining the sense of Shakespeare's works as living creative experiences which drove Gibson, his teacher-research partners and his peers to first develop the body of practice and literature commonly referred to as 'active Shakespeare'.

Active and theatre-based Shakespeare: Definitions and context

Though the tradition of active approaches to teaching Shakespeare has a history almost as long as public education itself (Irish 2016), the term became popularized in the late twentieth century via the Shakespeare education work of teachers, scholars and practitioners, including Rex Gibson and Peggy O'Brien. Gibson, working and writing on this topic in the 1980s and 1990s, called his own methods 'active' as a contrast to the more passive desk bound and transmissive teaching of Shakespeare he and his teacher colleagues experienced as common at the time. He describes active methods as comprising 'a wide range of expressive, creative and physical activities'. Like his contemporary O'Brien of the Folger Library on the other side of the Atlantic, Gibson was an educationalist, interested in finding the most effective pedagogy for supporting young people's learning. As teachers, Gibson and O'Brien's starting points were the classroom not the rehearsal room, but they invoked theatre practice in support of their aims. Gibson explains that active methods 'recognise that Shakespeare wrote his plays for performance, and that his scripts are completed by enactment of some kind'. His vision is that active methods 'release students' imagination' giving 'force and substance to the discussion, writing and design work that students undertake'. He finds pedagogical value in how active methods 'dissolve the traditional oppositions of analysis and imagination, intellect and emotion', because in this way, young people develop personal responses which are 'informed, critical and appreciative' (1998: xii–xiii). O'Brien reached similar conclusions, explaining: 'The man wrote plays. So is this about acting? No, it's about *doing*. . . . Make no mistake: learning Shakespeare through *doing* Shakespeare involves the very best kind of close reading, the most exacting sort of literary analysis' (1993: xii, italics original). This is Shakespeare very much in the mould of Dewey's 'living artist'. Within their active Shakespeare writings and practice, Gibson, O'Brien and those following them have been clear about two key principles that have become increasingly accepted and understood in education research more broadly: (1) encouraging young people to bring their own prior knowledge, ideas and values to bear on a shared experience of understanding the text; and (2) intellectual and emotional learning are not distinct and are often best brought together through embodying the text.

The field of active Shakespeare grew alongside the field of drama education in the late twentieth century and recent decades have seen a proliferation of toolkits, guides and programmes focused on more active and dramatic approaches (including O'Brien 1993; Gibson 1998; Stredder 2004; Rocklin 2005; RSC 2010; Winston and Tandy 2012; Banks 2014; Thompson and Turchi 2016; Long and Christel 2019). In the UK, these approaches gained traction in the wake of a broader creative turn in education and cultural policy under the New Labour government of 1997–2010. This included Ken Robinson's influential report on the importance of creativity in schools (Robinson et al. 1999); a general commitment to a dynamic, if contested, 'what works' culture in educational policy and practice (Hammersley 1997; Hargreaves 1997); and an overarching investment in collaborative creativity as an economic, social and educational good (Neelands and Choe 2010). More specifically it led to the publication of a government document 'Shakespeare for all ages and stages' (DCSF 2008) encouraging theatre-based approaches to Shakespeare across a child's school career. This picture should not, however, be seen as suggesting that active or theatre-based approaches are the norm in classrooms either in the UK or globally. As others have noted (Coles 2013; Elliot 2016; Semler et al. 2023), despite the toolkits and resources available for active theatre-based study, most young people continue to experience Shakespeare more as a literary text to be read than to be performed. The 'sea-change' towards 'a pedagogy of performance, or active methods' claimed by Gibson (1996: 142) perhaps created waves rather than floods. Policy contexts change, as do developments and trends in teaching practice, and these impact the cultural framing and practice of active Shakespeare education work. These are influences we explore further in Chapter 2.

Against a backdrop of policy and pedagogical shifts, theatre organizations can be seen to have increasingly owned and capitalized on the narrative of 'active approaches to Shakespeare' and the term has developed under this range of cultural and creative educational practice. The Folger (under O'Brien's leadership) defines its practice as the 'Folger Method'; the Globe Theatre (following Gibson's influence) uses the term 'Creative Shakespeare'; the RSC (following Cicely Berry's influence) uses the term 'Rehearsal Room Approaches'; while Coram Shakespeare Schools Foundation, curators of the UK's largest youth Shakespeare festival, speak of a 'playful ensemble' approach. While these and other organizations seek to make their practice distinctive, there are many overlaps based on the two key principles of valuing prior knowledge and the embodiment of text identified earlier. In Part Two, we present a curated conversation between these organizations and other practitioners in the Shakespeare education arena.

An early title for this book, 'Active Shakespeare', was chosen as a term that will be most familiar to teachers and practitioners in the wake of the body of work we acknowledge earlier. The term has become a catch-all for a pedagogical approach that recognizes Shakespeare's plays as scripts to be analysed through performance rather than reading. Our preferred term in talking about these active, dramatic, performance approaches within the classroom, however, is *theatre-based practice*. In choosing this term, our intention is not to exalt theatre practice over other English or language arts techniques but to recognize and celebrate the overlap of best practice across disciplines. We use the term 'practice' rather than 'approaches' to endorse teaching as a high-skill profession in which an expert teacher will adapt from any toolkit of approaches to weave lessons that best serve their students. Used well, theatre-based practice underpins creative and collaborative approaches to close, critical reading, allowing a dialogic exploration of Shakespeare's plays as a social and artistic resource, as well as literary heritage. This supports Thompson and Turchi's assertion that the purpose of teaching Shakespeare's plays is 'to increase a student's independent facility with complex texts' (2016: 7), not least because 'Where better to talk about complex identity issues than through complex texts?' (2016: 13).

This book is predominantly about the teaching and learning of Shakespeare in formal education. There are overlaps with youth theatre, extracurricular projects, and higher education study, but our focus is an exploration of Shakespeare's value on the curriculum for five to eighteen-year-olds. In 1996, Gibson noted that 'Shakespeare studied by students under nineteen years of age, goes largely unremarked in the major journals. When "teaching Shakespeare" is addressed, the focus of attention is undergraduate level or higher' (1996: 141). Despite Shakespeare's dominant position in school curricula, education remains a relatively small corner of the Shakespeare studies field and much of what is published still tends to focus on higher education. With the notable exceptions we draw on, when Shakespeare scholars do write about school Shakespeare, it is often without a robust engagement with the parallel domains of education research, and especially the world of drama education. We hope this book will contribute to redressing that imbalance.

We should also add that in focusing on embodied theatre-based practice, we do not explicitly deal with digital resources for teaching Shakespeare. Many organizations working with schools on Shakespeare found themselves catapulted into creating online offers during the periods of lockdown resulting from the Covid-19 pandemic and are continuing to assess the strengths and weaknesses of those ways of working. We acknowledge this important and growing area and its key crossovers and implications for theatre work – some of which is explored in our interviews in Part Two. Within the remit of this book, however, we recognize digital pedagogy as a growing area of specialized literature in its own right (Bell and Borsuk 2020; Henderson and Vitale 2021) and focus on the multi-modal embodied pedagogy that is our specialism.

Rhetorics of cultural value

Our aim in this book is partly to consolidate and reflect on active and theatre-based Shakespeare within schools, theatres and cultural organizations. It is also to respond to both the continued challenges in deploying these practices within mainstream schools and curricula and to the critiques of them. Although there is, in many contexts, a growing support for teaching Shakespeare as performance texts, there is also a lingering assumption from some policymakers, academics and English teachers that at best such work simply makes the plays more accessible and enjoyable, and at worst distracts from the serious business of literary analysis and appreciation. Sarah Olive, for example, questions the 'naturalization of Shakespeare as theatre', rather than this being one possibility among 'Shakespeare as poetry, as artefact, or as the object of textual study' (2011: 254). Jane Coles argues that an idealized reading of the 'democratizing' access to Shakespeare that theatre-based approaches often purport to grant do not take enough consideration either of the underlying political and cultural forces at work in the construction of Shakespeare's cultural value or of the narrow and high stakes testing regimes schooling increasingly operates within (Coles 2013). Olive and Coles set out some useful challenges to the Shakespeare education industry. We will unpick these contentions further but our main argument is that theatre-based practice, at its best, acknowledges and accounts for these differing pedagogical and cultural considerations and opens up a space to critically explore them . To work with Shakespeare as theatre does not preclude, indeed should invite in, understanding of his place in history, in culture, in international influence and in literature, along with paying careful attention to how Shakespeare uses language and how societies have used Shakespeare. As Joe Winston asserts, desk-bound literary criticism and critical cultural exploration are part of a good rehearsal process (2015: 114). It is therefore our position that theatre-based practice is not about reductive binaries of Shakespeare as performance against Shakespeare as literature, or Shakespeare 'in a drama studio' against Shakespeare 'at a desk', but a question of approaching Shakespeare in such a way as to, in Dewey's terms, retain his status as a living artist. This is the central precondition of a lively, relevant twenty-first-century teaching of Shakespeare which remains in vital conversation with the specific and globalized concerns of young people. As we explore in this final section of our introductory chapter, this is, at heart, a question of perceptions of Shakespeare's educational and cultural value. Through charting the parameters of education policy and practice debates, we demonstrate how Shakespeare education practice and approaches are ultimately informed by positions on the nature and function of culture within education.

The current stated aim of the National Curriculum in England is to provide pupils with 'an introduction to the essential knowledge they need to be educated citizens. It introduces pupils to the best that has been thought and said, and helps engender an appreciation of human creativity and achievement' (DfE 2014: 3.1). The transmissive nature of this aim is clear: young people are to be *provided* with what they need to *appreciate* what others have done. The phrase 'the best that has been thought and said', often at the centre of considerations of cultural education within the UK and elsewhere, comes from nineteenth-century schools inspector and writer Mathew Arnold. Arnold's essay *Culture and Anarchy* (1869) was seminal in influencing ideas and definitions of culture that ripple through to learning today. The idea of not just 'the best' but 'essential knowledge' landed in the National Curriculum thanks to the influence of American academic E. D. Hirsch, author of *Cultural Literacy: What Every American Needs to Know* (1988). As will be explored further in Chapter 2, Hirsch and his followers position themselves against Dewey and the progressive movement for what they perceive as undervaluing of knowledge. Jerome Bruner's progressive conception of 'discovery learning', for example, is often misinterpreted as unstructured play, whereas its core principle is that if knowledge is 'discovered' through the learner's own cognitive efforts, that discovery has come about by relating new knowledge to old, making it more secure because more personal (1996: xii).

As the only compulsory author for study on England's National Curriculum, Shakespeare is enshrined as 'essential knowledge', 'the best that has been thought and said' to be 'appreciated' as *the* icon of 'human creativity and achievement'. If ever an art product achieved Dewey's classic, untouchable status, this rhetoric is telling us Shakespeare has. No wonder teachers and students can feel daunted. A survey of fourteen-year-olds' attitudes to Shakespeare, carried out across state schools in England in 2007, found that only 35 per cent believed it was important to study Shakespeare and only 23 per cent agreed with the statement 'Shakespeare's plays are relevant to events in the modern world' (Winston and Strand 2015: 134–5). Many young people leave school thinking of Shakespeare as another piece of education broccoli, put on their plates as good for them: to be swallowed to help them pass exams but ignored when it comes to enjoying their lives. Teachers are similarly alienated, often finding themselves as wary of Shakespeare as their students. Feeling they need to have all the answers when their students are confused by archaic language and sixteenth-century cultural references, they can end up relying on offering a pre-digested analysis rather than a live engagement drawing in the prior knowledge of their students.

A way forward can perhaps be seen in the less-famous context of Arnold's statement on 'the best'. The 'anarchy' Arnold was responding to in his essay was a sense of growing individualism and commercialism that he saw as damaging the social cohesion of the nation. A shared culture was his answer to this threat, defined as 'a pursuit of our total perfection by means of getting to know, on all matters which most concern us, the best that has been thought and said in the world, and through this knowledge, turning a stream of fresh and free thought upon our stock notions and habits'. Arnold's focus was almost certainly more in line with Hirsch's ideas of cultural literacy than Dewey and Bruner's commitment to art as living experience, but a sense of challenge is here. Arnold called for a knowledge of 'the best' as a way to enrich lives and develop 'all sides of our humanity'. His words can be interpreted as a progressive call to action. We might also note that he says 'pursuit': a journey, not a destination; a continuous striving for understanding, rather than merely building a collection of knowledge; something to pursue, not something that is provided to be passively appreciated. This idea of pursuit can be seen reflected in the findings of an influential report from Harvard's Project Zero into excellence in arts education, entitled 'The qualities of quality' (Seidel et al. 2009). The report finds that what constitutes quality in the arts is hard to define because it is inextricably linked to personal identity, values and meaning. It involves judgements but cannot be easily measured and 'is a constant and persistent quest and not an end game' (2009: i).

Notably, Arnold also writes 'the best that has been thought and said *in the world*', encouraging a broader perspective on what constitutes that 'best'. He then exhorts us to use our learning to turn 'a stream of fresh and free thought upon our stock notions and habits'. More critical, pluralistic, fresh and free thinking about 'stock notions and habits', which includes questions about what constitutes 'the best' and who decides, is something we propose as a third principle of theatre-based practice, alongside valuing prior knowledge and embodied approaches. In this, we explicitly seek to move away from simplistic claims of Shakespeare's universality: that his works and cultural significance speak openly and equally to all people globally and across time through universal human themes; an argument which has been referenced in previous active Shakespeare texts (Banks 2014; Gibson 2016). On one level, this is an engaging claim which makes a simple and robust statement about the value and accessibility of Shakespeare's texts to all learners. On the other hand, research and scholarship have demonstrated how a universalistic perspective on Shakespeare ignores its particular historical and cultural positionality (Thompson 2011) and also the history of European imperialism (Eklund and Hyman 2019) which has deeply informed our 400-year cultural engagement in Shakespeare's works. As Thompson and Turchi (2020b) state, teaching Shakespeare under a guise of 'universality' rings increasingly false with our students, and is actively triggering to those who experience exclusion and oppression due to their race, class, gender or sexuality.

Theatre-based practice has been recognized by both educational and Shakespearean scholars (Thompson and Turchi 2020a; Coles and Pitfield 2022; Dadabhoy and Mehdizadeh 2023) as a valuable way to fruitfully disrupt the concept of universality when teaching the plays. In their analysis of teachers' use of drama-based practice with Shakespeare in English classrooms, Jane Coles and Maggie Pitfield observe that 'reading through drama is a pedagogy that acknowledges difference, and in [teachers'] . . . hands it becomes an effective means of avoiding illusory claims to Shakespeare's "universalism" along with manufactured forms of "relevance"' (2022: 82). Building on the recognized issues with a universalistic approach to Shakespeare, Ambereen Dadabhoy and Nedda Mehdizadeh propose the concept of *salience* over 'relevance'. They argue that relevance as an educational concept ultimately requires students to meet the text as a fixed expression of human experience and offer the exploration of salience as a more student-led approach that invites young people to look for moments which 'leap' from the page to meet them in their contextualized lived realities (Dadabhoy and Mehdizadeh 2023). They advocate theatre-based practice as a key way to identify and explore the salience of Shakespeare for their learners, stating:

> Performance can be an important method through which students can reinforce and support Shakespeare's salience to their lived experiences. Shakespeare's plays are performance scripts that mandate engagement through embodiment. When instructors shift students' orientation toward these objects by building performance into their courses with attention to students' identities, they will find that students begin to reevaluate their relation to Shakespeare's works. (Dadabhoy and Mehdizadeh 2023: 66)

In this book, we align ourselves with salience as an orienting concept with theatre-based practice, inviting the prioritization of learners' resonances with the text over established 'universal' themes. We locate ourselves in opposition to deficit and acquisition-based models of Shakespeare's cultural value based on his perceived universalism, and in alignment with approaches grounded in the search for his active salience for learners, based on a dynamic encounter with the texts as living art. For this reason, we suggest it is necessary to move away from Hirsch's notion of cultural literacy when undertaking theatre-based practice with Shakespeare. As we explore further in Chapter 2, the terms 'cultural literacy' and 'cultural capital', both in frequent use in cultural and educational conversations, are insufficient for describing the value system that drives active Shakespeare principles as we have set out here. We focus instead on the concept of 'intercultural democracy' as the guiding principle in navigating rhetorics of Shakespeare's cultural value, in line with the growing influence of research developed from concepts of decoloniality, intercultural communication, and cultural intelligence.

Summary

In this book, we seek not only to map and consolidate the uses of active, theatre-based Shakespeare education practice over the past decades but also to critically explore and reassert their pedagogic and cultural value in the twenty-first century as a practice of intercultural democracy. Over the following chapters, we explore how Shakespeare's language and also his cultural positionalities offer a unique site for such work when his plays are explored as scripts incomplete without the playful criticality that theatre-based practice invites.

We argue that treating a play as a text posing questions to be inhabited by contemporary human beings, answers Dewey's enduring invitation to 'active, imaginative creation' as well as the growing need for pro-social skills; critical thinking; collaborative resilience; and appreciation of diverse cultural perspectives in an increasingly uncertain and divisive world. Throughout this book, it is our core contention that if a cultural inheritance – in this case Shakespeare – is to be useful for young people in building their future, they need to learn how to creatively and critically interact with it to assess how best to use and develop it. Shakespeare's texts offer complex metaphorical layers to support development of complex active communication skills *if* we position him as a living artistic resource and site of received, but dynamic and contestable, knowledge through which young people can develop meaning.

In this introductory chapter, we have set up the questions we want to explore of what teaching, learning and performing Shakespeare has to offer school-age young people as we move deeper into the twenty-first century. Responding to considerations of contemporary and historical education practice, policy and research, we have proposed three key principles of theatre-based Shakespeare teaching for creating a pedagogy of intercultural democracy in schools. Namely that it should encourage young people to

1) bring prior knowledge, ideas and values to bear on a shared experience of understanding a literary text;
2) combine intellectual, social and emotional learning through embodying the text; and
3) develop criticality in questioning a cultural inheritance and how that canon can in turn raise questions about today's world.

In Part One of this book, we build on the theoretical basis outlined in this introductory chapter to examine how and why the playful work of theatre-based practice is valuable, not just for enjoying and understanding Shakespeare but in developing the creativity, criticality and collaboration now heralded as the skills and attributes most useful for successful life in the modern world. Part Two offers a curated journey through extracts from interviews with ten leaders and practitioners from major theatre companies and other organizations working primarily with Shakespeare. Here we find a diversity of approaches but a commonality of values around using Shakespeare as a high-quality resource for exploring the questions young people have and for building the skills and competencies they need. In Part Three of this book, we turn to reflections and explorations from teaching practitioners with a series of invited chapters on how the principles of active and theatre-based Shakespeare have informed and impacted their teaching and the educational experiences of their learners.

PART ONE

Perspectives from multidisciplinary research

1

The pedagogy question

Progressive principles

Theatre-based or active Shakespeare practice is often defined by its format, particularly when placed in contrast to 'desk-based' approaches: if learners are on their feet, performing or exploring the text with their voices and bodies this is *active* Shakespeare. The implication being learning which occurs sat down, verbally or internally, is *inactive*. Yet, as we began to discuss within the introductory chapter and will explore in more detail over the following chapters, theatre-based and active Shakespeare as a field of practice can be more helpfully and richly understood through a range of pedagogic principles rather than a set of exercises or approaches. In this chapter we set out the core principles underpinning this practice, including the diverse ways the growing body of theatre-based Shakespeare literature interprets and applies them, and end with a consideration of the core competencies these principles ask of a teacher.

Experiential learning: The classroom as rehearsal room

One of the most commonly cited and obvious rationales for theatre-based Shakespeare education practice is that the plays were written to be performed and experienced as performances. Leaving aside the very much still-live debate on whether it is more formally correct or educationally useful to define the plays as theatrical or literary texts; a foundational aspect of much theatre-based Shakespeare writing is that the classroom space should be considered and used as an 'authentic' theatrical space. Jonathan Bate, for example, in relation to his education and research work with the RSC, explains: 'Our idea was that the effective classroom bears analogy to the effective rehearsal room; that the rehearsal room is a learning experience; that in some senses the director is like a teacher ... who brings on a class, the acting company, through collaborative work, through asking questions, playing games, through trust, through exploring ideas together and respecting different opinions' (cited in Winston 2015: 11). This concept brings with it certain underlying pedagogic considerations of both rehearsal rooms and classrooms as active and generative spaces. When Peggy O'Brien states 'The most significant work in the entire world goes on in schools . . . what goes on daily in the mind of a student is the future creating itself' (2006: xi), we can gain a sense of the social and educational value that theatre-based Shakespeare practitioners place on these generative hybrid performance/learning spaces.

As Jonothan Neelands and Jacqui O'Hanlon have also discussed (2011), the idea of the class/rehearsal room as a model for authentic engagement with the texts chimes with Dewey's concept of experiential learning:

> First, that the pupils have a genuine situation of experience . . . secondly, that a genuine problem develop within this situation as a stimulus to thought; third, that he [a pupil] possess the information and make the observations needed to deal with it; fourth, that suggested solutions occur to him which he shall be responsible for developing in an orderly way; fifth, that he have the opportunity and occasion to test his ideas by application, to make their meaning clear and to discover for himself their validity. (Dewey 1916: 167)

Neelands and O'Hanlon argue that the 'rehearsal room' education practice of the RSC offers an authentic 'situation of experience' via actively engaging with the text as actors and directors, with the 'genuine problem' offered through the challenge of making sense of the language and stories. Theatre-based practice therefore makes a claim to 'authentic' education experience through this Deweyan idea of genuine problems that generate problem-solving. Within this there is also the claim towards authentic experience through the specific use of exercises and activities drawn from the professional rehearsal room. Fiona Banks, for example, states that 'most' approaches used by Globe Education started their life in the theatre's professional rehearsal rooms (Banks 2014). Shakespeare's Globe is an interesting example here because their pedagogic model also draws on the idea of historical authenticity – establishing resonances between their contemporary educational practice and Early Modern rehearsal and performance approaches. Banks quotes the theatre's first artistic director Mark Rylance reflecting that performing Shakespeare within the reconstruction Early Modern playhouse was an 'exciting challenge'; the equivalent of playing on Mozart's original violin. Banks goes on to emphasize the Globe as an inherently experimental learning space, asking what can be understood about Shakespeare's playtexts when performed in one of the spaces they were originally written for: 'The Globe theatre is like a massive classroom where actor can be both student and teacher' (Banks 2014: 14).

Similarly Edward Rocklin, in his exploration of the use of what he terms 'performance approaches' to teaching Shakespeare with US English Literature university students, draws links between a classroom and an 'Elizabethan theatre/stage' (2005: 6). Citing Ralph Alan Cohen on the use of original staging in the Shakespeare classroom, Rocklin argues circular or 'U-shaped' configurations within the performance-approach classroom unlocks an enhanced understanding of Shakespeare's words. There are social as well as educational implications within these ideas of the Shakespearean classroom as a historically and artistically authentic and generative cultural space. The key educational claim outlined in this section, however, is that theatre-based practice is predicated on an experiential pedagogy because it draws on authentically historical and professional approaches to interpreting Shakespeare's playtexts and maximizes on the 'inherent' pedagogy of rehearsal and performance spaces.

Constructivism and progressivism: The text is completed through action

Building on the basis of the plays as fundamentally intended for and best interpreted through performance are the implications of the material nature of the plays as dramatic texts. Throughout theatre-based Shakespeare writing is the explicit or implicit perspective that, as an object of study, the playtexts are in very real terms brought into being or completed through embodied and verbal action. This is commonly expressed through the metaphor of the difference between a piece of sheet music and a final orchestral performance to emphasize the added richness and depth of understanding which can be built on theatre-based exploration of the texts. In this section we will critically consider the implications of this metaphor.

In order to do this we will first explore how this premise places theatre-based practice within the pedagogic realm of constructivism; an approach to pedagogy which sees the nature of knowledge not as fixed and external but as interpersonally and socially 'constructed' via communal and collaborative approaches to learning which take account of education's active relationship to broader society and social norms. The ideas of twentieth-century constructivists such as the Russian social psychologist Lev Vygotsky (1978) have become a core component of contemporary western educational practice and are particularly relevant to the practice of theatre-based Shakespeare teaching. Rocklin is usefully specific on the constructivist implications of this approach when he states: 'when they [students] perform they do not "add" the physical reality to the words as we "add" decoration to our clothes; rather, they fully incarnate what is only potentially present in the words of the play' (Rocklin 2005: 50). Theatre-based practice is emphatically not therefore a high-octane 'add on' to the study of Shakespeare, as has been claimed elsewhere (Wilson 1997), but expresses a specific constructivist understanding of the nature of knowledge and textual interpretation. This constructivist understanding of knowledge also implies a progressive perspective in relation to the role and status of learners. As Rex Gibson states in *Teaching Shakespeare:* 'Through such participatory and co-operative activity [enacting the playtexts], students both discover and create meaning. They become agents of their own learning as they take responsibility for their own inquiries and investigations' (2016: vii). As well as the constructivist perspective on the nature of knowledge, in Gibson's statement we can also see a progressive educational position being expressed: that learners come to educational experiences with existing identities, positionalities and knowledges and these have purpose and value within educational endeavours. To summarize the key points of this chapter so far therefore: the core pedagogic claims of theatre-based Shakespeare are that it offers a historically and aesthetically authentic experience which invites a constructive approach to knowledge and a progressive perspective on the positionality and capacity of learners.

Radical and liberal implications

Within active and theatre-based Shakespeare writing, both liberal and more radical or critical interpretations of these pedagogic foundations exist. The liberal interpretation consists of highlighting the potential for learners to utilize and develop their creativity and imagination; to have an authentic, emotional engagement with the text; and to encounter it from a position of experimentation, curiosity and discovery, those being the Enlightenment ideals of rational and autonomous intellectual endeavour (Rousseau 1762).

These liberal values can be seen in Gibson's assertions that active methods 'accord a greater degree of responsibility to them [students] than traditional ways of teaching' (2016: 4) and that 'in such activities, the development of critical thinking accompanies imaginative and emotional growth as students speculate, reason, predict and hypothesize' (2016: 6). Banks similarly emphasizes the divergent exploration and problem-solving capacity of theatre-based approaches, stating they 'draw on and value imaginative engagement, they require suspending judgment, asking "what if?" Creative approaches often require students, like actors, to turn detective' (2014: 5). As Banks goes on to emphasize, this process of active inquiry is frequently associated with deeper and more strongly retained learning, citing the oft-quoted experiential learning Confucian proverb 'I hear and I forget. I see and I remember. I do and I understand.'

This notion of the theatre-based Shakespeare classroom as a space of explorative knowledge co-construction holds implications about the relationship between knowledge, learning and identity which comprises another common thread within theatre-based Shakespeare writings: the progressive education focus on learner autonomy. For example, James Stredder highlights a level of autonomy within theatre-based approaches: 'In the process of learning, our students also require a feeling of personal control, of being at the centre of their learning and the creation of meaning' (Stredder 2009: xxiv) Povey et al.'s term 'author/ity', is useful here, as it focuses specifically on the constructive 'authorship' of the playtext the learner is seen to undertake within theatre-based practice:

> Teachers and learners sharing this way of knowing work implicitly (and, perhaps, explicitly) with an understanding that they are members of a knowledge-making community. . . . As such, meaning is understood as negotiated. External sources are consulted and respected but they are also evaluated critically by the knowledge makers . . . with whom author/ity rests. Such a way of knowing opens up the possibility of understanding knowledge as constructed and meaning as contingent and contextual and personal. (Povey et al. 1999: 234)

The concept of author/ity therefore draws out resonances between a 'reader response' approach to text, a progressive approach to learners and the wider social justice potential of this work. It takes us away from granting Shakespeare *authority* because of his *authorship* and emphasizes the empowerment implicated in a co-constructivist approach to the text where learners are invited to share author/ity through their own authorial responses to the text. Gibson picks up on the social and social justice implications of a pedagogy concerned with learner author/ity when he states: 'the recognition that learners actively make meaning has cultural implications. Each student brings their own culture to each lesson. That rich variety of culture is a resource that Shakespeare lessons can celebrate and enjoy rather than dismiss' (2016: 10). Theatre-based Shakespeare teaching can therefore be understood as an approach in which an explicit valuing and welcoming of students' cultural diversity is grounded in the underlying epistemology of the pedagogy.

This welcoming of inclusive author/ity from multiple sources is explicitly extended to teachers within much theatre-based Shakespeare writing. The Folger's *Shakespeare Set Free* series, for example, emphasizes that the Folger Method represents 'the combined and comprehensive knowledge of many fine working teachers' (O'Brien et al. 2006: xiii). Gibson and Banks similarly emphasize the value of teachers being led by their own interests and preferences in working with the playtexts, and across theatre-based Shakespeare writing there is an emphasis on the exercises and programmes being offered in a spirit of suggestion or invitation. Banks talks about a 'recipe book' to be tinkered with and foregrounds the differing perspectives of a cast of Globe Education Practitioners throughout her book, while Rocklin frames the method outlined in his book as an accordion fully stretched, with the different segments to be compressed and isolated as needed.

Rocklin draws these meditations on learner and teacher author/ity into the realm of identity and theatrical role-taking, reflecting on 'the multiple roles I ask my students to play, as well as the multiple roles I play myself' (2005: 5) In this way, the author/ity implicit in theatre-based Shakespeare education's understanding of knowledge formation is linked to theories of the complex relationships between identity, self and community within theatrical performance. This can be seen, for example, in sociologist Erving Goffman's work on the presentation of self in everyday life as the enacting of specific social 'roles' (Goffman 1990) or in performance scholar and anthropologist Victor Turner's explorations of the 'plural reflexivity' of identity possible through dramatic exploration and action. Turner gives the example of how while the character of Hamlet can only brood on his own motives, *Hamlet* the play can reflect on broader themes within the text and beyond (1987: 106). As Thompson and Turchi have highlighted, and as we will continue to explore, theatre-based Shakespeare work can therefore be seen as a route into contemporary explorations of personal and social identity (Thompson and Turchi 2016).

Theatre-based Shakespeare work gives both teachers and learners author/ity to inhabit a set of creative roles around and through the playtexts. Rocklin refers to this as a 'complex ensemble' including playwright, player and playgoer and goes on to highlight the variety of learning which can come from teachers and learners occupying each of these perspectives (Rocklin 2005). Through this liberally progressive reading of the constructivist nature of theatre-based practice a *relationality* with the playtexts and by implication with Shakespeare himself as playwright is assumed.

Dewey writes of the tension between 'living' and 'isolated' art: whether an artist is put on a pedestal or brought into direct conversation with the perspectives, knowledges and contexts within the classroom. Theatre-based practice can revitalize both the art and the artist, bringing Shakespeare back into contact with the 'human condition' and 'human consequences' and connecting to ideas of historical and theatrical authenticity. 'Shakespeare was not writing plays for posterity, but texts for performance by people he knew well. He relied on their competence, composed towards their capacity', argues Thomson (2002: 140). In the theatre-based Shakespeare classroom learners are invited to literally and figuratively step into that relational role Shakespeare held with his players. The process of meaning-making and knowledge creation in active Shakespeare practice relies on learners' competence and capacity: 'students learn Shakespeare by meeting him on his own ground – inside the play' (O'Brien et al. 2006: xii). The egalitarian metaphor of the Shakespeare rehearsal room evoked by theatre-based practice implies the possibility of a less monumental, more interpersonal relationship with the texts and their author.

A more socially critical interpretation of a constructivist and progressive theatre-based Shakespeare pedagogy pushes more radically on the educational and cultural implications of social constructions.

Within this pedagogy therefore, alongside celebrating opportunities for author/ity, there is the recognition of constructions of inequality and exclusion within society and how Shakespeare as a set of playtexts and a cultural institution intersects with them. Along with all the explorative plurality and reflexivity of role and identity discussed earlier come the tools and the critical capacity to interrogate our current social context through the framework of the playtexts and the pedagogy. As Hillary Eklund and Wendy Hyman summarize in their edited volume *Teaching Shakespeare Through Social Justice* 'social change and pedagogy are baked into dramatic form itself. The study and teaching of plays, therefore, afford a clear opportunity to engage in conversations about social justice' (2019: 8). This leads to a recognition that theatre-based Shakespeare shares key pedagogic DNA with the practice of critical pedagogy. In this more critical reading of theatre-based Shakespeare pedagogy is the rich and radical potential to use this active practice to identify, critique and push back against the normative geometries of power implicated in Shakespeare's text and his cultural status (Kitchen 2023). Stredder highlights:

> All practical work is, pre-eminently, production. This notion of producing or 'making' the characters or the narrative of a play is attractive, both to progressive pedagogy (it is creative, stimulating, participatory, offering ownership) and to the rigours of modern critical theory (where meaning is actively produced by reader/audience and situation, rather than universal or inherent; and where the language and conventions of the text generate multiple meanings, rather than a single, harmonized perspective). (Stredder 2009: 14)

Shakespeare studies as a broader field of practice is currently engaging with the implications of this. In addition to Eklund and Hyman's volume, for example, is an Arden Shakespeare Handbook exploring the literary, performance and educational implications of Shakespeare and social justice (Ruiter 2020); while explorations of theatre-based practices such as classroom contracting and the use of tableaux are recognized as supportive of anti-racist Shakespeare pedagogy (Dadabhoy and Mehdizadeh 2023). Similarly, applied and educational drama scholarship is increasingly focusing on critical questions of social justice (Adams Jr 2013; O'Connor 2014, 2016; Gallagher et al. 2020). Often this work focuses on problematizing liberal framings on the civilizing and transformative potential of arts education (Finneran and Freebody 2016; Freebody and Finneran 2021; Nicholson 2011). As Michael Finneran and Kelly Freebody state, 'critical pedagogical and theoretical perspectives allow us a chance to provide a counter-narrative to the received idea that simply by intending to do "good", drama work will automatically always do "good"' (2016: 184). This critical scholarly perspective from applied and educational drama brings to theatre-based

Shakespeare practice a lens to both interrogate and develop the social justice potential of the work. This is not to state that a theatre-based practice is *necessary* to undertake either a liberally or radically social justice-focused approach to the teaching of Shakespeare, but that these social and educational theories are foundational to theatre-based practice. We would also state moreover, based on this analysis, it would seem like a conscious and rather odd omission to seek a constructivist, progressive and socially just approach to Shakespeare *without* ever actively treating the plays as theatrical playtexts.

Embodied cognition: Learning through doing

In the previous section, we focused on how social science research and critically conscious approaches support the constructivist and progressive pedagogical principles underpinning theatre-based practice. In this section we explore how scientific studies offer support for the embodied cognition that lies behind that embodied practice.

Sarah-Jayne Blakemore states: 'Education changes the brain, and therefore neuroscience is fundamental to teaching and learning' (2019: 178). However, she also reminds us: 'It is crucially important to understand that science doesn't produce facts, it produces findings – and these findings can be overturned by further research' (2019: 180). Approaches promoted for the classroom increasingly claim scientific backing, but those claims often represent simplified interpretation of findings rather than indisputable facts. Fads such as brain gyms and learning styles come and go as they are debunked from the claims they promise; even though they may offer a core nugget of truth if we accept their place in a more complex picture. Every teacher knows the classroom is a hive of 'variables' because every child is unique, bringing their own variabilities of experience, ability, interests and inclinations. The 'big data' of replicable findings from studies involving significant numbers can be highly informative, but individual living humans will always present exceptions. A reflective teacher needs to be open to, but critical of, how they use pedagogical 'solutions' in their own classrooms. As Adey and Dillon warn: 'Many myths in education arise from over-simple categorization and stereotyping . . . teachers have been subjected to an increasing barrage of instructions, guidance, advice and statutory regulations all designed by an administration that acts as if the fine details of classroom life can be fully controlled' (2012: xxiii).

Bearing those caveats in mind, there are a number of key findings from neuroscience and cognitive research that have gained sufficient consensus to make them usefully informative for the theatre-based education community. This section briefly surveys, under the umbrella concept of embodied cognition: Systems 1 and 2, neural plasticity, the social brain, theory of mind (ToM), mirror neurons and conceptual metaphors.

Mind as function of body

What science philosopher Mark Johnson calls the 'the illusion of disembodied mind' (2007: 2) has been a foundation of education systems that promote the superiority of reason over feeling and mind over body, leading to learning being cultivated as the passive, sedentary process captured by Paulo Freire's famous metaphor of the 'banking system' of a transmissive style of teaching (1970). More broadly, psychiatrist Ian McGilchrist warns against a trend in Western cultures, 'towards the ever greater repudiation of our embodied being in favour of an abstracted, cerebralised machine-like version of ourselves' (2009: 120). The concept of *embodied cognition* (Varela et al. 1991) is defined by Shapiro and Stoltz as 'concerned with the interaction of the mind, body and environment in explaining how knowledge is grounded in sensorimotor routines and experiences' (2019: 26). It is reflected in the 'cognitive turn' of performance studies (McConachie and Hart 2006) and is at the heart of theatre-based pedagogies that pay attention to the role feeling, experience and reflection play in constructing meaning.

Antonio Damasio explains how 'The mind exists in and for an integrated organism', since 'our minds would not be the way they are if it were not for the interplay of body and brain during evolution, during individual development, and at the current moment' (2006: xxvi; 2012). What we see, hear, touch, taste, feel and think is determined by our very personal sensory contact with the world around us, interpreted by our completely unique mental schema of that world. In any moment, our brain is performing billions of adjustments to what we perceive, fuelled by circumstantial evidence from external and internal sensory input and interpreted by the cumulation of our lived experiences; a tiny fraction of which is fed through to the conscious awareness of our minds. Embodied cognition, or knowledge developed from 'sensorimotor routines and experiences', adds up to who we are and how we learn.

Neuroscientists are increasingly able to describe how we create the personalized mental schema in our brains that make sense of the sensory input we receive, and how that input is emotionally coloured according to the nature and nurture forming our biases. A sense of a more primitive system of response that is constantly alert to threats and opportunities in our environment but subject to the judgements of an executive function is now part of a common understanding of behaviour. This understanding, however, can lean into another simplified iteration of the superiority of a rational mind over an emotional body. Daniel Kahneman's use of the metaphorical terms *System 1 and System 2* (2012) is useful in keeping a sense of the complex ecosystem of feedback loops of physiology, perception, response, cause and effect, constantly in play. He differentiates fast thinking System 1 as subconscious, instinctive responses caused by evolutionary inheritance interacting with learning from lived experiences. While slow thinking System 2 engages conscious effort, requiring focused attention to evaluate the options provided by System 1 and in performing less familiar tasks. System 1 is the 'automatic system'; System 2 is the 'effortful system'.

It can be highly useful for educators to understand that System 2, the system that focuses attention, monitors behaviour, checks biases, keeps us polite and pro-social – all the behaviours we expect in a classroom – requires effort which is easily depleted. For too many young people, their capacity for this effort may already be depleted by factors such as stress or malnourishment. The brain takes shortcuts to protect us whenever it can and those shortcuts can lead to the host of biases humans are subject to. As Maslow first suggested in 1943, there is a hierarchy of physiological and psychological needs that need to be fulfilled before new learning can be effective. System 1 needs to be happy before System 2 can step in to ensure pro-social behaviour and productive learning.

Key to the formation of Systems 1 and 2 and the individual mental schema we all carry, is *neural plasticity*: the brain's remarkable ability to adapt, change and develop throughout life. For children, social, nurturing environments are vital in supporting cognitive development and language acquisition (Blakemore and Frith 2005; Fitch 2010). In adolescence the brain undergoes huge changes in how it processes information and what it pays attention to. Blakemore suggests this 'might be a period of relatively high neural plasticity, in particular in brain regions involved in decision making, planning and social cognition' (2019: 188). This suggests there are opportunities for education to harness that plasticity and the accompanying 'heightened creativity and novel thinking, energy and passion' (2019: 194) of teenagers into pathways that support them to better understand themselves and the world around them.

The social brain

Continuing advances in studies of cognitive evolution use the shorthand of *the social brain* to describe the composition of features in human brains that seem responsible in allowing us to read others' intentions and to assess the possible results of our possible responses (Trimble 2007: 173). A theme running through this book about the value of theatre-based practice is the importance of sociality in how humans learn. The dynamic formation of the cognition resulting from our embodied interactions with our environments is highly affected by our understanding of ourselves relative to others. Carrington and Bailey (2009: 2313) describe *theory of mind* (ToM) as 'the ability to think about mental states, such as thoughts and beliefs, in oneself and others [which underlie] social interaction and allows people to make sense of the behaviour of others'. In figurative terms, ToM means being able to imagine yourself in someone else's shoes and understand how they might see the world differently to you. This ability is related to the apparently uniquely human ability of intentionality. Other species communicate for various pragmatic reasons and read intentions in others for their own benefit; as far as is currently known, however, only humans *intend*, indeed seem driven, to share information, thoughts and ideas with each other (Fitch 2010).

Intentionality and ToM develop in complexity as children grow older (Westby and Robinson 2014). In a classic experiment, most children aged four to five are able to distinguish that if someone else has seen an object put in a box but not seen the object removed, that person will expect the object to still be in the same box (Wimmer and Perner 1983). In other words, by four or five years old, children understand that other people have different perspectives on the world to them. The complexity of this understanding grows through adolescence and studies show how it can be affected by a myriad of genetic and environmental circumstances including neurodiversity and adverse experiences (Blakemore and Frith 2005, Atherton et al. 2019). Blakemore summarizes key research that for the majority of children, 'an understanding of other people's minds develops gradually over the first five years of life' (2019: 110) but goes on to offer descriptions of recent research that has found how ToM abilities differ in development after that age. In the 'Director Task', for example, participants are asked to follow directions to move objects around shelves. The 'director' is positioned opposite the participant and so has a different view of the shelves, some of which are open to both views and some of which have a backing which means the director cannot see that shelf. If the director says, 'move the small ball up one shelf', the participant needs to understand which ball the director sees as being the smallest. The participant may know there is a smaller ball on a backed shelf, but the test is about their facility to recognize that this is not the ball the director means. Variations of this experiment have demonstrated that although ability improves through adolescence, many adults still make errors on around half of all attempts, suggesting that, even with conscious effort, understanding someone else's perspective is not an easy task (2019: 111–18).

Humans are innately co-operative and deeply social learners but that sociality and co-operation hang in fragile balance. Experiences inside and outside the classroom can operate to nurture innate abilities to understand others' perspectives or suppress that understanding. As we explore further in Chapter 3, childhood is a highly sensitive time when the stories we hear can make us more open and tolerant of difference or closed and infected by stereotypes. Young people are subject to increased pressures in their social media-dominated world to 'take sides'. Dialogic engagement with complex texts may encourage development of counter-narrative ToM capacities for empathy and a socially critical understanding of what Gibson calls 'the other-sidedness of things' (1993: 80). Mathew Williams explains: 'If you cannot bring yourself to imagine what it is like to be a member of the outgroup, you can only conceptualize "them" as a collective, meaning the individual is lost . . . it only takes a few steps to dehumanize all of "them"' (2022: 28).

An ability to inhabit the emotional world view of others is something we practise every day through *mirror neurons*. The phenomenon was identified in 1996 (Rizzolatti et al.) and further study has revealed how we seem to understand each other by unconsciously, but closely, observing physiological changes that reflect emotions and mirroring them. This creates in our own bodies an approximation of how that other person feels. Shaun Gallagher argues that mirror neurons create an instinctive, subconscious response, a resonance and reaction 'to the joy or the anger, or the intention that is in the face or in the posture or in the gesture or action of the other' (2008: 449). McGilchrist explains that 'communication occurs because, in a necessarily limited, but nonetheless crucially important sense, we come to feel what it is like to be the person who is communicating with us' (2009: 122), while Michael Trimble concludes that mirror neurons are 'an unconscious system for monitoring the intentions of others' (2012: 108–9). Gallagher suggests that because we learn how to interpret and share meaning through these sensory interactions with others, the more varied the social contexts we are exposed to, the more we can learn, and understand, about others.

The question all this raises is the extent to which theatre-based practice can offer Gallagher's varied social scenarios for young people to experience, both through its collaborative approaches and through creatively interpreting the scenarios in the texts. Robin Dunbar has explored ToM specifically in relation to Shakespeare. He explains the demand required from an audience asked to follow multiple mind states in the plays; for example in understanding that Iago wants Othello to think that Desdemona loves Cassio. He proposes that actors and playwrights require even higher levels of ToM since they must understand that the audience thinks Iago wants Othello to think that Desdemona loves Cassio who is actually thinking of Bianca (Stiller, Nettle and Dunbar 2003). The ability to predict and monitor the behaviour and intentions of others has obvious advantages for successful living for a highly social species, not least for the development of empathy, trust and collaboration. Our interest is in how theatre-based practice can be optimized to support this development, including how it can feed into Turner's 'plural reflexivity', mentioned above, that allows the students to engage with and benefit from the multiple perspectives inherent in a playtext.

Conceptual metaphors

Language gives us the ability to express and share any thoughts and feelings we have and by this definition is uniquely human. Any typical child born anywhere in the world has the ability to learn any language but will rapidly, and with little conscious effort, learn the lexicon, syntax, dialect and references of the culture/s most immediately around them (Fitch 2010). A consequence of our being in the world as embodied beings with embodied cognition is that the language through which we explain the world to ourselves and each other derives from sorting, understanding and describing our sensory experiences. We do this through comparisons. Shakespeare understood this intuitively and his language oozes with analogy, metaphor and antithesis, rooted in the imagined sensory experiences of his characters and released in the visceral connotations of those experiences through the body and voice of an actor.

Embracing embodied cognition within a pedagogy leads to embracing the metaphorical nature of language and appreciating it as far more than aesthetic flourish. George Lakoff and Mark Johnson's seminal work *Metaphors we live by* (1980) accelerated investigation of a now widely accepted understanding that metaphor forms the conceptual basis of how we understand the world. Our brains sort and store new knowledge and experience by connecting to and comparing with other knowledge and experiences we already have. This associative thinking results in an average of one metaphor every ten seconds of speech or writing (Storr 2019: 44) and cognitive scientist Douglas Hofstadter's metaphorical maxim that: 'Analogy is the very blue that fills the whole sky of cognition' (2001: 499).

Lakoff and Johnson propose that infinite complex metaphors arise from cultural and environmental experiences that build from approximately 150 universal primary metaphors. For example, with the primary metaphor *affection is warmth,* the connection between the two conceptual domains of 'affection' and 'warmth' is easy to understand: from birth we associate a sense of affection with the warmth of, particularly, our mother's bodies. This association supports a subconscious understanding of a metaphor such as 'Juliet is the sun' (*RJ*, 2.1.58), where Romeo contrasts the warm glow of his physical encounter with Juliet (both the living encounter in his memory and the hoped for one in his imagination) with the cold light of a chaste moon goddess. Another primary metaphor *love is a journey* is brought to life as a complex metaphor in every comedy and many tragedies, encapsulated in Lysander's line, 'The course of true love never did run smooth' (*MND*, 1.1.136). *Understanding is seeing* compares the two separate conceptual domains of cognition and vision but relies on the physical connection that much of our cognition comes from vision, so we 'see a solution', 'close our eyes to a problem' or think from 'a point of view'. We learn from embodied experiences that eye focus reflects security because we know we can feel either safe or threatened under the gaze of another. From the primary metaphor *knowing is seeing*, we derive metaphorical language such as being 'looked after', 'watched over' or 'spied on'. In *King Lear* we find layers of use of this primary metaphor from Kent's exhortation to 'See better, Lear, and let me still remain / The true blank of thine eye' (*KL*, 1.1.155), to the blinding of Gloucester enacted before us as both literal event and metaphorical symbol, which leads him to see more clearly his relationship with his sons.

The language we share emanates from our visceral interactions with the world around us as we internalize physical sensations, abstracting them through metaphors into the imaginative reality of symbolism. *Power is up* is another primary metaphor evident throughout Shakespeare. Ask any group to make a still image with a royal leader and the leader immediately becomes apparent as they both take and are given status. As young children we internalize the understanding that those who have authority over us are taller, so that even when we have grown and powerful figures are no longer physically bigger, the symbolism of the metaphorical reality remains. Alongside this, we learn from our own bodies that we feel more powerful when we stand tall, shoulders back, than when we sit hunched over: the first position reflecting a confidence in not being hurt while the second protects our vital organs from harm. When Cassius describes Julius Caesar as bestriding the world like a colossus (*JC*, 1.2.134-136) the point about his power is viscerally understood by Brutus and by us. Activities that invite students to understand Shakespeare's language through physical movements and gestures tap into this innate ability to find meaning through conceptual metaphors. In summary, the embodied nature of theatre-based practice respects young people as living crucibles of intentions, perceptions and experiences, and asks them to bring their personal knowledge and feelings, engage their imaginations, use their social brains to negotiate meaning with those around them, and find analogies with Shakespeare's words.

Ensemble

In this section, we explore the history and pedagogic implications of the concept of ensemble as a core feature of theatre-based Shakespeare pedagogy. As well as discussing a specific intellectual and practical genesis of the concept from a 2005 to 2010 RSC-Warwick research partnership, this section will draw on the concept of ensemble as a 'bridging metaphor' between drama, theatre and performance-based pedagogy to explore how the broader history of theatre, arts and creative education has influenced theatre-based Shakespeare education approaches.

Ensemble Shakespeare via the RSC and Warwick University

From 2005 to 2010 the Creativity and Performance in Teaching and Learning (CAPITAL) Centre, a collaborative research and practice partnership funded by the large-scale New Labour higher education innovation programme Centres of Excellence in Teaching and Learning (CETL), ran between the University of Warwick and the RSC (University of Warwick 2021). This research-led exploration into the rich interconnections between the performative and the educational centred largely on the implications of 'ensemble' as a concept in both. Alongside outcomes such as collaborative university modules, workshops, research studies and performance projects, this work led to a range of publications discussing ensemble's potential within theatre-based Shakespeare education (Neelands 2009a, 2009b; Neelands and O'Hanlon 2011), as well as educational settings more broadly (Monk et al. 2011; Neary et al. 2014). In particular, work at the CAPITAL Centre catalysed the pedagogic and logistical development of the RSC's long term flagship educational partnership programme, the Learning and Performance, as Winston details in his book on the company's education work (2015). Largely coinciding with RSC Artistic Director Michael Boyd's tenure, in which he sought to rediscover what he saw as the collaborative ensemble-led genesis of the company, the work and output of the CAPITAL Centre became instrumental in popularizing the concept of 'ensemble approaches' as a core tenet of theatre-based teaching practice both within the RSC and beyond (Enciso et al. 2011; Pigkou-Repousi 2020).

At the 2004 Equity and Director's Guild conference, which focused on ensemble practices, the following definition of the term was given: 'Ensemble theatre occurs when a group of theatre artists (performers, artistic directors, stage management and the key administrative staff) work together over many years to create theatre' (2004: 3). This definition encompasses the collaborative and egalitarian process of theatre-making as a whole (though other working definitions of theatrical ensemble might also focus on plot and storytelling structures, with 'ensemble production' often referring to the lack of a single clear main character and the use of multiple intersecting plots). An ensemble can also refer, particularly in musical theatre contexts, to the chorus or general body of the cast beyond the principal players. There is across all of these understandings of the term, however, a recognition of theatre as a collective art form, whether as a specific element of the performance or in the overall process of theatrical production.

At the 2004 ensemble conference, Boyd discussed in his keynote speech his plans to return the RSC to founding director Peter Hall's commitment to ensemble theatre approaches. Hall, Boyd noted, had been heavily influenced by Brecht's Berliner Ensemble and Boyd himself acknowledged how he had been 'profoundly sheep-dipped' in European socialist ensemble theatre traditions during his time as a trainee under Soviet theatre director Anatoly Efros in Russia (Equity & Directors Guild of Great Britain 2004: 16). Building on this unequivocal aesthetic and political basis, Boyd posed the question: 'Can an ensemble . . . act in some sense as a . . . better version of the real world on an achievable scale which celebrates the virtues of collaboration?' (Equity & Directors Guild of Great Britain 2004: 17).

This was a question Neelands took up in his writing and research on ensemble approaches to teaching Shakespeare, exploring how the collaborative principles of a theatrical ensemble could translate to learning environments. Through this work, Neelands explores the implication of ensemble approaches in light of long-held notions of theatre as a socially transformative practice. He charts the origins of this in Ancient Greek Theatre, through Victorian notions of culture as redemptive and into twentieth-century political and social theatre movements (Neelands 2009b). Through these theatrical discourses and alongside similar constructivist and progressive educational principles outlined earlier in this chapter, Neelands emphasizes what he sees as the pro-social quality of ensemble-focused teaching, positioning active, rehearsal-room approaches to education as an opportunity for not only artistic but social development. That performative education approaches can be socially transformative is one of the central tenets of this area of practice (Finneran and Freebody 2016). Neelands, however, emphasizes that the pro-social potential of ensemble pedagogy is only an 'idealized abstraction' which he argues must be realized in the lived reality of classroom experience. For Neelands this requires the 'uncrowning' of the teacher and an aspiration at least, to distribute some power among the group (Neelands 2009: 183).

Alongside this sense of democratic value, there is also within theatre-based Shakespeare education writings a sense of ensemble approaches as holding a historical authenticity. Banks highlights elements of ensemble-focused theatre practices commonly attributed to the Early Modern period such as the use of cue sheets, where the practice of actors rehearsing from scripts containing only their own lines and short cue sentences is read as prompting actors' inter-reliance and active listening skills; and the company tradition, where troupes worked together over a period of years suggesting a theatrical art form characterized by performers' reflexive and collaborative engagement with the text (Banks 2014). As we explore further in the institutional and practitioner interviews of Part Two, these Early Modern rehearsal practices are presented within Banks' book alongside an appreciation of the Globe theatre as an egalitarian space, which invites active participation from its audiences via the shared light and circular space of the open-air venue (Banks 2014). To summarize, ensemble theatre practices can be understood as offering an aesthetic, democratic and historical grounding for theatre-based Shakespeare education work.

Ensemble as a bridging metaphor

Neelands refers to the concept of ensemble as a 'bridging metaphor', stating 'The ensemble serves as a bridging metaphor between the social and the artistic, between the informal uses of classroom drama and professional theatre' (Neelands 2009a: 182). Neelands cites this in part as a move to reconcile opposing viewpoints within the drama education community, with lines roughly drawn between proponents of drama education practitioner Dorothy Heathcote's process-led approaches to drama work, grounded in the notion of drama as a student-led tool for learning and social discovery (Bolton 1998); and David Hornbrook, who advocated for the primacy of school drama teaching as imparting training and knowledge of theatre as an artistic and professional form (Hornbrook 1998). It is worth noting that the cohesion of theatre-based Shakespeare work has suffered from the rift of this fracture; in practice drawing from both methodologies but in terms of scholarly and professional literature struggling to find an established home. Thus, the concept of the ensemble is offered as a shared touchstone, not just across the 'process drama' versus 'theatre as art' divide but also across educational, community, academic and theatrical scholarship and practice with Shakespeare's works. The ensemble, whether in the classroom, rehearsal room or lecture hall, is literally a community of practice, a group defined by not (only) their shared identity or location but their shared work of educational, artistic and cultural production. In Neelands's writings, he draws on the model of the Ancient Athenian polis, and the key role which theatre played in its civic processes (McGrath 2001; Neelands 2009a), charting a compelling narrative of theatrical performance as a crucible of democratic contestation and community, an engine of civic life. In much theatre-based Shakespeare literature, Shakespeare, with the texts' diverse characters, stories and linguistic complexity, is positioned as a rich and potent fuel for this engine, inviting explorations of how we want to live and relate to each other in the world. Neelands argues that acting within the performing arts and humanities allows students to develop the skills and resources to fully 'act' in public and civic life, drawing on Nussbaum's concept of 'narrative imagination': 'This means the ability to think what it might be like to be in the shoes of a person different to oneself, to be an intelligent reader of that person's story and to understand the emotions and wishes and desires that someone so placed might have' (2010: 95–6). This ToM associated concept of 'narrative imagination' and the analogous 'social imaginary' (Castoriadis 1997) point towards readings of theatre-based Shakespeare education as part of a public and civic theatre-making process (Etheridge Woodson 2015; Hickey-Moody 2013).

Yet, as Jennifer has explored elsewhere (Kitchen 2021, 2023) there are issues with this institutional model of the educational ensemble grounded in an Ancient Athenian model of democratic citizenship. As Neelands himself concedes, the Ancient Athenian polis was grounded in imperialistic and patriarchal principles; and held a limited membership in historical reality (Neelands 2009a: 186). Feminist pedagogic theory (Lambert and Parker 2006; Noddings 2013; Porter 1996; Segal 2017) offers a more 'care-led' model of ensemble-based active citizenship applicable to ensemble-led, theatre-based Shakespeare work, which veers away from monolithic institutional models of democracy and leans into more relational ones. Across the past few decades, applied and educational drama scholarship, always interested in the intersections between the educational, artistic, interpersonal and social and how critical social theory could chart these interconnections (Grady 2003), has increasingly taken a critical social 'turn', throwing a critical light on the long-held claims of individual, interpersonal and social benefits to the practices (Finneran and Freebody 2016; Freebody et al. 2018; Freebody and Finneran 2021; Hughes and Nicholson 2016; Snyder-Young 2013). Drawing on feminist principles of the radical political power of love, care and joy (hooks 2003; Segal 2017) drama education research has highlighted the power and potential of care-led teaching practice through performance art (Gallagher 2016; Gallagher et al. 2020; Thompson 2022). This holds implications for the application of ensemble principles within theatre-based Shakespeare practice, inviting us as it does to attend to the interpersonal and relational nature of classroom discourse; offering an alternative to the formalized, institutional relations mandated by much western schooling practice.

Ensemble as a metaphor for theatre-based teaching practice therefore does more than invite our exploration of the interpersonal and collaborative nature of Shakespearean texts, their original performance context and contemporary theatrical processes; it points towards exploration of the educational environment as civic, relational and care-informed. While we should be wary of making any firm transformational or transcendent claims of the ensemble-led environment, it does point towards the possibilities of creating a 'third space' (Etheridge Woodson 2015; Rodricks 2015; Thomson et al. 2012) where we can potentially begin to untether ourselves from some of the more restrictive and oppressive power relations of everyday life and institutions and engage our social brains in critical and care-led social imaginaries of how things might be otherwise. This concept of a third space can be seen reflected in Liam Semler's concept of 'ardenspaces'. Taking his cue from the experimental and transformative space of the Forest of Arden in *As You Like It*, Semler (2016) proposes the need for ardenspaces as opportunities for more creative, democratic engagement with Shakespeare away from the dominant systematization in formal education. Theatre-based ensemble pedagogy is therefore a practice for the creation of 'ardenspace'.

The effective teacher

Having discussed the pedagogical principles of theatre-based practice as underpinned by progressive and constructivist approaches, working through embodied cognition, and operating within a consciously and effectively care-led ensemble environment, this final section focuses on the teacher competencies that enable this work and maps them against the three principles of theatre-based practice identified in the introduction of working with prior knowledge, employing embodied approaches, and encouraging a dialogic and critically conscious cultural engagement.

Teaching as a practice

A great deal of education research has explored what good teaching means and much of it has found the pedagogical and social competencies of a teacher to be at least as important as their subject knowledge, and more important than structural factors such as facilities and materials. The 2000 Hay McBer report concludes: 'Respect for others underpins everything the effective teacher does' (2000: 1.3.7), while the 2016 OECD report *Teaching Excellence* recognizes the 'intangible qualities that are difficult to quantify' in how teachers work with their students (2016: 3) and asserts that the 'quality of education can never exceed the quality of teaching and teachers' (2016: 12). In his assessment of the value of effective teaching, Ken Robinson (2013) offers an analogy with Peter Brook's famous (1968) assertion that 'theatre' requires an actor to walk across an empty space and a spectator to watch. Where Brook argues that theatre happens in this human interaction, and that set, costume, props, lights are merely extras, sometimes enhancing, sometimes distracting, Robinson argues that classrooms, books, uniforms, smartboards are merely extras to the collaboration of teacher and students that creates learning. Effective teachers make teaching practice their own by adapting responsively to their students. They are 'reflective practitioners' (Schön 1983) or 'students of their own impact' (Hattie 2012: 17), who operate intuitively with awareness that they 'make thousands of decisions every day about the process of helping learners to learn' (Lucas and Spencer 2017: 11). Teaching is a highly skilled profession and effective teaching is an art that weaves professional attributes and pedagogical techniques into a personal and personalized practice. A core contention of this book is that personal adaptation is the difference between theatre-based *practice*: a reflective, constantly shifting and active process, and theatre-based *approaches*: a set of tools to use.

Dewey argued that the traditional transmissive approach of 'formation from without' must be balanced with the personal experiences of 'development from within', and that the art of teaching lies in managing this balance (1938: 17). Frances Dolan observes this dilemma from the perspective of the university Shakespeare seminar: 'Other teachers have sometimes shared with me their concern that allowing students to make connections to the present encourages relativism, a cavalier disregard for the otherness of the past, sloppiness. This is not an anxiety I've ever shared. I prefer chaos to silence any day and those often seem as if they're pretty much the alternatives' (2009: 194). The chaos versus silence Dolan suggests may well be recognized by teachers of literature as the alternatives of a drama versus desk-bound approach to the plays. Teachers often feel they have insufficient training to use theatre approaches with their students or are sceptical that such methods provide sufficient depth of analysis for examination requirements. They can feel that the silence of students apparently imbibing knowledge is preferable to the chaos of apparently unassessable and undisciplined discovery. However, what Lucas and Spencer have called 'a great shift taking place' (2017: 1) has seen an increase in recognition that learning is built through connections and that relativism need not be cavalier or chaotic but harnessed to develop the competencies needed to interact critically, creatively and progressively with inherited knowledge.

John Hattie's extensive and influential investigation of education research published in 2009 led to his concept of 'Visible Learning' (2012), a metaphor which captures his conclusions that metacognition is central to good pedagogy because 'achievement in schools is maximized when teachers see learning through the eyes of students, and when students see learning through the eyes of themselves as teachers' (2012: xii). This level of metacognition requires students to make connections between what they know, what they need to know, and awareness of how they make those connections. Building on the constructivist and cognitive concepts introduced earlier, Hattie explains: 'It is not the knowledge or ideas, but the learner's construction of the knowledge and ideas that is critical. Increases in student learning follow a reconceptualization as well as an acquisition of information' (2009: 37). The role of the effective teacher in this vision is to lead and activate a student's learning through a relationship of trust. Hattie argues that trust is built when students recognize a high level of competence and integrity in their teacher, alongside a personal regard and respect for themself as an individual. This trust is key to Neelands's ensemble concept of uncrowning discussed in the previous section and allows for feedback to nurture a growth mindset (Dweck 2006). Bruner puts this more strongly: 'Any system of education, any theory of pedagogy, any "grand national policy" that diminishes the school's role in nurturing its pupils' self-esteem fails at one of its primary functions' (1996: 38). A recent 'State of the Nation' report on young people's mental health and well-being finds a convincing correlation between young people's reported well-being and their happiness at school (DfE 2023). Part of a teacher's expertise is then in creating the climate of the best theatrical and care-led ensembles where vulnerability and risk-taking are celebrated so that students can be brave in voicing their thoughts and ideas, and in asking for help when they need it (Brown 2017).

Another of Hattie's findings is that 'succeeding at something that you thought was difficult is the surest way in which to enhance self-efficacy and self-concept as a learner' (2012: 52). This is where Shakespeare's reputation for difficulty can be an advantage, very often conferring a boost to students' confidence when they are able to feel ownership of his work through the understanding theatre-based practice can bring. It requires teachers to take risks in their encouragement of students to take risks (Irish 2011; Lucas and Spencer 2017) but in this way, learning becomes intrinsically worthwhile for the student rather than merely valuable for the extrinsic rewards gained from socially conforming and passing tests. A complex web of factors in and out of school affect a young person's self-esteem but the role of education should be in mitigating those factors as far as possible through effective collaboration at all levels to build productive communities of practice (Lave and Wenger 1991). Three qualities that most experts seem to agree are essential for effective teachers are being reliable, reflective and open.

Young people need the structure and support provided by reliable adults, they need teachers who continuously reflect on how to support them better, and they need to learn with leaders who are open and interested in them and the world around them. This is the basis of a constructivist pedagogy that engages with Shakespeare as a living artist and builds on the progressive principles that bell hooks describes as 'a profound, ongoing commitment to social justice' (2010: 14).

Emphasizing that today's teachers are preparing today's students for unknown tomorrows, Andreas Schleicher calls for education systems to 'do more than transmit educational content: they have to cultivate students' ability to be creative, think critically, solve problems and make decisions', in ways 'that help people to live and work together' (2016: 9). Creativity, both in the arts and as a cross-disciplinary competence, has been gaining increasing attention as a subject of educational research for the last two decades (Craft 2001; Adams and Owen 2017) and has recently become an aspect of the Programme for International Student Assessment (PISA) comparative studies. PISA's 'Creative Thinking Assessment' (OECD 2022) builds from a position that: 'Experts agree that engaging in creative thinking can also improve a range of other skills, including metacognitive, inter- and intra-personal, and problem-solving skills, as well as promoting identity development, academic achievement and career success' (Boix-Mansilla and Schliecher 2022: 6). Boix-Mansilla and Schliecher recognize these as the skills needed for young people to 'navigate through an increasingly complex, volatile and uncertain world' (Boix-Mansilla and Schliecher 2022). In summary, we recognize teaching as a skilled professional practice that builds a climate of trust and community, encourages creative criticality and requires continuous active reflection that is curious about and respectful of individuals.

The teacher/director parallel

As mentioned in the first section, the potential for using theatre-based practice to teach Shakespeare in schools is often identified with the analogy of a classroom as a rehearsal room. As with all analogies, the differences provoked are at least as interesting as the similarities. A major difference is that directors work with a cast, while teachers work with a class. The relationship between a professional director and actor is generally between adults and can assume a level of training and motivation. By contrast the relationship between a teacher and student entails inequality of age and experience and can include a wide spectrum of ability and motivation. In the classroom, therefore, theatre practice becomes 'theatre-based': it aims for the dialogic explorations and risk-taking of a good rehearsal room but must take account of what is possible and what best serves the students.

In their preparation, directors draw on knowledge of Shakespeare, whether of social historical context, performance history, narrative or rhetorical effects. They bring that knowledge to the company, first to frame an idea or a design and then to support actors to explore that concept and make their own choices. For a teacher, the concept equivalent would be a well-structured scheme of work, containing a line of enquiry with key questions or lenses that are narrow enough to provide focus for the time allocated but broad enough to allow exploration and interpretation. Perhaps this scheme of work culminates in an ensemble performance where students take on the roles of design, directing and acting. More commonly, it might employ many of the investigative processes of the rehearsal room but culminate in written tasks. An ensemble director or teacher allows and encourages questions about a text to emerge, but pragmatically time and resources require them to make choices about which questions to pursue. Part of their expertise is the leadership skill to make decisions, both ahead of the process in shaping the scheme of work/rehearsals, and responsively during that time to draw out the potential of their students/actors; always actively listening for the questions of most salience for each individual and the collective. A director monitors learning and provides feedback through 'notes' which are immediate formative feedback given in constructive dialogue. Monitoring what feels right in a rehearsal process can be compared to monitoring the quality of learning as it happens in the classroom. Hattie places a great deal of emphasis on the value of immediate, dialogic feedback for progress, in comparison with summative assessment which he regards mainly as justification for grading (2012: 127).

Perhaps most important for the effectiveness of both teacher and director is their ability to create a climate which builds curiosity, compassion and courage to explore identity, agency and purpose. Brook describes an ensemble ethos as 'the force that can counterbalance the fragmentation of our world' (1996: 66). This seems a worthy aim to pursue. He explains how 'deadly theatre' results from a 'deadly' director, who can create work that is admired and respected but is complacent, relying on 'old formulae, old methods, old jokes, old effects' (1968: 44). The 'deadly director' and the 'deadly teacher' both know how to get the job done but there is wasted potential in the lack of personalized challenge for the actors/students. Brook observes how the busyness of theatre 'trundles on' so that 'we are too busy to ask the only vital question which measures the whole structure. Why theatre at all? What for?' (1968: 44). Under constant change and pressure, the busyness of school also trundles on, with barely time for teachers to ask 'Why education at all? What for?' Directors and teachers need to keep asking these questions, restlessly chasing a sense of theatrical and pedagogical quality as cultures turn and shift. The answer to the questions: 'Why Shakespeare at all? What for?' shifts with them. The parallel between a teacher and director of Shakespeare we propose is then primarily in *how* they lead their students/actors on a journey of discovery: shaping the constraints of that journey while encouraging both individual connections and collectively understood meanings to emerge.

The competencies of an effective teacher of theatre-based Shakespeare

The three competencies we propose as those exemplified by effective teachers of theatre-based Shakespeare are informed by Boix-Mansilla and Schleicher's forms of expertise required for educators of global competence (2022: 73–6); Hattie's five dimensions of an expert teacher (2012: 26–7); and Lucas and Spencer's four-step process to cultivating creative capabilities (2017: 9–14). Our competencies relate specifically to our three key principles that theatre-based practice should: (1) invite prior knowledge, ideas and values to bear on a shared experience of understanding a literary text; (2) combine intellectual, social and emotional learning through embodying the text; (3) develop criticality in questioning a cultural inheritance and how that canon can in turn raise questions about today's world.

> *Understand students as individuals within a social learning ecosystem*: Our shorthand for this is *ensemble*. This means being curious about each of your students and the unique model of the world they bring: acknowledging their backgrounds and their skills; inviting into the classroom their interests, knowledge and lived experiences; and encouraging them to be curious in the same way about each other. It means creating a classroom climate that helps them feel comfortable to take risks, connect new learning to old and build bridges to broader cultural interests.
>
> *Continuously develop pedagogical practice*: This means understanding learning as a social process that involves emotions and intellect, mind and body, heart and head. It means continuous reflection on how to facilitate better learning for your students, being interested in developments in education research, and cultivating informed but not rigid opinions about why and how we should teach Shakespeare. It means being consciously aware of the perspectives and values you bring into the room in how you respond to your students in each moment.
>
> *Create conditions for creative and critical interaction with received knowledge*: This means treating Shakespeare as a living artist to talk back to, whose work is a moral playground where we can explore complex issues, conflicting views and diverse experiences. It means seeing language as a means of communication rather than an expression of fixed ideas, and Shakespeare's words as a resource to playfully explore how language works. It means teaching students to listen actively and encouraging them to find confidence in their own voice.

2

The cultural value question

This chapter explores questions of Shakespearean cultural value and how this applies to classroom contexts, referencing contemporary debates of Shakespeare's cultural positionality and questions of culture's definitions and functions within education. In the previous chapter, we explored the underlying pedagogic theories and implications of theatre-based Shakespeare education practice. There we focused largely on 'Shakespeare' as a body of theatrical and poetic works. However, the teaching and learning of Shakespeare is typically considered in much broader and significant cultural terms than a working knowledge of the plots, characters, themes and theatrical and literary techniques of a group of plays and poems from an Early Modern writer. 'Shakespeare' as a social and cultural construct, beyond 'Shakespeare' the man or 'Shakespeare' the textual canon, carries an arguably unparalleled cultural weight. It is important to note there is a broad and ongoing area of scholarship and discussion on this topic (Olive 2015; Rumbold 2008, 2011; Rumbold and McLuskie 2014; Shellard and Keenan 2016). In particular there has been an acceleration in cultural value debates within the early twenty-first-century UK context, driven by questions of funding and policy over arts, cultural and education policy (Belfiore 2011, 2012; Rumbold 2008) and a range of major policy drives and reports to explore the implications of arts, culture and creativity for both education and society (Robinson et al. 1999; Fleming 2010; Thomson et al. 2012, 2015; Neelands et al. 2015; Bull et al. 2017; Cultural Learning Alliance 2017). While this chapter draws on the research, policy and practice of this area of scholarship, it cannot be comprehensive in scope but will instead focus on discussions of Shakespearean cultural value as they relate to schools and education. Specifically, we explore four different and interconnecting frameworks of cultural value – cultural literacy, cultural capital, cultural democracy and intercultural democracy – and how they are leveraged in Shakespeare education contexts.

Cultural literacy

In 2019, the UK school-inspecting body Ofsted announced they would be looking in their visits for how a school's curriculum contributes to learners' acquisition of *cultural capital*, a term they define as 'The essential knowledge that pupils need to be educated citizens, introducing them to the best that has been thought and said and helping to engender an appreciation of human creativity and achievement' (DfE 2019). This statement builds on the well-established and continuing discourse of the Conservative government's education policy, summed up by Michael Gove's 2013 statement that 'The accumulation of cultural capital – the acquisition of knowledge – is the key to social mobility'. This acquisitional approach to cultural knowledge and experiences currently remains central to UK educational policy following the Conservative party's regain of power via the coalition government of 2010. In the following section, we explore the original definition of cultural capital and posit the UK government's current policy is more directly informed by the notion of cultural *literacy*. We then unpick the use (and misuse) of this concept within current education policy and its implications for the teaching and learning of Shakespeare through theatre-based practice, in more detail.

One key issue, as much news and professional media has identified, is that in Ofsted's definition, and in other UK DfE documents, there is a fundamental misunderstanding of the meaning of 'cultural capital' as a working concept (Enser 2019; Mansell 2019). In the simplest terms: 'cultural capital' is a term coined by sociologist Pierre Bourdieu to describe the non-economic capital which ruling elites valorize and reproduce in order to maintain the social status quo. The concept closest to what Ofsted describes is actually 'cultural *literacy*', a term coined by educational scholar E. D. Hirsch, whose work became wildly influential in 2010's UK education policy (Hirsch 1983; Eaglestone 2021; Hodgson and Harris 2022). This distinction is important and worth exploring in detail because the two terms, and the theoretical perspectives associated with them, suggest very different understandings of the value and social mechanisms of cultural experience and cultural knowledge. Because of this, they offer very different positions on the cultural nature and cultural value of Shakespeare within education. In this section, therefore, we begin by focusing on the concept closest to Ofsted and the Department for Education's intended meaning: cultural literacy.

'Cultural literacy' was a term popularized by Hirsch in a 1983 *American Scholar* paper and 1987 book *Cultural Literacy: What Every American Needs to Know*. The education research, policy and teaching resources developed from this original concept are now collated under the US-based Core Knowledge Foundation (2022) which gives its stated aim as working towards 'educational excellence and equity built on strong foundations of shared knowledge'. It is a term which has prompted much debate and polarization within the educational world, so it is worth returning to

Hirsch's original arguments to explore it further. In 1983, Hirsch presents the issue of falling literacy rates within US education. He identifies the problem as a lack of shared cultural knowledge upon which to ground the technical literacy skills of reading, writing and comprehension. The chief cause of this problem, he suggests, is the increasing move towards a 'formalist' or skills-based literacy curriculum, which concerns itself solely with technical issues of instructional approach and leaves choices of literary and cultural *content* to individual teachers and school communities, in the name of pluralism and inclusion. Hirsch argues against this 'technocratic' approach to literacy education, as he sees it, stating: 'A rich vocabulary is not a purely technical or rote-learnable skill. Knowledge of words is an adjunct to knowledge of cultural realities signified by words, and to whole domains of experience to which words refer' (1983: 160)

Hirsch's proposed solution to this problem is to rearticulate, explicitly within a curriculum, a set of canonical texts and knowledge which will allow learners to effectively develop 'the translinguistic knowledge on which linguistic literacy depends' (1983: 165) or, as a recent *Times Educational Supplement* article describes it, holding a higher level of 'Cultural literacy means that the things we encounter simply make more sense' (Enser 2019). This line of argument reads as a purely pragmatic one. Hirsch, however, argues firmly within this paper that the very aim of popular literacy is a deeply political position and that the development of a cultural literacy canon could only take place in a 'political arena'. Moreover, there is a parallel thread through his proposition of a cultural literacy canon beyond simply providing a shared cultural basis for technical literacy skills. He argues it is essential for the development of a cohesive democratic citizenship: 'Without appropriate, tacitly shared background knowledge, people cannot understand newspapers. A certain extent of shared, canonical knowledge is inherently necessary to a literate democracy' (Enser 2019: 165).

In fact, Hirsch argues, the creation of a cohesive and specific national civic culture has always been part of the mission statement of US education. It is worth pausing at this point to acknowledge how much of this line of argument can be said to run roughly in parallel with many of the pro-social claims of active and inclusive Shakespeare education, that cultural education not only enhances learners' individual educational outcomes but contributes to a functioning civic society. However, there is a further element to this second, civic strand of Hirsch's cultural literacy, which accounts for much of its critique and controversy, for Hirsch goes on to posit explicitly that an overly pluralistic national culture threatens the project of a cohesive national identity and functioning civic society: 'American culture, always large and heterogeneous, and increasingly lacking a common acculturative curriculum, is perhaps getting fragmented enough to lose its coherence as a culture' (1983: 167).

This fear of American culture and curriculum becoming fragmented and incoherent due to overly 'diverse cultural influences' thus treats diversity as a challenge to both education progress and national identity. Hirsch is shockingly unequivocal about this within the article. For him a permissive, pluralistic approach to curricular cultural influences is a threat of such weight that decisive action is needed. He directly acknowledges and fully accepts the then-imagined accusations of his detractors that a pre-determined cultural canon 'is nothing but cultural imperialism (true), which submerges cultural identities (true) and gives minority children a sense of inferiority (often true)' (Hirsch 1983: 161). From this unequivocal statement we can only take that Hirsch sees a furthering of cultural imperialism and submersion of 'minority' cultural identities as necessary to combat poor educational outcomes and national cultural incoherence. Unsurprisingly, this is where many in educational and cultural contexts part company with Hirsch and take sharp exception to cultural literacy as a theory and practical proposition.

Hirsch's own admission of the concept's oppressive cultural imperialism is so bare-faced we will leave aside further development of this critique within this book and point towards where other scholars have undertaken this more detailed work elsewhere (Gray 1988; Eaglestone 2021). For our purposes, we want to pull back to the implications of the popularization of cultural literacy approaches within western educational policy and consider its specific implications for Shakespeare education.

As stated in the opening of this chapter, the recent UK education policy concern with cultural education can be seen as within the tradition of cultural *literacy* because it focuses on an acquisition-based understanding of culture for civic coherence in its definition of 'the essential knowledge that pupils need to be educated citizens'. The further mention of 'the best that has been thought and said', as we discussed within the introduction, is a direct citation of Victorian cultural commentator Matthew Arnold. As we explored there, what is often missed within references to Arnold's famous essay is the emphasis on 'turning a stream of fresh and free thought upon our stock notions and habits'. The 'best that has been thought and said' was never intended to be a static definition but allowed, in theory at least, for its growth and change through 'fresh and free thought'. Similarly, alongside his unequivocal cultural imperialism, Hirsch is clear that a cultural literacy canon should never be universalistic or static but specific to its national context and open to inevitable change and development over time.

This is where we can most directly consider the implications for Shakespeare education within all of this. On the one hand, if we are looking for a model of cultural education which firmly cements Shakespeare within it, cultural literacy is a viable option. Taking up its thread of the 'translinguistic knowledge on which literacy depends', the linguistic and literary legacy of Shakespeare's texts are so fundamental to our use and understanding of spoken and written English they would win a lifetime's place on any curricular canon concerned with English literacy. Yet where is the scope for engagement in the work's living artistry within this? Shakespeare as a lodestone of canonical knowledge implies something inert and foundational that cannot be disturbed. This becomes particularly problematic when the racialized (Dadabhoy and Mehdizadeh 2023) and gendered (Williams 2018) language within the plays is left unexamined and positioned as foundational to a shared cultural inheritance.

Coles and Pitfield utilize Evan's (1989) term 'incrustation' in reference to this issue: 'the sense in which Shakespeare becomes weighted down by socio-cultural layers of signification'. They reflect: 'One of our ongoing concerns is whether active Shakespeare pedagogies sufficiently acknowledge "Shakespeare" as a complex cultural sign, one that represents a site of struggle, even alienation, for many young people' (Coles and Pitfield 2022: 34). This is a concern we recognize, and argue for this reason that the model of cultural literacy does not offer enough scope for exploring the complexities and potential alienations of Shakespeare as both text and a cultural signifier in diverse contexts to be a fruitful theoretical basis for constructivist and progressive theatre-based practice. To frame Shakespeare's value within a cultural literacy perspective foreshortens both the possibilities for dynamic engagement with the texts as living artistry and as sites of inclusive and pluralistic cultural discovery.

The framework of cultural literacy, its enduring popularity within twenty-first-century educational policy and practice, however, should give us critical pause: to what extent do we as teachers and practitioners rely on the assumption that Shakespeare is an 'implicit' and 'automatic' part of cultural education? How often do we directly consider what ideas, identities, traditions and people are either excluded or required to assimilate under the mission for a cohesive national civic identity? While this book and the practice of theatre-based Shakespeare education cannot answer those questions definitively, we suggest they are important ones to hold and interrogate as we go forward.

Cultural capital

As we touched on in the opening of this chapter, cultural capital is a much-referenced and much-misunderstood concept within educational and arts policy and practice. Bourdieu (1986) coined the term to define the process by which the ruling elite leverage and naturalize a particular set of cultural and aesthetic values in order to maintain and consolidate its power. It is, at its core, a Marxist critique of social power, extending his analysis of the centrality and functionality of capital into non-economic forms. Bourdieu did not identify cultural capital so educators could seek to maximize it for their learners but in order to recognize and deconstruct its social power and to begin to release learners from its tyranny.

The most common misreading of this critical theoretical model is to take it as purely descriptive: that the accretion of cultural capital allows for personal development and increased social opportunities. Ergo, building not unreasonably on this descriptive premise, a core aim of educational, artistic and cultural institutions should be to ensure all citizens, particularly the young, and particularly those without existing easy access to these institutions and experiences, gain that access, in order to generate as much cultural capital as possible and thus maximize their life chances. As discussed in the previous section, this interpretation of cultural capital is actually much closer to the concept of cultural literacy: that personal flourishing and active citizenship within a cohesive nation state is maximized when individuals amass knowledge of a clearly defined cultural canon. So why is this misreading an issue, and what is its relevance for our focus on the purpose and possibilities of theatre-based Shakespeare education? First, as discussed earlier, cultural literacy as a concept is explicitly exclusionary and culturally conservative. It is built on an assumption of a cultural deficit, that is, some learners are deficient in cultural knowledge, skills and experience. As many cultural and educational commentators have observed, this dismisses and devalues alternative and diverse forms of cultural experience and knowledge, and can alienate many young people entering western schooling from marginalized and racialized communities (Blackledge 2009; Yosso 2005). Educational commentators have argued against the 'closing the gap' policy discourses of cultural experience which arise from this deficit model of cultural value (Times Educational Supplement 2019). Inevitably, Shakespeare as a cultural signifier becomes co-opted into this deficit model. As Coles and Pitfield explain: 'Underpinning much of the debate about the curricular value of Shakespeare runs a discourse of deficit, particularly in relation to learners' cultural lives outside school. In effect, this rests on assumptions that the majority of young people lead culturally impoverished lives and that a canon-rich curriculum will serve to compensate for this (2022: 33).

Research has explored the impacts of this deficit narrative within Shakespeare education and youth community work, highlighting the oppressive outcomes for racialized young people in particular (Thomas 2017; Barnes 2020; Dadabhoy and Mehdizadeh 2023). The rhetoric of Shakespearean cultural encounters as 'transformational' over-ascribes agency to the texts and minimizes the active (inter)cultural interpretation undertaken in youth and educational work with Shakespeare.

Despite the significant issues with a normative, 'deficit' reading of cultural capital as a concept, the facts on youth access to many cultural institutions and experiences are stark (Neelands et al. 2015). Evidence from the Cultural Learning Alliance in the UK for example demonstrates a 61 per cent drop in students taking 'performing and expressive arts' at GCSE between 2010 and 2019 (Cultural Learning Alliance 2019). In the wake of successive unfavourable funding and economic conditions, from the

2008 economic crash through Brexit and the financial impacts of Covid-19, many creative and cultural educational experiences and programmes have suffered, reduced or stopped completely (Walmsley et al. 2022). In light of this, to mourn these losses and fight their impact in order to secure increased opportunity and access to cultural experiences and institutions is instinctive for many educators. 'Cultural capital' as a descriptive unit of analysis therefore offers a tempting metric to measure these processes of loss and gain.

Yet retaining a Bordieuan understanding of cultural capital as a socially critical concept – one that defines the current mechanisms of cultural control, rather than a descriptive guide for cultural liberation – helps retain a sense of reflexive balance between the impetus to provide increased and egalitarian 'access to' Shakespearean cultural education and a recognition of the alienating cultural discourses 'incrustated' around and within these texts. Theatre-based education practice through its embodied, discursive and explorative approaches offers a rich framework for recognizing and navigating this balance and invites a focus on facilitating engagement with author/ity for learners (Cheng and Winston 2011; O'Connor 2014; Winston and Strand 2013; Dyches 2018; Dernikos 2020). The progressive and constructivist pedagogic grounding of theatre-based practice, as we explored in Chapter 1, primes us as teachers to prioritize the identities, experiences and knowledges in the room and draw on this as a starting point for encounters with Shakespeare. This is not to claim the opportunities of that priming are always fully taken up, as Neelands has it: drama 'by itself does nothing' (2009a: 13). This is where critical social models such as Bourdieu's cultural capital can prompt more nuanced and inclusive grapplings with the paradoxes and challenges inherent to a Shakespeare education practice that aims to develop criticality towards questions of what constitutes cultural value.

Cultural and intercultural democracy

If cultural capital as a critical theory can help identify the exclusionary power dynamics incrustated within canonical texts such as Shakespeare, cultural democracy is a concept which can offer a more egalitarian and diverse model of cultural value and cultural production. Cultural democracy has, from the late twentieth century onwards, been proposed as a more actively diverse vision of cultural production. Often contrasted with the notion of 'democratising culture', which is the aim to increase access and appreciation of *existing* 'elite' cultural forms, cultural democracy proposes a radical revaluing of *all* citizens' diverse and 'everyday' cultural production and creativity (Evrard 1997). As David Micklem, co-founder of arts participation charity 64 Million Artists frames it, cultural democracy is defined by moving from the consumer model of democratizing culture –

concerned with increasing the access and consumption of centralized pillars of cultural value – to a citizenship model, which is focused on a grassroots valuing of existing, diverse processes of cultural production (Micklem 2019).

As Kuttner has observed, the proposition of cultural citizenship: 'the right and capacity of people to develop and pass on diverse cultural traditions and identities while participating effectively in a shared cultural and political arena' (2015: 70) has increasingly been a focus for cultural scholars across the past thirty years. By enshrining the right to develop diverse cultural traditions and refusing to see this as incompatible with a 'shared cultural and political arena' this networked and quintessentially plural model of cultural value offers an alternative to the deficit frameworks of cultural literacy and reductive, acquisitive understandings of cultural capital. There are also clear resonances here with the constructivist and progressive pedagogic frameworks of theatre-based education practice: a shared engagement with Shakespeare, particularly through the embodied, contextualized work of performance, is not incompatible with equally valuing and making space for other aesthetic and cultural traditions. This is a model with the potential to reposition Shakespeare from a centralized cultural monolith more towards a 'living artist', in networked conversation with a range of parallel cultural texts and activities.

Calls have been made for remodelling cultural policy and practice around a cultural democracy framework. The 2017 King's College Report *Towards Cultural Democracy* made this case, laying out the argument that 'it is only when "substantive freedom" is realised in relation to culture – real, concrete freedoms to choose what culture to make, as well as what culture to appreciate – that people are genuinely empowered in their cultural lives' (Bull et al. 2017: 5) The King's report frames this within an ecological understanding of culture, highlighting as key findings of their eighteen-month research process that 'beyond the professional arts . . . there are many versions of culture being created together around the UK – often in ways that go unnoticed'. And that therefore, 'Recognising the full diversity of *cultural creativity* in society – and its ecological nature – is an essential step' for democratic legitimacy in cultural policy (Bull et al. 2017: 4).

Yet, despite this invocation of an interconnected cultural ecology model, there are two key issues with the aim and conceptualization of cultural democracy as presented here, when considering its implications for inclusive theatre-based Shakespeare education. First, throughout the report, the proposed ecology is often given a tellingly binary shorthand, for example 'world class arts'/'diverse everyday creativity'; 'the creative industries'/'everyday participation' or even 'old things'/'new things'. This, in practice, retains much of a 'two-tier' model, despite citing the progressive concept of cultural capabilities (Sen 2006; Nussbaum 2010) and expressly rejecting the principles of a deficit cultural model. Second, this de facto two-tier model, presented in these anodyne terms (old things/new things), avoids reckoning with the cultural weight these 'old things' can carry and neutralizes the precise imperialist, misogynistic nature of much of that cultural weight; to take just one example, the fact that as of 2021, 88 per cent of artists in the UK National Portrait Gallery were men (Brown 2021). We would argue that any grassroots-focused policy to increase and diversify cultural production needs to fully acknowledge the scale, nature and history of the current cultural imbalances, and offer a framework for directly reckoning with that history. Otherwise, any institutional or political drives for more 'diverse' and 'everyday' cultural production are unlikely to engender substantive change.

Jennifer has written on this issue within a Shakespeare education context via the concept of domestication (Kitchen 2015), exploring the tendency for the more radical and critical social justice elements with theatre-based and pro-social Shakespeare education practice to undergo a similar neutralization process when applied within mainstream western educational contexts. This was observed in a 2010 evaluation of the RSC's Learning and Performance Network (LPN) programme, which noted that between the 'hub' schools, who worked more directly with the RSC, and 'cluster' schools who worked more with their respective hub, that while finite outcomes of involvement with the LPN such as knowledge of Shakespeare plots and vocabulary, and performance skills, continued to be valued, what faded was a commitment to the pro-social value of Shakespeare (Thomson et al. 2010: 26). Furthermore, the sense of the rehearsal text as something actively and collaboratively interpreted over time was more limited or absent in some cluster schools (Thomson et al. 2010: 22–6). As Coles and Pitfield have argued, based on their analysis of discussions in UK secondary English classrooms, the normative cultural weight of Shakespeare's exceptionalism poses a significant challenge for teachers to create genuine space within the mainstream western classroom to acknowledge, critique and challenge this. 'That students are rarely provided with formal curriculum space to unpick the way canonical texts relate to their personal histories and beliefs means that the curriculum is likely to remain disconnected from students' lives, the point of it never made clear' (2022: 40).

For these reasons, we would argue that cultural democracy as a model for Shakespearean cultural value poses rich potential for Shakespeare's work to be treated with less cultural reverence, and more as a 'living' art within a networked cultural ecology in which there is more space for multiple and previously marginalized cultural voices and forms. However, what some interpretations of cultural democracy have missed is a substantial focus on or explanation for *how* culturally democratic approaches are to address the 'incrustation' of canonical cultural signifiers such as Shakespeare, or account for what the creative and practical interface between a more diverse field of cultural production and existing cultural monoliths, such as Shakespeare and the attendant Shakespearean cultural industry, might look like. In order to explore this in more detail we turn now to the concept of interculturalism.

'Interculturalism' as a concept has, broadly speaking, grown in response to the early twenty-first-century argument that 'multiculturalism', the 'melting pot' society to which Hirsch makes critical reference, is deemed to have failed as a model of social and cultural policymaking in the western world (Cantle 2012; Torres and Tarozzi 2020). Interculturalism has therefore been offered as an alternative model of relations, suggesting this can fulfil the need for responding positively to the demands of globalization and offer models of how to function as international citizens on a global scale (Cantle 2012). Broadly defined, interculturalism can be seen as an approach to social and educational policy that focuses on the dynamics and mediations of integration via new, more international models of citizenship (Torres and Tarozzi 2020). Without having the space to unpick these policy and scholarship discourses in detail, and recognizing interculturalism as a 'sliding signifier' (Torres and Tarozzi 2020), we nevertheless offer the term here as a guiding concept by which educators can seek to prepare learners for 'a world in which they will work and live among people of diverse cultural origins who hold different ideas, perspectives and values; a world where trust will have to bridge those differences; and a world in which their lives will be affected by issues that transcend national boundaries' (Schleicher 2016: 16). In short, interculturalism, we suggest here, offers a framework to conceptualize the cultural interfaces, explorations and discourses which a cultural democracy approach hopes to achieve by fostering a more diverse field of cultural production.

Shakespeare education, particularly the embodied and discursive nature of theatre-based teaching practice, has often been aligned with notions of intercultural learning and encounters (Cheng and Winston 2011; Yandell and Brady 2016; Yandell et al. 2020; Kitchen 2022). Duncan Lees has explored the shared implications of theatre-based and intercultural practices of teaching Shakespeare in English as Additional Language (EAL) teaching contexts (Lees 2021, 2022). As Lees argues, the embodied, active nature of theatre-based practice 'is also inherently intercultural, as processes of (de)familiarization and mediation encourages learners to reflect more deeply on their linguistic and cultural assumptions and identities' (Lees 2022: 131). For Lees, much of the value of Shakespeare's texts' is not in their canonical centrality, but in their unabashed 'strangeness' (Blank 2014) arguing an intercultural, theatre-based approach foregrounds the processes of defamiliarization and embodied exploration possible for learners with these 'strange' texts.

Interculturalism and the resulting intercultural dialogue therefore require an interest in what happens in the progressive spaces between our intersecting and constantly evolving cultures, constructed as they are through time, space, race, gender and class (Cantle 2012). This perspective on cultural value and cultural relations, we argue, reaches substantively further than models of cultural democracy in that it provides a framework to imagine the interface by which diverse and emerging cultural forms speak *to* and *through* existing pillars of cultural canon. This gives shape and weight to the ecological, networked models of cultural discourse imagined within cultural democracy as laid out within the King's report (2017).

What, therefore, are the implications of a theatre-based Shakespeare practice driven by a focus on a discursive intercultural production of cultural value? Kate Flaherty deftly draws our attention to the resonances between developments in Shakespearean scholarship and Shakespearean pedagogy both driven by a 'performance turn'. Drawing on Sonia Massai's (2005) model of 'Shakespeare as a permeable field of production whose share and possibilities are constantly organised through the agency of "new entrants"' (2013: 75) Flaherty emphasizes how local and diverse engagements and interpretations with Shakespeare are: 'Not just distant iterations of the real subject of scholarly attention but are, much more compellingly, by their very locality, constitutive of the dynamic cultural field called "Shakespeare"' (2013: 75). This offers an intercultural model of Shakespeare education, scholarship and performance whereby, unlike cultural literacy and descriptive cultural value models 'Shakespeare' is not established as an unshakable foundational pillar of meaning-making to be protected and appreciated by learners inherently deficit by contrast but as a shifting, dynamic and at times problematic global cultural touchstone. As Flaherty states, this holds implications for our view on not only Shakespearean cultural value but the actors and processes of Shakespearean cultural production.

As we have mentioned, within Shakespearean scholarship, education is often seen as a marginalized area of study and practice, and even this is framed by the frequent assumption that 'education' refers exclusively to higher education. Education in school contexts, and especially theatre-based education, is often ignored or dismissed. When it does become the focus of discussion, there is sometimes the implication that something reductive and faintly distasteful is happening (Wilson 1997; McLuskie 2009), as when Schupak comments in relation to classroom editing of the plays 'of course, one winces at the very thought that any of Shakespeare's texts could be subject to such cavalier treatment' (2018: 173). Flaherty's intercultural community of cultural production offers a radically alternative framework in which we can see every classroom and youth encounter with Shakespeare as directly constitutive of 'Shakespeare' as a field of creative, scholarly and cultural production.

This claim might be read as well-meaning cultural relativism, a disingenuous refusal to acknowledge the bodies of expertise which have grown around Shakespeare's work across hundreds of years. A discursive, intercultural model of Shakespeare's cultural value, however, one that is genuinely informed by the progressive and constructivist principles that knowledge and meaning are generated by the combination of experiences and identities within the room, points us to cultural relativism as a critical and progressive site of exploration. Educational scholarship has termed this a 'student as producer' model (Neary and Winn 2009; Neary 2019) in which learners are seen as emerging members of an evolving community of practice, immediately co-producing intellectual work alongside more established members through enquiry-led, constructivist and collaborative pedagogies. This unequivocally points towards the egalitarian potential of theatre-based Shakespeare, a pedagogic practice which – just as it positions Shakespeare as just one representation of living art in a networked field of cultural production – also positions its teachers and learners squarely within a broader network of cultural production; a network which prioritizes enacted meaning-making over static, stale or centralized claims to cultural capital. While drawing on a pluralistic cultural democracy model of cultural value, the focus here on intercultural exchange granularizes both the opportunities and challenges of actively and discursively grappling with Shakespeare's incrustation within this more egalitarian model.

This framework of Shakespearean cultural value and cultural production, which is inclusive of critical, global reworkings of the texts in the broadest sense (Dyches 2018; Stornaiuolo and Thomas 2018; Hartley et al. 2021; Julian and Solga 2021), is also increasingly being recognized in literary and higher education Shakespeare scholarship: 'Our knowledge changes constantly. We don't just transmit a stable body of knowledge, because it doesn't exist. We constantly remake it and we do so in a collaborative way' (Dolan 2009: 189).

This is, in short, a model for educational practice which begins by establishing on behalf of learners a valued space and voice through which to engage both with Shakespeare and with our world *through* Shakespeare. It has been our experience as theatre-based Shakespeare practitioners in a variety of international contexts, as we will continue to argue throughout this book, that working through a model of intercultural democracy provides a pedagogic framework for contending with both the oppressive incrustation of his texts as cultural signifiers and the sometimes challenging or alienating narratives of the historical texts themselves; and moreover using this conscious exploration as a catalyst for contextualized and contemporary questions of literature, arts, culture and identity. It is by prioritising intercultural exchange within our theatre-based classrooms and by genuinely working on the principle that the people in the room with us have just as much author/ity, in Povey et al.'s use of the term, to interpret Shakespearean texts as any celebrated scholar or creative practitioner that we have best been able to realize our third principle of theatre-based practice: to develop a criticality in questioning our 'cultural inheritance' and how that canon can in turn raise questions about today's world.

In the following, and final, section of this chapter, we turn from critical explorations of cultural value models to a closer exploration of how they have played out in educational policy and practice.

Shakespeare as an icon of literary heritage

Shakespeare's pre-eminence is usually attributed to his exceptionalism with his name frequently seen as connoting 'genius' regardless of any familiarity with his work. Bate goes so far as to suggest, 'the opinion that Shakespeare was a genius is as close to fact as we are ever likely to get in aesthetics' (1997: 157). Alongside this, as discussed earlier, 'Shakespeare' has become a social and cultural construct and that makes it hard to disentangle the quality of his work from the myriad cultural influences on how we view him. Although Shakespeare's exceptionalism is an outcome of probability: a serendipitous confluence of one individual's unique skills, talents and experiences colliding with a host of other intersecting factors, his standing as an icon of literary heritage is so widely accepted that it can be useful to consider how that standing came about.

The debate around Shakespeare's value in our education systems has paralleled the growth of literature as a subject for study. Since the eighteenth century, material knowledge of Shakespeare has been viewed as a marker of educational quality. As the popularity of literary anthologies grew, so did Shakespeare's presence in them. By 1814, Jane Austen tellingly has Edmund Bertam in *Mansfield Park* declare, 'His celebrated passages are quoted by everybody: they are in half the books we open and we all talk Shakespeare, use his similes, and describe with his descriptions' (Austen 1814: 259). While Bertram represents a certain stratum of society, Andrew Murphy offers evidence that for working-class families able to access education from the growing Sunday School movement, 'quotations from Shakespeare become a standard element of the reading books' (Murphy 2008: 30–5). As the demand for a more literate population followed the growth of industry in Victorian Britain, Shakespeare's inclusion in anthologies and adaptations also continued to grow (Bottoms 2013). The value of studying literature became about the cultural capital of familiarity with those works selected as worthy and the ability to competently read aloud from them.

Victorian educators also, however, seem to have assumed that simply by reading Shakespeare and other suitable authors, young people would imbibe appropriate attitudes and good behaviour. Mathew Arnold, he who ensured Shakespeare's reputation as foremost among 'the best that has been thought and written', described how 'in all but the rudest natures', readers would 'be insensibly nourished' by their reading and 'their taste will be formed by it' (1863, cited in Shuman 2000: 58). Peter Barry summarizes these early values for teaching literature as 'a distinctly Victorian mixture of class guilt about social inequality, a genuine desire to improve things for everybody, a kind of missionary zeal to spread culture and enlightenment, and a self-interested desire to maintain social stability' (2002: 14). It is interesting to reflect on the connections here with the cultural literacy/capital confusion explored earlier, where a modern class guilt continues to believe that equality results from social mobility when less advantaged children learn the core knowledge that allows them to 'share' the intellectual currency of the more privileged classes.

As compulsory education grew during the twentieth century, Shakespeare's privileged place as the foremost icon of literary heritage did not waver, but confidence in his accessibility for young people of any background and ability did. In his homeland, he was mainly studied only by a select few, until restored to a central role by the National Curriculum in 1989. That newly prescribed Shakespeare, however, meant prescribed tests and late twentieth/early twenty-first-century battles over how Shakespeare was to be taught and tested replaced questions of whether he should be taught at all. The current state of play in England is a requirement for sixteen-year-olds to have studied at least two Shakespeare plays and to have been 'taught to . . . read and appreciate the depth and power of the English literary heritage', with that 'appreciation' being measured through external examinations. Being taught to appreciate Shakespeare as the only mandatory author echoes cultural literacy mandates of a 'right way' to respond to the 'right kind' of literature. Back in 1887, Edward Freeman, professor of history, anticipated the continuing tensions around testing responses to literature when he objected to the establishment of English as a subject at Oxford: 'We are told that the study of literature "cultivates the taste, educates the sympathies and enlarges the mind". These are all excellent things, only we cannot examine tastes and sympathies. Examiners must have technical and positive information to examine' (cited in Barry 2002: 14). As Tracy has written elsewhere (Irish 2016), the current value of Shakespeare in our classrooms seems muddled when we expect his work to teach our young people universal values, develop them culturally, emotionally, intellectually, socially and spiritually, and reduce their responses to what can be coded in marking an essay or written examination; particularly in light of the increasing capabilities of AI.

Since at least the early twentieth century, voices such as Harriet Finlay-Johnson (1912), Henry Caldwell Cook (1918) and the English Association's call in 1908 for Shakespeare to be heard through 'the living voice' have encouraged understanding of the texts as plays to be performed, with the argument this gives increased opportunities to explore the social, emotional, and spiritual as well as cultural and intellectual aspects of these complex literary texts. Many opportunities now exist for literature teachers to engage with theatre-based pedagogy; however, those opportunities are not without challenges, subject as they are to practical issues such as time, space and training, but mainly, as we find in Part Three, teachers' passions and motivations. While the curriculum may not require it, the question for teachers of Shakespeare persists: Is there room for engaging creatively and critically with this marker of excellence, so that students can challenge and construct, as well as appreciate, his cultural value?

Many have seen the value of art in how it communicates beyond what the artist may have intended. Dewey questioned 'the authority of tradition and convention' (1934: 313) and was suspicious of anyone imposing judgements of quality on others. He believed the purpose of art should not be communication of abiding values but of possibilities and cites Aristotle in this tradition as saying: 'It is not the business of the poet to tell what has happened but the kind of thing that might happen – what is possible, whether necessary or probable' (cited in Dewey 1934: 295). Literature deals in possibilities and the value of complex texts is to stimulate inquisitive engagement with the possibilities the world presents. Bruner describes classical literature as 'talking to dead authors'; a valuable site of interaction providing the objective of the encounter is 'not worship but discourse and interpretation' (1996: 62). Bakhtin similarly sees the value of literature as encouraging dialogue through engaging a reader with the different perspectives of the characters an author creates, something he describes as 'a living contact with unfinished, still evolving reality' (1981: 7). A curriculum emphasis on examining Shakespeare as a test of reading an icon of literary heritage without critical, creative interaction seems at best reductive and unambitious, and at worst the way to alienate young people from Shakespeare as a living artist.

In this chapter, we began by exploring different models of cultural value and considered what each could offer in terms of underpinning and explaining theatre-based approaches to teaching Shakespeare. We found a misreading of the concept of cultural capital (Bourdieu 1986) to be the current predominant metric of Shakespeare's value in education systems, and argue this metric is better described by the culturally conservative and exclusionary model of Hirsch's cultural literacy. We then considered how these different cultural value models are echoed in how the study of literature is and has been constructed within education systems and why Shakespeare has become exceptionalized in his role as icon of literary heritage.

Across all of this, we have centred on the exploration of the central tensions in a Shakespeare for acquisition (to pass assessments and as a cultural capital vitamin) and a Shakespeare for inquisition (to be playfully pulled apart in a creative and critical engagement with heritage). We propose that greater value can be found if acquisition is entwined with inquisition; that we need formal education to result in more than passive acquisition of knowledge, rather it should stimulate enquiry, collaborative engagement, emotional literacy and metacognition about how we learn and communicate. We propose resolutions in how theatre-based practice works with Shakespeare as a living artist to facilitate spaces for intercultural dialogue and critique. As will be found in Part Two, organizations promoting theatre-based practice with Shakespeare find that young people gain 'ownership' of Shakespeare's text not through a passive acquisition but as the result of a collaborative inquisition of the text that does not replace close reading skills but deepens them.

3

The literature question

In the introduction to a report calling for more diversity of the literature studied in schools, Bernadine Evaristo describes literature as 'a curator of our imaginations', enabling 'self-contemplation and self-questioning, and a very deep and intimate engagement with the world' (in Elliot et al. 2021: 4). It is a resonant description. The report goes on to raise important questions about the models of the world young people absorb from the preferenced reading offered by schools and argues for greater representation of different authors with different world views in consciously exploring identity relative to the white male gaze of standard canonical texts. Scrutiny of Shakespeare's place in that canon and his perspective as a white male author of his time and place has grown exponentially since feminist, post-colonialist and cultural materialist criticisms first took hold in the 1980s. Having explored the broader pedagogical underpinning of theatre-based Shakespeare, the very live questions surrounding the cultural capital society invests in him and the intercultural dialogue young people can bring to him, these last two chapters of Part One move into addressing the place and purpose of Shakespeare as a literary text on the curriculum. What is unique about the ensemble he offers of story, drama and poetry, combined with a 400-year history of social and artistic engagement? How is that useful for developing young people's literary and literacy skills? Is there still value in exploring his white, Anglo-centric, Early Modern, male gaze? Can this help us with intercultural democracy and stepping into others' shoes? In this chapter, we consider Shakespeare through the lens of literature; focusing on his roles as a storyteller, dramatist and poet, and the value of his artistry in diffusing those classroom literary divides. We explore how treating Shakespeare as a performance text is not adjunct to but concomitant with literary study in treating plays as 'curators of imagination' with which students can actively, inquisitively and deeply engage.

Shakespeare the storyteller: Why do we need stories?

Shakespeare gives us stories that have been shared across generations and around the world, and there are many who claim Shakespeare's cultural value lies in being a collection of universal tales. Any internet search will reveal a plethora of novel and short story adaptations for every age group; with the most enduring of these, *Tales from Shakespeare*, first published more than 200 years ago (Lamb 1807). Storytelling (oral and performance storytelling for most of our species' existence) is a deeply human process that helps create and define who we are. Trimble explains the evolution of creativity as 'a basic neurobiological force' (2007: 210) that compels us to explore and manipulate, not only the world around us but, by extension, also the worlds we can imagine. Stories simultaneously abstract, simulate and stimulate our social experiences.

Social questions

In *The Science of Story-telling*, Will Storr describes humans as a hyper-social species whose stories are crucial to the complexity of negotiating and maintaining social relationships. Whether learning about the heroes and villains who came before us, gossiping with friends about contemporaries around us, or weaving a narrative of our own actions for ourselves in thoughts and diaries, we are manipulating language and making sense of our world by telling stories. Stories are social grooming that allow us to make connections and share reflections on the behaviours of others, for good or ill. They can provide the comfort of belonging, but also establish stereotypes; they are not only how we define an identity but also how we form new perspectives. Storr tells us: 'Story is both tribal propaganda and the cure for it' (2019: 210). Chimamanda Ngozi Adichie tells us: 'Stories have been used to dispossess and to malign but stories can also be used to empower and humanize' (2009). Bruner researched stories as playful sites where problems are to be found not solved. He explains how the *problem-finding* of questioning received knowledge is the way human knowledge progresses and proposes stories as sites of possibility to rehearse problem-finding by exploring 'what might be and why it isn't' (1966: 159).

Two fundamental human questions can be found at the heart of all the stories we tell: 'Who am I?' and 'What is my place in the world?' These questions are complementary but there is also a very human tension in them between the individual and the collective, the need to define ourselves but also to find belonging and purpose through our interactions with others. Bruner found that young children readily relate to stories from different cultures by finding the shared humanity behind the superficial differences; for example by bringing their own experiences of kinship to bear on stories from Inuit culture. He concludes: 'What the children were learning about was not seagulls and Eskimos, but about their own feelings and preconceptions that, up to then, were too implicit to be recognisable to them' (1966: 161). We can consider how in studying *A Midsummer Night's Dream*, children are not so much learning about magic and mayhem in an Ancient Greek wood, as testing out ideas about love and friendship. Psychologists Raymond Mar and Keith Oatley explain it is 'psychological realism, not the superficial characteristics of the setting, that determines whether we can learn useful social information and processes from a work of fiction' (2008: 185).

'Who am I?' and 'What is my place in the world?' are key questions for young children and teenagers. Blakemore explains how 'adolescence is the period of life in which we develop a profound sense of who we are, and particularly of how we are seen by other people' (2019: 201). Young people are particularly attuned to how they fit as a character in the story of their lives and, potentially therefore, particularly open to how literature offers possibilities and opportunities to reflect on their identity and values through finding and exploring the problems stories can raise. Exploring the social educational value of stories, Bruner concludes: 'It is through our own narratives that we principally construct a version of ourselves in the world, and it is through its narrative that a culture provides models of identity and agency to its members' (1996: xiv). For Bruner, stories become 'a communal tool' for sense-making (1990: 45) and a way of 'trafficking in human possibilities rather than settled certainties' (1986: 26). He evaluated narratives for their success in describing not what is 'true *of* life' but what is 'true *to* life' (1996: 122). In *Macbeth*, we can recognize the humanity of characters, even in their darkest moments. The story of *Macbeth* abstracts our sense of love and fear, loyalty and ambition, guilt and pride, courage and cowardice and weaves all that and more into a tale that is not true *of* the life of Scottish thanes but is true *to* lives that deal in power. An inquisitive exploration of this tale can then stimulate us to question where we stand and to wonder 'What if?' What if I heard those prophecies? What if someone I loved asked me to do something bad? What if my leader were behaving tyrannically?

Mar and Oatley describe narratives as offering 'focused examination of social experience with other daily concerns placed in the background', recognizing how fictional stories 'allow for prediction and explanation while revealing the underlying processes' of social relations that young people need to learn (2008: 183). Blakemore's work on mapping of brain functions suggests that in day-to-day life, whereas adults seem more likely to tap into areas of the brain storing memories of social experiences, children and adolescents may be relying more 'on a simulation based strategy in which they *imagine* how they would feel in a particular situation' (2019: 126–7). Adults have more life experience to draw from for the 'social scripts' that allow them to predict and attempt to control new situations. Young people are still evolving their social understanding and perhaps are more reliant on narratives that are true *to* life, to help them explore social questions. If this is the case, the quality of those stories can be seen as key in offering a variety of social scenarios and simulations that contribute to building the neural pathways that will make the adult that young person becomes (Gallagher 2008).

A moral playground

Throughout human history, stories have been used didactically to nudge, the young especially, into certain ways of behaving. Examples of good behaviours rewarded and bad behaviours punished are common, with wealth and beauty typically bestowed on those who are brave and dutiful, while devils and demons torment those who go astray. Heroes are to be admired for defending our values, villains are to be despised for attacking them. Our curiosity to keep hearing, reading or watching a story is triggered by innate tendencies to search for patterns of cause and effect: we need to see how characters resolve their problems and understand why they behave as they do. We can take great cathartic satisfaction from seeing villainy revealed and punished, or hope from seeing a villain redeemed. Storr tells us, 'Just as our storytelling brains are wired to valorize pro-social behaviour, we're designed to love watching the anti-social suffer the pain of tribal comeuppance' (2019: 148). However, stories also allow us to see other models of the world. We might find a character's actions wrong according to the written or unwritten rules of the society that we inhabit, but if we imaginatively step into their shoes, we might find understanding of what makes sense to them in their own world, their *habitus* (Bourdieu and Wacquant 1992: 127). We seek patterns in stories but we delight in complexity and variation. We crave justice that is fair, but often find this means some rules get broken, and that the most interesting characters do not divide simplistically into good and bad.

There is a long history of Shakespeare's nuances being smoothed out to suit the moral worldview of a particular group. *Tales from Shakespeare*, mentioned earlier, was written in a growing tradition of seeing Shakespeare's plays as sources of universal truths from which moral guidance could be drawn. The authors declared the plays to be 'a lesson of all sweet and honourable thoughts and actions' (Lamb 1807: xv) with no recognition of the racism and misogyny very apparent to us today. Antonio in *The Merchant of Venice*, for example, is described as 'the kindest man alive' (Lamb 1807: 72) while Katherine in *Taming of the Shrew* is praised for becoming 'the most obedient and duteous wife in Padua' (Lamb 1807: 145). Nuance is woven into the fabric of Shakespeare's storytelling. Antonio may be kind to his friends, but he is far from kind to Shylock. Katherine's final speech can be interpreted as ironic or the result of abuse rather than dutiful. In *Romeo and Juliet*, Shakespeare adapts Arthur Brooke's narrative poem, illustrating the consequences of teenagers not doing as their parents tell them, into a live debate of 'What if?' and 'If only'. In his plays about kings, he adapts from semi-historical sources to raise not just issues of succession but how a leader should rule, and why they want to. Shakespeare often used distances of time and culture in his stories to allow more imaginative moral play and a key part of his value is that we use him in the same way. In Michael Boyd's words, a 400-year-old play raises a series of questions to explore in the 'moral playground' of theatre practice (Irish 2009). These questions can include: How did people feel about these situations then? How do we feel now? What's the same? What's different? What's different about how we feel here compared to how people feel over there? What should be different? How can we make it different?

Every culture tells stories that turn 'us' into heroes and 'them' into villains. Adichie warns of the danger of 'single stories' (2009) which can lead to stereotyping when we learn only one aspect of people unfamiliar to us; while Madeleine Sayet asserts, 'The stories we choose to pass down shape our collective possible futures' (2023). Williams (2022) offers a fascinating investigation into the deep human need to create in-groups and out-groups; the stories we tell that dehumanize 'them', and the System 2 cognitive effort we need to question those stories and embrace the nuance and complexity of 'us'. Without varied and complex stories to virtually inhabit and find shared humanity across superficial difference, we are isolated in our own models of reality. Adichie warns of a growing tribal 'social consensus', in our media age, that stifles freedom of expression (2022). She argues that if we cannot, with compassion, share *all* our stories, using any discomfort about them as fuel for discussion and negotiated understanding rather than censorship, we continue to risk the simplification of knowing only single stories. If analogizing and storytelling support young people in making sense of the world and their place in it as research suggests, continued attention to the impact of literary texts in the classroom for supporting or combating the biases we naturally develop seems crucial.

Some critical pedagogues have argued that the texts of Shakespeare, grounded as they are in their patriarchal, euro-centric Early Modern English context, and inculcated through generations of use to leverage, naturalize and reinforce oppressively misogynistic, heteronormative and imperialistic views, require a radical approach to their stories through study, interpretation and performance. Re-storying is the decolonizing practice of confronting and working through the exclusionary and colonial past (and present) of a text and retelling its story in a way that makes space for the knowledges, experiences and perspectives in the room (Bissonnette and Glazier 2016; Dyches 2017; Stornaiuolo and Thomas 2018; Dyches et al. 2021). This can be understood as a process of re-articulating existing stories, texts and cultural objects with the explicit aim 'to better reflect a diversity of perspectives and experiences, [and as] an act of asserting the importance of one's existence in a world that tries to silence subaltern voices' (Thomas and Stornaiuolo 2016). In exploring the centrality and power of story both within Shakespeare and within our social lives, re-storying seeks to move beyond acquisitionary or even inquisitorial re-telling and invites radical and whole-hearted reinterpretations looking towards social justice. Examples of this in performance include Aimé Césaire's *Une Tempête* and Toni Morrison's *Desdemona*, while Nora Williams's education project 'Measure (Still) for Measure' offers learners the opportunity to radically edit and adapt *Measure for Measure* through theatre-based practice, attending to questions of sexual violence and coercion in the text (Williams 2018).

All this offers a challenge to educators of Shakespeare. Is it enough to appreciate Shakespeare's works and how they have been interpreted and admired by others as great literary achievements? Or can we invest them with the plurality of voices our classrooms bring and interrogate the thought experiments his stories offer to question the judgements we and those around us make? Can we playfully engage in the present to develop responses, re-storyings and counter-stories to Shakespeare's stories from the past to shape attitudes for the future? This is the story site of exploration Shakespeare can offer: a moral playground full of characters to be infinitely reinterpreted.

In this section, we have explored how human minds understand the world through stories and how Shakespeare's stories both draw from and provide common story sites which can be used to explore and express intersectional perspectives. We have presented Shakespeare's writing as a treasury of stories, often reworking old tales and tapping into universal themes of human endeavours and conflicts. We have also, more importantly, explored how they can offer space for inhabiting different perspectives and for imaginative interpretation of intentions and understanding, offering opportunities for the creation of rich and radical re-storyings. We now move on to examine the difference in this space afforded by taking storytelling into a performative format.

Shakespeare the dramatist: Why do we need theatre?

Stories offer simulations, thought experiments and embodied metaphors which generate and test ideas proposed by our hyper-social human cultures. We have evolved to learn about ourselves and our place in the world by being instinctively interested in others: what we need from them, what they need from us, what their intentions might be. Characters give us abstracted, distilled versions of ourselves and others and help us explore and rehearse our responses. Our stories can shine a light on how things are and what should change (Boal 1985). As a situation investigated through a plurality of voices, story as drama allows us to viscerally step inside and put the thought experiments of the story into four-dimensional living, breathing bodies.

Shakespeare through drama offers young people the opportunities to speak and hear how the text works, discover different possible perspectives, try out different possible identities and re-story for the worlds they live in today.

Embodied present

David Edgar argues that drama 'is able to concentrate experience so effectively because of a characteristic it shares with music' (2009: 10). That characteristic being a control of tempo in how audiences experience the art form. You can put down a book, come back to a painting, stop a film, but you cannot leave a live event and pick up where you left off. Even if you return the following evening to watch the second half, the audience, the artists, the world, you, will all have changed.

Boyd has called this theatrical communal journey 'a collective encounter hanging in the air between us' (2008) and experiences of pandemic lockdowns have perhaps given us new perspectives on valuing the shared humanity of live, in-person, collective events. Theatre guides us on a journey in real time but manipulates our sense of time as it does so to craft a collective experience. An RSC production of *Macbeth* in 2018 gave a graphic metaphor of this by displaying a large digital countdown to the moment of Macbeth's death. Behind the scenes, the stage crew slowed or sped up the count to ensure zero arrived at the exact right moment of action. Edgar explains how the craft of theatre concentrates 'the chaos of life, removing its profuse redundancy and exposing its underlying synchronicities, rhythms and shapes' (2009: 201).

Theatre might also be seen as more affected by real time than other arts because performance requires contemporary bodies. Who we see, or can imagine, inhabiting those characters and how that affects which characters we feel able to relate to is instrumental in how we interpret a text. Theatre companies are becoming more conscious of the impact of representation with, for example, new casting policies being implemented around gender, race and disability by the RSC and the Globe. Consciously or not, the artistic team of any new Shakespeare production is affected by the social and political movements of their own time and can only reflect on the words, actions and social history of the plays through the lenses their *habitus* allows. Because a production aims to be received in the public forum, it must make account of itself there, sharing its ideas with an audience who each bring their own *habitus*. As Stephen Greenblatt describes, theatre is necessarily a social event, influenced both by the time of its production and of its reception because the 'artistic form itself is the expression of social evaluations and practices' (1994: 33). Shakespeare as theatre means Shakespeare in the complex embodied present of contemporary people in contemporary times.

Ewan Fernie explains how the relatively new critical movement of Presentism has been viewed suspiciously in Shakespearean academic circles as dissolving historical difference, but argues that it can instead allow a more responsive approach to what difference means (2005: 179). In their exploration of the cultural value of Shakespeare, McLuskie and Rumbold dismiss what they describe as 'idiosyncratic reflections on the contemporary political situation' that audience members bring to productions. They give the example of Libby Purves's review of the Histories Cycle at the RSC (2005–8), describing her 'startling imaginative leap . . . to the complex politics of fundamentalism in Pakistan', which they do not accept as 'coherent intellectual analysis' (2014: 136). For Purves, her social brain made intuitive analogies that extended her empathy and illuminated her understanding both of the situation portrayed on stage and the contemporary situation in Pakistan. We would argue that for Purves, as for the young people we want to draw into a community of Shakespeare practice, any imaginative leap is to be welcomed in raising questions, finding problems and inviting in prior knowledge. Through the dialogic, embodied exploration of theatre-based practice, that imaginative leap can then be explored to find how coherent the analysis it brings up might be.

Embodied action

In a novel, we (usually) have contextual support: descriptions of setting and tone; asides about relationships and intentions; authorial commentary. Modern play scripts often give detailed descriptions of settings and actions which can be adapted, even ignored in performance, but will always affect any study of the play. Shakespeare gives us very little beyond the words his characters speak. E. M. Forster notes how in a play 'all human happiness and misery does and must take the form of action, otherwise its existence remains unknown' (1985: 84). That action, however, is the result of how and why characters say what they say. Playing out that action in our minds as we read dialogue requires a great deal more cognitive effort without authorial description of what the action is. Many people's negative experiences of studying Shakespeare at school stem from becoming lost in the cognitive load of keeping track of the interplay of actions and emotions, unsurprisingly when the text allows for so many possibilities of what those actions and emotional responses might be.

Mar and Oatley (2008) suggest we get to know protagonists in novels better than people in real life, even, perhaps, better than we know ourselves, because of the different perspectives we gain from other characters, narrative commentary, and especially from the patterns about their behaviour that we are guided to observe. Without the narrative commentary of a novel or story, actors must instead search out clues. They examine what a character says about themselves and what other characters say about them and note any patterns and variations. From these clues, they create informed, imaginative inferences about who their character is, their place in the world and their motivations. Theatre-based activities designed to recreate this work in the classroom deepen textual analysis and reduce cognitive load through experimenting with possible embodied actions to find meaning in a character's words.

A concern we recognize as a common misapprehension of theatre-based practice is that it leads to a Bradleyan conception of characters as real people. Coles, for example, observes English teachers using active approaches and notes, 'What becomes important is experiencing the apparently authentic feelings, motivations and preferences of people who inhabit the play, rather than exploring roles, ideas and situations in a more abstract sense' (2013: 252). The work of an actor is not to somehow shapeshift into an agreed form of Juliet or Macbeth as real people but through exploration to breathe life into what David Mamet (1998) describes as 'black marks on a page' and find their own truth in the possibilities of who that character can be. Actors work to gain a deep understanding of a text, how it works and what it might have meant to Shakespeare's original audience, while allowing an interplay of metaphorical imagination around what and how it might mean now. Actors necessarily engage in a dialogue between Shakespeare's culture and their own, exploring the ambiguities and nuance of the language to create and convey shared meanings in performance. In studying a play, cognitive ease comes with getting the text into moving bodies. Watching others bring the text to life is good but embodying those texts for yourself brings a far deeper, more visceral embodied cognition of a character's dilemmas and engages innate curiosity in solving the puzzles of who these people are, how they belong, why they do what they do, and what they want. Reading and talking about stories can help us appreciate others' perspectives, but theatre helps us understand other points of view and develop divergent critical interpretations in a multi-sensory, embodied way. As Jacques Rancière describes: 'Drama means action. Theatre is the place where an action is taken to its conclusion by bodies in motion in front of living bodies that are to be mobilized' (2009: 3).

Embodied democracy

The purpose of a play is to put bodies on a stage and as soon as our social brains and our senses are engaged we apply and develop symbolism about what we see as we read a performance from our own unique perspectives. Many have observed that education can never be a neutral space and teachers must be alert to the power dynamics and ethical issues their classrooms create. Many have also recognized that studying complex texts, perhaps especially drama texts, provokes questions about those dynamics and issues. Bruner confesses a revelation, early in his career, about the power of drama after hearing 'the intensity of the discussion of moral philosophy' from a group of fourteen-year-olds and urges that 'we consider more seriously the use of this most powerful impulse to represent the human condition in drama and thereby, the drama of the human condition' (1986: 163). Cicely Berry describes the purpose of theatre to 'provoke us and make us want to talk, to discuss, to think – to communicate through language' (2008: 13). Within what Augusto Boal (1985) called the 'container' of theatre, absorbing theory of mind tensions arise from considering characters' attempts to read each other's intentions: what Tybalt or Mercutio think about Romeo's behaviour; what Macbeth thinks Banquo thinks about the witches; what Polonius thinks Hamlet thinks about Ophelia. As audience, we love engaging in this imaginative speculation. With literary characters, just as we do through gossip about people we know, we can speculate about motivations and judge behaviours, implicitly recognizing how issues of status and vulnerability play into what we observe. The advantage with fictional characters is that not only is there no one to offend, we see only a distillation of behaviour, without the background noise of messy reality.

Understanding and sympathy for both sides of a dramatic conflict can become significantly deeper and more nuanced when young people inhabit the characters, exploring objectives and motivations through theatre-based activities designed to open up possibilities of interpretation and allow each actor to find their own connections. To get a text on its feet in performance, puzzles have to be solved. A technique we have found useful is to offer a provocative statement as a lens and invite participants to stand along a line according to how far they agree or disagree with the statement. For example: 'Children should do what their parents tell them to do' or 'Success is more important than friendship'. The spectrum of responses that arise serves both to demonstrate difference in terms of the views that may be held in the room, but also the questions this abstract moral statement raises; 'It depends . . .' or 'But what if . . .' are often where responses end up. We then engage students in various activities designed to familiarize them with a scene and finally give them another statement to respond to. For example: 'Hermia should marry Demetrius as her father wishes' or 'Macbeth should kill Fleance to prevent Banquo's children taking the throne'. This second provocation makes the first generalized statement into a specific example, an embodied metaphor, and tends to provoke a far richer discussion as participants attack and defend the characters they have imaginatively invested with intention and purpose. They often naturally employ language from the text to illustrate their points and make analogies with personal experience (Irish and Gonsalves 2023).

Importantly, moral discussion ensues based on the values, embodied experiences and social questions the participants bring into the room and develop as they listen and respond to each other. The role of the teacher is to facilitate the discussion, aiming to encourage and ensure all voices are heard, and asking well-placed questions to develop what is said. There are many ways to explore text through the lenses of statements and questions, set out in the various available Shakespeare toolkits. As just one further example, students can be asked to stand relative to symbolic representations of characters according to how sympathetic they feel towards that character. Discussion can then be facilitated around these positions. *The Tempest* scene between Prospero, Caliban and Miranda brings immense baggage in terms of colonial attitudes, sexual violence and patriarchal control. If students imaginatively and actively step into these characters, they then have specific but fictional examples to draw from to explore issues that can feel salient in their own lives. They can slip easily into discussion about contemporary power dynamics of race, gender and class; the protective and controlling instincts of parents; and on into constructive questioning of societal norms and cultural assumptions. Edgar calls drama 'a zone in which we can experiment with our dreams and our dreads, our ambitions and our impulses – murderous as well as virtuous – in conditions of safety' (2009: 202).

Brook describes how theatre practice must be alive and political but is the opposite of politics – that while politicians are required to smooth away nuance and defend big ideas, good theatre provides space to explore possibilities. He explains how: 'In life the heat of conflict makes it almost impossible to enter into the logic of one's adversary, but a great dramatist can without judgement launch opposing characters against one another, so an audience can be at one and the same time inside and outside them both, successively for, against and neutral' (1998: 140). Through creating these models of experience, theatre-based practice may not directly effect change, but can stimulate dialogue affecting young people's models of reality with tiny moments that may shift outlooks and build confidence. Brook goes on to propose that through an engagement with alternative sympathies and attitudes illustrated on a stage, 'spectators can be given a moment of perception beyond their normal vision' (1998: 141). This recalls Vygotsky's influential observations on how 'play creates a zone of proximal development [ZPD] of the child. In play a child always behaves beyond his average age, above his daily behaviour; in play it is as though he were a head taller than himself' (1978: 102). This extension to a child's daily world, as they creatively imitate the adult roles they see around them, allows children to develop their language abilities and to grow cognitively, emotionally and socially. Vygotsky's concept of the ZPD informs how the collaborative and creative social play of drama and theatre-based practice supports young people to playfully step into perceptions beyond their normal vision as they reach for the heights of Shakespeare's complex texts. This imaginative engagement with the plurality of possible perspectives can expand a sense of intercultural democracy rather than becoming numbed by wrangling over the rights of different interest groups. Implicit in theatre-based practice is an embodied democracy that each voice should be understood, not just merely heard.

This section has explored what makes drama distinct from other literary media in how it tells stories, and how Shakespearean drama in particular can engage empathy and imagination when young people inhabit, and watch others inhabit, his words. An experience of Shakespeare in performance with a facilitated awareness of how situating the text in contextually bound living bodies raises questions and can profoundly deepen the problem-finding skills of young people, leading to creative re-storying and thoughtful analysis. The format of drama texts offers enjoyable challenges for creative and critical interpretation. Using theatre-based practice with texts designed for the theatre eases the cognitive load of making sense of texts without authorial commentary and invites students to bring their personal embodied experiences to bear on exploring how they themselves might respond under the 'true *to* life' given circumstances of a narrative.

Shakespeare the poet: Why do we need poetry?

Shakespeare's poetic language is paradoxically both the barrier to engaging students with his work and what makes that engagement worthwhile. Stredder notes how facility with Shakespeare's language is often associated with cultural exclusivity, which can lead to mockery of its poetic 'airs and graces', but he also notes that 'Through speaking language it becomes our own' (2009: 116–117). This value of a sense of ownership in learning is a recurrent theme in this book. In this section, we focus on how speaking Shakespeare's poetry aloud, in a moment, for a reason, allows young people to feel for themselves, not just the pleasure of articulacy, but also the purpose. Complex texts feed our curiosity by offering our brains the stimulation of poetic forms: patterns of words that distil an intensity of feeling, and images that light up our associative memories. Susanne Langer describes drama as 'essentially an enacted poem' (1953: 314) capturing how playwrights employ poetic designs to compose complex human thoughts into lines of text which actors flesh out with momentary emotion. When used dramatically, poetic language offers opportunities and challenges to find out more than just what happens next. In the nuance and ambiguity of Shakespeare's poetic language lie all the possibilities that an actor can choose from to manifest 'black marks on a page' into action. This section is not about explaining Shakespeare's poetic forms. The Shakespeare library offers various detailed and thoughtful explorations about his use of verse (e.g. McDonald 2001; Rokison 2014) and the Arden Performance editions offer authoritative explorations of the possibilities those forms offer. Instead, we examine the value of poetry in the theatre-based Shakespeare classroom and how rhythms, patterns and imagery are integral to Shakespeare's dramatic storytelling.

Mysteries and musicality

As discussed in Chapter 1, the imagery of Shakespeare's language stimulates our visceral connections to cognitive or conceptual metaphors. Sometimes imagery connects immediately but often Shakespeare gives a simpler version as well. For example, when Orlando says, 'What passion hangs these weights upon my tongue?' (*AYL*, 1.2.246), he conjures a relatable image of inability to be articulate around someone we are attracted to, but he also follows it up with 'I cannot speak to her'. The juxtaposition of these phrases supports a more sensual as well as intellectual understanding. When Rosalind describes her feelings for Orlando, she says, 'that thou didst know how many fathom deep I am in love! But it cannot be sounded. My affection hath an unknown bottom, like the Bay of Portugal' (*AYL*, 4.1.194–196). Her associative imagery of 'fathoms sounded' may be unfamiliar but a love so deep it has an 'unknown bottom' is not just clear but comically relatable.

Associative, analogous thinking is essential in how we process the world, and so too are the prosodic elements Shakespeare employs in offering his images. Intonations, rhythms and poetic devices are recognized as essential and universal in human communication. Research from various disciplines has built on Darwin's propositions for the musical origins of language and found many overlaps in how we are affected by music and prosody (Trimble 2007; Fitch 2010). In that light, the much commented on 'musicality' of Shakespeare's language can be seen as an integral part of how his language works to achieve social, emotional communication and comes alive when the text is spoken aloud with intention. Berry compares Shakespeare's text readily to music. She describes a 'primal need' in all of us for cadence and rhythm (2008: 6) and believes character emerges from how the rhythms of thoughts 'knock against each other' (2008: 2). Rhythm is regarded 'as a biological given of our bodies and our autonomic functions, from breathing and heartbeat to the rhythm of our brains' (Trimble 2007: 201). A line of pentameter is considered the amount that can be voiced, on average, from one breath. The iambic metre underpinning Shakespeare's verse is often compared to the rhythm of the human heartbeat. Brain imaging studies are showing that functional shift (a common Shakespeare technique) excites rhythmic energy pulses in the brain (University of Liverpool 2006) and that vowels are central to the sense of rhythm that allows brains to process speech (University of California 2019). As linguistic science progresses, we may yet learn more about how and why we respond to the qualities of Shakespeare's texts, but we currently know enough to recognize that a predilection for rhythms and patterns in language is in our DNA. Our brains are alert to patterns in every aspect of our lives, so that variation is what really grabs our attention. Understanding Shakespeare's metre is about understanding what Berry calls 'the infinite variety of movement within a single line of iambic pentameter' (2001: 113); in other words, that his structures are there to support, not define, how text is spoken or understood. Shakespeare rarely lets metre trip along for long without variation and actors are vigilant to the clues those variations, or lack of them, could offer in reflecting possibilities for characters' status, feelings and intentions.

Tuning young people into the images and rhythms of Shakespeare's text is key to unlocking the power of his language. It is the basis of many activities advocated by the organizations and practitioners we meet in Part Two and the teachers in Part Three. Theatre-based practice calls for playful engagement with Shakespeare's language and encourages young people to bring their own intonations and colloquialisms into that playground. While good practice judiciously edits text, building from short extracts to full scenes as students gain confidence and ability, it does not smooth away complexity by simplifying language. As Stredder explains, if we don't build students' confidence with the language, they may feel outsiders to it, 'either resenting their exclusion, or superstitiously respecting qualities they have not personally experienced' (2009: 117). The delight of Shakespeare is complexity, ambiguity, nuance; what John Keats evocatively summarized as 'negative capability'. Keats (1818) coined the phrase in reference to Shakespeare as meaning 'when a man (sic) is capable of living in uncertainties, mysteries, doubts', rather than being dominated by an 'irritable reaching after facts and reason'. Gibson proposes negative capability as one of his principles of studying Shakespeare and describes how it 'invites and encourages imaginative exploration and creative dissent in the knowledge that interpretations can never be fully complete, never the final word' (1998: 25).

While they are the very essence of poetry, 'uncertainties, mysteries and doubts' are hard to measure. The testing systems which currently dominate formal education seem to accommodate Shakespeare more easily as a literary icon standing on a pillar of the 'facts and reason' of received knowledge. Examination boards say they want creative engagement with text; however, the overall systems under which teachers operate often make busy teachers feel that particular measurable responses are required. For example, in England, the AQA 2019 examination report for GCSE Literature declares, 'It was pleasing to see a marked reduction in the unhelpful and obstructive use of subject terminology', explaining how students' use of terminology often limited rather than supported their discussion of imagery. The report concludes, 'This reductive view of a literary text, reducing it to parts of speech, has been clearly identified as unnecessary and unhelpful, and fortunately is on the wane' (AQA 2019). What the report does not acknowledge is how and why so many teachers feel they have to teach their students to sprinkle such often barely understood terminology in their work. Perhaps better systems and better assessments might promote a more creative approach that allows for students to appreciate terminology as a shorthand for concepts they have understood, rather than a rote learning of terms – an idea we explore further next and in Chapter 4.

Antithesis and nuance

Binaries are the foundation of our sensory motor experiences from our earliest experiences of light and dark, warm and cold, empty and full. As a result, either/or thinking is deeply embedded in our Palaeolithic brains:

fight or flight, right or wrong, love or fear, but we are also deeply adept, when allowed and encouraged, at understanding the shades in-between. Antithesis permeates Shakespeare's plays from the conceptual level of generational divide or ambition versus honour to the phrase level of 'My only love sprung from my only hate' (*RJ*, 1.5.137) or 'Vaulting ambition which o'erleaps itself / And falls on the other' (*Mac*, 1.7.27–28). Boyd names Shakespeare's main stylistic tool as antithesis, 'unresolved antithesis – an argument which is never resolved is why his work has survived to this day' (2008: 8). Shakespeare gives us heroes and villains, comedies and tragedies, high and low status but with opportunities to challenge and disrupt our binary biases. He has villains state their villainy: 'I am a plain dealing villain' (*MA*, 1.3.29), 'I am determinèd to prove a villain' (*R3*, 1.1.30), or question it 'How am I then a villain?' (*Oth*, 2.3.343), 'as if we were villains on necessity' (*KL*, 1.2.121). However, as Richard's 'determinèd' crystallizes, the text provides ample nuance for any actor to explore (as the teaching adage goes) the drivers of bad behaviour rather than bad people.

Nuance is the swathe of difference between binaries that gives antithesis its power. It was undoubtedly a concept, but not a word, that Shakespeare was familiar with, apparently entering English from French in the eighteenth century with an etymology connected to *nubes*, the Latin for cloud. With that hint, a Shakespearean metaphor of nuance might be Henry VI's description of the progress of the battle of Towton:

> The battle fares like to the morning's war,
> When dying clouds contend with growing light,
> What time the shepherd, blowing of his nails,
> Can neither call it perfect day nor night.
>
> (*3H6*, 2.5.1–4)

A shepherd knows the difference between day and night, his survival depends on it, but even he can't tell the precise moment when night becomes day and day becomes night. Our brains are adept at blending concepts across binaries (Fauconnier and Turner 2002) in this case of time, temperature and weather, to understand holistically the nuance of dawn and dusk. Even more amazingly, we can take that visceral understanding from everyday existence into understanding the nuances of a king's comparison with the moving fates of a battle.

In order to best appreciate the text, some Shakespeare teachers advocate what McDonald called 'solitary engagement with the words on the page' (2009: 38). Our argument, set out in the drama section earlier, is that while some find great pleasure and meaning in reading Shakespeare, many others find the words come to life more easily through theatre-based activities. With the aforementioned passage, we can teach subject terminology to talk of the regularity of the blank verse; the antithesis of the verbs 'dying' and 'growing' and the nouns 'day' and 'night'; the alliteration of 'clouds contend', or the assonance of 'growing' and 'blowing'. The words to talk about these patterns, however, are only worthwhile and memorable, once a student has made the imaginative leap to being that shepherd on a cold morning watching the clouds fade as the sun rises. Then they can debate qualitatively the meaning of Henry's metaphor, reaching for the terminology to help express their thoughts as they make theory of mind inferences about why a king, whose own wife has told him to stay away from the fighting, might be thinking about a shepherd.

Shakespeare's poetry gives rise to the symbolism of performance including bodies and costume, gestures and props, accents and music. McLuskie and Rumbold's (2014) discussion of the RSC's 2005–8 Histories Cycle again offers an interesting example of a perspective very different from our own. They state: 'The plays' complex narratives of dynastic conflict were presented with great clarity, but the overall effect of sound and colour was of a total theatre that did not depend on interpretive reading' (2014: 134). The implication here seems to be that the company randomly imposed symbolism on 'the truth' of the texts. McLuskie and Rumbold go on to say: 'The moments of recognition that connected audience to action came from memorable visual images' and they give examples of Joan of Arc reincarnated as Queen Margaret; the future Richard III playing with a pig's severed head; and Edward IV's white coronation robes becoming stained with Henry VI's blood. However, they dismiss these moments as 'spectacle' without consideration of how those interpretations, and the embodied metaphors they offer, were found through the process of investigating the imagery of the text in rehearsals. Any staged image is crafted to create associations for an audience with the understanding that many possible layers of resonances may result (Eco 1992). Rancière describes beautifully the optimal experience of a young audience member: 'She composes her own poem with the elements of the poem before her' (2009: 13), suggesting that each student, if engaged, cannot help but conceive their own cognitive associations as a production weaves with their senses and memories. Storr explains how associative thinking is what 'gives poetry its power', playing with 'our associative networks as a harpist plays on strings' (2020: 42). Four hundred years of Shakespeare study has not answered every problem to be found in the plays, nor exhausted every way the words can be spoken and heard. We can never fully know a Shakespeare play because its meanings are in constant dynamic shift with the diversity of any culture it sits in; and that offers each student an invitation to compose their own poem as Rancière suggests. Our role as educators is not to determine the meaning young people make but to help them reflect, question and learn as they make that meaning.

Berry believed that an actor needs to be bold to fill Shakespeare's heightened text but she insisted this is not about making the poetry sound 'beautiful': 'We do not want the listener simply to appreciate it; we want him/her to recognize its necessity' (2001: 3). Shakespeare's language is poetry but it is also language in action being used by one character to affect another. The forms, sounds, rhythms and patterns are not true *of* life, nobody, even in Elizabethan England spoke with such composition, but they are true *to* life. His choices concentrate and craft to convey a quality of meaning: rhythms and repetitions are there to drive and energize; imagery is there to connect and illuminate. Here we find Vygostsky's ZPD in action: when young people playfully engage with Shakespeare's complex text, they become a head taller as they do so. The heart of Shakespeare's exceptionalism is his poetry, and his exceptionalism for the classroom is the potential in his writing to allow each young person to feel their own exceptionalism as they inhabit his language and make it their own.

Building from an understanding of the fundamental human drive to express and understand the world through stories, this section has concluded its exploration of Shakespeare as literature by examining how we use words in all our storytelling to engage and delight. We have looked at how the heightened poetic language of Shakespeare is both aesthetically pleasing and also pragmatic as language in action used to provoke and affect. In the next chapter, we move on to explore how interaction with the material Shakespeare offers is useful in developing the communication competencies of young people.

4

The language question

It is not easy to find an agreed universal definition about the purpose of education. There is general agreement that it should increase equality of opportunity, transmit a core cultural body of knowledge and prepare students for adult life. Even these aims, however, are shot through with possible controversies as we have found so far: What does equality mean? How are opportunities provided? What constitutes core knowledge? How do you best prepare for the unknowns of the future? It seems hard to disagree with Bruner's succinct purpose for education that it should aim for 'more effective, less alienated, and better human beings' (1996, 118); however, the epistemological questions of how we do that need continuous reassessment. From a global perspective, Schleicher expresses concern that young people's curiosity and creativity are dampened by education systems that require compliance and teaching to the test. He says, 'Too much of what happens in today's classroom is geared towards having students reproduce what they have learned, rather than extrapolating from it and applying their knowledge creatively to novel situations' (OECD 2022). Nussbaum goes further in claiming, 'a catalogue of facts, without the ability to assess them, or to understand how a narrative is assembled from evidence, is almost as bad as ignorance' (2010: 94). Better creativity, criticality, collaboration and communication seem a common call from employers and from the demands of daily life if young people are to survive and thrive in ever-changing environments.

In the last chapter, we found Shakespeare's stories to be a playground of possibilities for social, moral and linguistic exploration. We explored how the stories we encounter not only affect our sense of identity and belonging but also open up possibilities of what the world is and could be. In this final chapter of Part One, we focus more explicitly on the centrality of language in learning generally and how Shakespeare's texts specifically can provide material to support young people in developing their own language skills as they respond to Shakespeare's. We briefly zoom out to consider how and why humans use language and survey the high value placed on communication skills for learning, employment and life. We then zoom back into the Shakespeare classroom and explore the social and pedagogical value of theatre-based Shakespeare in building confidence, resilience and enjoyment while developing the speaking and listening skills that are also the foundations of reading and writing. We finish with a call to action that education should focus more on Bruner's call for 'more effective, less alienated, and better human beings'.

The humanity of language

Exploring the uniqueness of humans, Adam Rutherford concludes, 'It is in the teaching of others, the shaping of culture, and the telling of stories, that we created ourselves' (2018: 17). Yet while schools are readily concerned with the dizzying pace of our tool-making manifested in technology, often taken for granted are the deeply human skills of language development and communication foundational to the teaching, culture-building and storytelling that make us what we are. To understand how the language in Shakespeare's plays works to communicate meaning we need to situate it back in the body where it has evolved over millennia to make us such a hyper-social, hyper-communicative species.

There is not yet a definitive understanding of how language evolved or how it conveys meanings. Homo sapiens have been around and biologically capable of speech for at least 200,000 years and it seems likely that the significant neural developments that characterize our species capitalized on existing gestural abilities to share information and innate musical abilities to share emotions, possibly resulting in a 'prosodic protolanguage' that eventually morphed into the sophisticated symbolic lexicons and syntax that characterize all human languages (Mithen 2005; Trimble 2007; McGilchrist 2009; Fitch 2010). The shift to verbal language may have coincided with the growth of cultural (rather than just practical) artefacts from around 50,000 to 80,000 years ago that indicate a significant development in conceptual and abstract thinking. Human communication employs a range of aspects beyond the culturally learnt words and signs of speech, such as gestures, expressions and intonations, that owe at least as much to the genes we share with birds and whales as other primates (Fitch 2010). Human speech, however, is unique. It relies on our instincts for social learning and cooperative expression, and allows us to share 'anything we can think . . . a boundless expressivity [that] sets our species off from all others' (Fitch 2010: 5). Verbal language, including sign language, was the human extension that brought the fine distinctions that have enabled us to build the complexities of human cultures. It gives us tools to think with, learn by and share with others.

Written language came much later, with a general consensus putting its first sustained use at around 5,500 years ago (in Mesopotamia). Until even more recently, reading and writing were primarily the province of a wealthier, educated elite. Literacy rates in England in Shakespeare's own time are estimated to be around 30 per cent for men and just 10 per cent for women, rising gradually into the 90s for both genders by the 1900s. Good literacy skills are now vital for everyone in modern societies but are dependent on the foundational skills of speaking, listening and storytelling. While literacy refers to the ability to read and write with fluency, it is also used to indicate ease and familiarity with a subject area. If we want young people to be 'Shakespeare literate', does that mean simply some knowledge of his life and work to appreciate his literary status or a wider remit that includes being theatre literate, rhetorically literate, emotionally literate and interculturally literate?

At the time of writing, the longer-term effects of the pandemic social distancing measures over 2020–22 are beginning to be seen in schools. Anecdotally, many teachers we know in the United States and the United Kingdom have spoken of a significant and disturbing increase in young people struggling with seemingly basic social behaviours. A UK cross-party report reviewed early evidence of the detrimental effects to learning that young people, particularly from disadvantaged homes, suffered through lack of social contact with peers and teachers (APPG 2021: 4). No doubt studies will further illuminate these experiences in time, but the pandemic generation seem to have missed out, not so much on leaning content as learning to be with others; on developing the 'soft skills' of communicating and collaborating. Even before the pandemic, however, teachers were noticing an increase in young people struggling to cope: sometimes with the reach of the technology that is now their birthright, sometimes with the daily realities of existing and thriving with other people, often with the overlap of both.

There is a general concern that in our globalized age of social media, nuance is lost as biases are entrenched in echo-chambers of social fragmentation. It can seem that as webs of knowledge and socio-economic and political influence become increasingly complex, the mass of opinions on social and often mainstream media become increasingly simplified. The rise in the mental health problems of older young people (DfE 2023) seems evidence that our Stone Age brains are grappling to keep up with the effects of high-speed technologies that strip away the communicative nuances that human beings subconsciously absorb in the real world, in real time, in real communities. Online technology is an amazing tool for building knowledge, culture and community but we need to balance it with the needs of our social brains for multi-modal human contact. A lifetime studying the co-dependence in our evolution of genetics and culture led E. O. Wilson to conclude that the problems humans now face are the combination of Palaeolithic emotions, medieval institutions and god-like technology (2017). We would never claim theatre-based practice or Shakespeare as the solution to such complex issues, but we are interested in how working creatively, collaboratively and critically with complex texts might be a step in the right direction.

What do employers want?

Preparing young people for the workplace has always been a key factor of mass education with basic standards of literacy and numeracy constantly revised and decried. The ever-increasing proficiency of AI brings a sharp new focus to this area when we consider that at the time of writing, a recently reported figure of 59 per cent of the global workforce using 'literacy skills daily at a proficiency comparable to or below that of computers' (OECD 2023: 9) has already been exceeded. Yet, while AI can do much, it cannot yet match human understanding and flexibility, especially with language, in making the contextual evaluations needed to find and share meaning and cooperate with other humans. The growth of AI, manifested through interfaces such as ChatGPT, does, though, make even more apparent a disconnect between what the twenty-first-century world of work needs and how young people are emerging from school systems. The best employers are increasingly calling for 'human skills' of resilience, flexibility and communication. Not just awareness and understanding of difference but the ability to value plurality and communicate across differences are skills increasingly valued in the workplace; variously described and developed from concepts of intercultural communication (Hall 1959) and cultural intelligence (Earley and Ang 2003). Reports from the world of business regularly highlight the need for a broad and balanced curriculum that develops these behaviours and attributes that enable young people to be 'work ready'. Currently around 40 per cent of employers in the UK find that they aren't (CBI 2019).

A 2012 report from the Confederation of British Industries (CBI) calls for a much broader approach in education that goes beyond the 'narrow definition of success' of the league tables of examination results. A 2019 report on 'Education and Learning for the Modern World' goes further. It establishes the 'essential and interconnected' attributes of character, knowledge and skills and calls for these three pillars to be given equal weight in schools. The report defines character in terms of resilience, flexibility, reflection and empathy, and skills in terms of understanding how to apply knowledge 'in real world scenarios through team work, leadership, problem-solving and communication' (CBI 2019: 6). This suggests that in our technological age, the most important skills young people need to develop are not what the traditional 'knowledge-rich' cultural literacy style curriculum offers, but constructive communication skills; more in line with the OECD's proposed global competencies for students 'to be able to use their knowledge, skills, attitudes and values to act in coherent and responsible ways that can change the future for the better' (Boix-Mansilla and Schleicher 2022).

There is currently a bias in many government policies and therefore school systems towards Science, Technology, Engineering and Maths (STEM) to ensure a continued pace of technological development. While we would never refute the value of these areas, we would support the countermanding push, from the CBI among many others, towards STEAM (the inclusion of the Arts). In the UK, opportunities for participation in arts and cultural offers are expected to form part of a broad and balanced curriculum, but, as noted in Chapter 2, when resources are focused on external measures of accountability, a decline in arts provision often follows. The Warwick Commission report on cultural value noted the symbiosis inherent in arts learning in calling for 'a curriculum that is infused with multi-disciplinarity, creativity and enterprise' if schools are not only to identify, nurture and train 'tomorrow's creative and cultural talent', but also 'produce creative, world-leading scientists, engineers and technologists' (2015: 15). While a growth in demand for creative skills supports our arguments for the place of theatre-based Shakespeare, we recognize that it is not unproblematic. As Nicholson carefully argues, a discourse of creative learning co-opted into marketable skills is not necessarily helpful for a pedagogy that values social learning and social justice (2011: 93–8). We also recognize that teachers of Shakespeare may prefer, or be expected, to focus on fulfilling the requirements of teaching literary analysis to support skills of reading, writing and appreciation of cultural heritage, rather than 'multi-disciplinarity, creativity and enterprise'. Our invitation is to consider the possible additional educational benefits of working creatively with Shakespeare's texts to develop young people's communication skills more broadly.

Multidisciplinary skills

The Education Endowment Foundation (EEF) toolkit offers a snapshot of the most effective ways to improve learning with access to the supporting studies that evidence these findings. The EEF concludes that some arts activities have positively impacted academic achievement, including 'the impact of drama on writing' and says, 'Wider benefits such as more positive attitudes to learning and increased well-being have also consistently been reported' (EEF 2023). More secure and quantitative evidence that arts participation can improve literacy has so far proved elusive as the area is so broad. At the time of writing, the RSC is undertaking a two-year research study, including random control trials, to investigate the effects of theatre-based Shakespeare on literacy and attitudes to learning. The study is further described by Jacqui O'Hanlon in Part Two. Many of the rationales for why that intervention might, or might not, succeed are explored throughout this book and we are deeply interested in the findings, acknowledging, along with the RSC research team, the difficulty of making any secure conclusions due to the variables involved.

While arts interventions overall are deemed low impact, the intervention that persistently tops the EEF table for high impact is 'metacognition and self-regulation'. Metacognition is perhaps best described as thinking about thinking; something Bruner says 'has to be a principal ingredient of any empowering practice of education' (1996: 19). It is paired with self-regulation as it builds on the abilities to reflect, think, plan and find intrinsic motivation to learn. These are effortful cognitive actions dependent on young people feeling both safe and engaged. Without that sense of safety, self-regulation abilities look to immediate survival rather than long-term gain and in the modern world that can translate into attention-needing behaviours that can lead to worse than being merely disruptive. Most often it leads to anxiety, disengagement and passive compliance.

Risk-taking is an important part of adolescence as young people test out the world and explore where they belong. Metacognitive development is crucial in developing better judgement about which risks to take, especially since risk-taking has been shown to be significantly affected by peer influence (Blakemore 2019). Even the apparently simple act of asking or answering questions in class poses social risks for young people because of how they think others may judge them. These common fears, resulting from our social brains, underline the value of building an ensemble classroom climate where young people feel supported by each other, as well as their teacher, to express their thoughts and feelings. Studies show that young people, especially twelve- to fifteen-year-olds, respond best to interventions designed to focus on values they prioritize and which give them a sense of agency (Blakemore 2019: 156). A pedagogy that is creative, collaborative, dialogic – that mitigates the risks of asking and answering questions and actively encourages everyone to be seen and heard – would seem to suit. Ensemble practice encourages discussion through lower stakes collaborative group learning where individual thoughts can be celebrated, supported and supportively challenged by collective responses (Winston and Strand 2013). Engagement with the thought experiments of complex texts does not stop negative risk-taking or anti-social behaviours; however, through developing collaborative and discursive skills and the principles of ensemble working, it can support metacognitive reflection, positive risk-taking and perhaps a negotiated consensus towards pro-social behaviours that can promote intercultural democracy. An adage used in drama, 'making the unconscious conscious' can be seen as a definition of metacognition. Drama practice stimulates young people to experience something and then, crucially, asks them to reflect on what they observed, how they feel, what they made, and how it worked.

In this section, we have briefly explored the origins of human language and its centrality to our lives in enabling learning and communication. We surveyed a growing call for creativity, collaboration and better communication in the workplace, noting caveats around commodifying these competencies. We now move into exploring how Shakespeare can support the development of language skills alongside the wider but hard to measure 'soft skills' of effective communication.

How sixteenth-century poetry develops twenty-first-century language skills

Gibson describes Shakespeare's language as 'both a model and a resource for students'. He argues, 'In its blend of formality and flexibility it offers unlimited opportunities for students' own linguistic growth' (2016: 6). For Stredder, 'the language seems to suggest and invite enactment'. It holds 'the motive and the cue for action' (2009: 118) that inspires students to make it their own. For Thompson and Turchi, 'The purpose of teaching Shakespeare's plays is to increase a student's independent facility with complex texts' (2016: 7). From a position of advocacy for theatre-based approaches, each of these pedagogies asks for more than the somewhat passive 'appreciating' literature required by England's National Curriculum. And in asking for more thorough exploration, investigation and interrogation, they promise more in terms of student outcomes of increased confidence and facility with use of language. In the last chapter we investigated the educational value of Shakespeare's texts in blending storytelling, drama and poetry into a moral playground for discovery. In this chapter so far, we have considered the calls from education experts, businesses and the public forum for more focus on communication skills in schools. We now move on to explore what it is about Shakespeare's language specifically that can help that development.

Embodied meaning

Cicely Berry's practice as an expert in voice and text has been highly influential in the development of activities that have become common currency in professional rehearsal rooms and in theatre-based practice for the classroom, at the RSC and beyond. Berry found a symbiosis in her work with theatres and schools and often spoke of a particular encounter in the 1970s as foundational in developing her ideas. This was a session on *Othello* with a group of teenage boys in an inner London school (2008: 28–9). Observing a lack of emotional engagement, she encouraged them to read a speech by Othello: 'Never, Iago. Like to the Pontic sea . . .' (*Oth*, 3.3.499) while holding on to each other, pushing and pulling as they did so. This movement created a physical in-the-moment analogy of feeling out of control that allowed the students to make an imaginative leap to understanding Othello as 'drowning in his feelings'. A more traditional approach to the text, with the teacher transmitting an interpretation, might decode Othello's reference to the Pontic sea by a literal glossing that strong currents carry water from the Black Sea through the Dardanelles strait, or an abstract glossing that Othello is driven forward by his anger like being carried in a strong current. This textual analysis offers sources for comparison but misses the opportunity for the students themselves to make deeper, visceral and personal links more likely to aid both their understanding and memory of the speech. English teachers may envisage the likely chaos of that activity rather than the gains, but more controlled versions are available! The principle of the activity is in moving and feeling a physical resistance as you speak the words, which takes you beyond the words themselves and into the feelings they represent. Shakespeare doesn't just have Othello say that his feelings will not change and keep flowing 'Like to the Pontic sea' and expect us to understand. He tells us of the 'icy current and compulsive course', knowing alliterative patterns catch attention and an image of ice cold water surging forward arouses sensory associations. The metre, the imagery, the patterning of the words carry us towards the phrase 'Swallow them up' to convey that sense that Berry's students found of Othello 'drowning in his feelings'.

Activities, like Berry's, which encourage gestures, movement and resistance utilize our embodied cognition and have been shown to help structure thought and support learning (Goldin-Meadow 2005). They can also make us more conscious of how words are symbols of concepts rather than having fixed meanings and how much speech, including sign language, relies on contextual understanding and cooperative interpretation to be understood. While it may be useful for an actor investigating character, or an academic investigating social historical references, to know that Othello is talking of the Black Sea when he says 'Pontic', metaphorically the word stands for far more than that simple fact. Wittgenstein told us: 'words have those meanings which we have given them; and we give them meanings by explanations' (1958: 27). Before him, Vygotsky told us, 'Word meanings are dynamic rather than static formations' (1934: 230). The meanings we associate with words are culturally and contextually contingent; even simply saying 'Put the book on the table' could mean a physical book on a physical table or the name of a book on an electronic table of titles. The meaning we give to a word in a moment of expression is just one aspect of all the connotations we have with that word swirling inside our brains. In *1984*, his dystopian exploration of linguistic determinism, George Orwell writes: 'Winston woke up with the word *Shakespeare* on his lips' (1949: 28). Orwell anticipates his reader will understand 'Shakespeare' here, not as suggesting any specific meaning, but as a shared cultural reference that sums up a world of internal associations that Winston dimly remembers.

As we have argued throughout this book, when Shakespeare's text is regarded, from a heritage perspective, as the best that has been thought and written, the epitome of beautifully crafted poetry, we construct it as a literary text that can make us think and feel in response to it, but which is to be read and treasured as complete in and of itself. If instead, we regard the text, from a divergence perspective, as thought in action, incomplete without a human body to mediate it, the experience of working with the text comes closer to understanding language as a process rather than a product of thought. As a performance text, Shakespeare's words are provocations, stimuli for audience and actor to complete thoughts we are perhaps otherwise unable to adequately express. When the biases of fear and loathing that many young people bring to Shakespeare are overcome, they often enjoy the feeling of articulacy to be found in speaking his text aloud. They find it viscerally satisfying to speak and emotionally satisfying in provoking a dialectical engagement with their own thoughts and feelings. Social and intellectual curiosity can then be brought into play as they explore the need for these characters to speak this particular text in this particular moment.

Normally, in life we reach for the right words to express our thoughts and feelings. The wider our vocabulary, the more options we have to choose from to find the words that feel most right in funnelling the sense of what we want to say into meaning to share with others. As the stakes get higher, finding the right words can feel harder. In moments of high emotion and extremity, Shakespeare gives his characters the words they need: the rich imagery and evocative patterns of speech to express heightened emotion in heightened language. Inhabiting Shakespeare's characters means speaking the text given, so that instead of searching for the right words, we instead consider what they can mean. Given the circumstances of the play, we imaginatively infer meaning. This process of reverse engineering is the work of an actor. Engaging with that work is the pleasure and profit of theatre-based practice, and relies on a symbiosis of the articulacy Shakespeare gives us and what we bring to him. In explaining the social value of exploring Shakespeare's language, Berry often quoted Thomas Kydd 'Where words prevail not, violence prevails'. Words as social grooming allow us to find ways of sharing space with each other and a key way we do this is by using what Lakoff and Johnson describe as using 'metaphorical imagination' to create rapport. They explain: 'When the chips are down, meaning is negotiated: you slowly figure out what you have in common, what it is safe to talk about, how you can communicate unshared experience or create a shared vision' (1980: 231–2). Developing young people's literacy in the widest sense of their ease with language is crucial for personal and social development, for, as Robin Alexander says, 'Language not only manifests thinking but also structures it, and speech shapes the higher mental processes necessary for so much of the learning that takes place, or ought to take place, in schools' (2008: 92).

Building vocabulary

Shakespeare is often celebrated for creating new words. The extent to which he made up these words, or captured their usage may never be known but McDonald suggests he 'contributed a substantial percentage', taking 'advantage of the plasticity and unruliness of the English language' at a time when it was finding its forms and rules (2001: 36–7). Neologizing is recognized by linguists as an essential and universal feature of our social brains as we reach to find expression. If we can reach for a word or phrase that already exists and already has currency we might find a satisfying sense of communication; children and artists especially, however, will playfully adapt language to suit their purpose.

Language is deeply connected to culture, to learning and to identity. Children instinctively absorb the sounds and gestures of communication around them in order to find belonging (Fitch 2010); but while they learn the rules of their tribe's standard communication, they also learn playful subversion as they experiment with different identities. Surveying how 'Individual diction and forms of speech do not vary because they need to for any physical, intellectual or practical reasons', David Bellos suggests that variations emerge 'as a differentiating tool – to differentiate not only where you come from, what rank and clan or street-gang you belong to, but to say "I am not you but me"' (2011: 350–1). Berry claims that 'speaking is in itself a positive, if not aggressive, act, for simply by making sound we are asserting our presence' (2008: 3).

Vygotsky observes that children can struggle to learn a new word as they acquire vocabulary, not because the sound is difficult but because they are not yet able to grasp the concept behind it. He quotes Tolstoy: 'There is a word available nearly always when the concept has matured' (cited in Vygotsky 1934: 9). Learning that Julius Caesar's former friends turn against him, whisper in corners about him and are called 'conspirators' because *conspire* means breathe together, can make sense as a concept if the prior knowledge of personal playground experiences are referenced. Encouraging play with Shakespeare's language allows children not just to enjoy new vocabulary but also to find words to convey concepts just within reach. The menace of King Lear's curse, 'into her womb convey sterility' for example, may not be fully understood, but his lament, 'How sharper than a serpent's tooth it is to have a thankless child' (*KL*, 1.4.236-7) perhaps gives words to an emerging concept that parents have feelings that can be hurt.

Language acquisition proceeds through and is encouraged by playful engagement. Many teachers informally report that working with theatre-based Shakespeare builds their students' vocabulary (RSC 2016); perhaps because they are encouraged to find pleasure and purpose in using words; perhaps enjoying playing with the qualities of the sounds and feeling a satisfaction in words that feel right to express what they want to express. Embodying and moving with those words opens up possibilities of connection in what Maxine Sheets-Johnson (1999: xviii) describes as 'languaging experience'. This wonderful phrase offers an example of how functional shift, much used by Shakespeare, grabs our attention in its playful approach to language. It also summarizes the process of progressive experiential learning: doing something, reflecting on that experience and reaching for the vocabulary to express the discoveries and knowledge gained.

Writing in role is a commonly used approach in theatre-based practice that leads many teachers to be pleasantly surprised at how it improves writing skills. Students are asked to retell events shown in, or inferred from, the texts from a particular character's point of view; but crucially, after they have been involved in activities that allow them to inhabit that point of view so that they have something to say: perhaps as the guard walking along the cold, dark battlements of Elsinore castle and feeling the eerie presence of a ghost; or as Macbeth writing his letter to Lady Macbeth having met the witches and heard their prophecies. Students absorb Shakespeare's words and phrases as they play with the scenes and gain an ease and familiarity that allows them to weave his words into their own writing, collaborating with Shakespeare to create new work.

Close reading

Literary metaphors can seem complex on the page but activities that find the physicality that roots them can bring better understanding. The role of a metaphor, as explored in Chapter 1, is to close a gap of understanding by comparing one thing to another. Understanding of Shakespeare's famous mixed metaphor, 'to take arms against a sea of troubles and by opposing end them', perhaps is deferred until we hear the phrase, 'To die, to sleep' (*Ham*, 3.1.62-66). Then we can understand that what Hamlet is proposing is that the only way to fight back against overwhelming force is to turn the weapons on yourself. The emotional power of the image depends on surprising us. How do you fight a sea? Oh, you can't. The comparison instead perhaps leaves us wondering how we might feel helplessly stranded in a wide open ocean or faced with an oncoming tsunami. Consciously, we have very little time to process that idea if we are listening to Hamlet speak, but in a good production, the actor playing Hamlet will have done their homework, understood the line and found an imaginative connection with the emotion the imagery offers. Because the actor understands what they are saying and why they are saying it, the non-verbal aspects of their performance help to make sense of the complex text in the moment for the audience.

This necessity of close reading for an actor is the process of theatre-based practice for the student. Actors/students might find physical gestures for key words and phrases: 'nobler', 'mind', 'suffer'; 'slings and arrows', 'outrageous fortune', to explore their meaning. They might paraphrase the text by finding personal, colloquial, alive 'translations' of the text, rather than smoothing away the nuance into standard English. They might try speaking the line in different ways: as if they want the audience to tell them what to do, understand their pain, or leave them alone. Many similar activities can be found in available teaching resources, but most importantly, none of these activities are about finding an objective right answer to how Hamlet feels or how an actor should deliver the lines. They are about young people gaining confidence in trying things out, being curious, asking 'What if?', sharing thoughts, and considering how Hamlet's words might find meaning today. As Thompson and Turchi observe: 'Highlighting patterns is not the same intellectual work as articulating how and why they matter' (2015: 15).

In addition to the educational value and possibilities of Shakespeare's language in the twenty-first century classroom, theatre-based approaches can clear space (literally and figuratively) for a playground in which to actively deconstruct its structural and aesthetic modes and place it in conversation with alternative texts. This is a valuable function of the practice because 'structures of social power are expressed in . . . aesthetic forms' (Copland and Olson 2018). Shakespeare education scholars and practitioners have offered a range of rich approaches here, such as Adhaar Noor Desai's close linguistic 'riffing' of the text (2019), Carla Della Gatta's use of assignments transporting Shakespeare's stories to other performative and literary genres (2019) or the text-pairing practices of the Folger's education team as described by Peggy O'Brien in Part Two and of the #DisruptTexts movement.

Specifically, this not only offers opportunities for learners to take 'ownership' and author/ity with Shakespeare's rich language and its connections to a shared humanity but also acknowledges and excavates the ways in which his language – and both historical and contemporary framings of them – can also be deeply and unequivocally inhumane; reproducing patriarchal, imperial, heteronormative discourses (Thompson 2011; Williams 2018; Kemp 2019). Playing with, through and at times against the language of the text can therefore develop learners' critical capacities, as Thomson and Turchi argue: 'in a social justice framework, Shakespeare's homophobic, anti-Semitic, misogynistic and racist lines are not ignored, minimized, or laughed at. Instead, they are the starting point for interrogating complex texts, contexts and identities' (2020b: 55).

Rhetoric

Rhetoric is the study of how words work on us and through us, affecting our perceptions, our thoughts and our emotions. Sam Leith describes it as 'language at play, language plus' and says we all use it all the time 'because it is either useful or delightful'. Leith also points out how commonly rhetorical devices are used when an imbalance of power is manifested through words (2012: 6–10). Words as power play is the very stuff of Shakespeare: through Portia's defence of Antonio, Benedict's 'merry war' with Beatrice, the pre-battle speeches of kings, and on and on. Shakespeare studied the rhetoric of classical writers and contemporary students of communication can benefit by studying him.

Engaging with rhetoric can be off-putting because of the vast glossaries of key terms that accompany any study. Just as with other linguistic terminology, however, rhetorical terms evolved to recognize the patterns of how we speak, rather than determine them. Learning the term for the repetition of a phrase at the start of lines (*anaphora*) can be deeply satisfying once we have recognized the effect of that pattern; learning the word first by rote and seeking examples afterwards is less so. Linguistic patterns such as groups of three, linked pairs, repetitions and rhymes are all around us, Shakespeare merely gives some great examples. In the classic example of Mark Anthony's funeral oration (*JC*, 3.2.74–108), a student can easily hear the catchy triad of 'Friends, Romans, Countryman' and the antithesis of 'bury and praise', 'evil and good', 'lives and interred'. Recognizing these patterns, they can consider how the triad is more effective because it is an ascending tricolon, or how the phrasing of 'I come to bury Caesar, not to praise him' affects the ear. They can discuss the musicality of the patterns and why claiming not to be doing what you really are doing grabs our attention, and perhaps then they can learn it has a term, *occulatio*. As with all activities in theatre-based Shakespeare the aim is to deepen close reading by experiencing the words in action, reflect on discoveries made, and then consolidate learning with useful specialist vocabulary.

Rhetoric records and formalizes the language play hyper-social humans learn in order to get others to listen; we learn to suit our words to our actions and to what others want to hear. Rhetorical terms are many and varied, but three key terms for understanding communication are the three appeals of *Ethos, Logos* and *Pathos*. *Ethos* is the idea that to get anyone to hear us, we have to establish trust. Classical rhetoricians knew what modern psychology has evidenced, that if we like someone, we are more likely to agree with their views (Kahneman 2012). If their words convey to us, 'you can trust me because I have similar experiences and thoughts to you', then, as Benet Brandreth puts it, 'we can offload the hard work of thinking for ourselves on to the speaker and simply agree with them' (2021: 45). *Logos* means following this through with reasons why your views are right. Notably, these need not be rational, instead they need to sound reasonable and convince your hearer that they are thinking sensibly by agreeing with you. If you've already established *ethos*, that becomes easier. *Pathos* means making arguments that appeal to emotions, suggesting images and analogies that make associations with things your hearer cares about.

Rhetorical devices are ways of communicating that we all use instinctively all the time but which advertising, media, and politicians use very deliberately. Understanding how others may be using rhetoric to manipulate us is a useful awareness to learn. We live in a world dominated by verbal language and respond readily to articulacy. We are subconsciously affected by how others speak and often do not recognize how their rhetoric, as well as their tone, manipulates us. Johnson suggests our trust in the objective truth of words can lead us to an 'illusion that meanings are fixed, abstract entities that can float free of contexts and the ongoing flow of experience' (2007: 80). Shakespeare's crafting of language includes his deep understanding of rhetoric, and the moral and linguistic playground of his texts provide ample material to explore how we are affected and can affect others through the arrangements of words we use.

In addition, as Brandreth proposes, 'The value of rhetoric for unpicking a text is not that it suggests the answers but that it shows us where important questions are being asked' (2021: 85). He explains how the argument a character puts forward through their use of *ethos*, *logos* and *pathos* is 'an expression of the speaker's understanding – true or flawed – of their status with and relationship to the listener, of what they think matters to that listener, of what they think the circumstances are in which they speak' (2021: 71). Interrogating the character's use of language gives us clues to that character's model of the world. To understand how best to persuade someone to our point of view, we need to understand theirs and what they think of us. Through inhabiting the texts, students can play with what a character's objectives and intentions might be and investigate how Shakespeare's characters attempt to get what they want with the words that they have. They can explore when they think characters succeed, when and why they fail, and reflect on what this can mean about how people use language in the real world. Brandreth summarizes: 'Learning about rhetoric in the context of Shakespeare in performance, one becomes equipped with a powerful framework for thinking and for understanding language in general, for analyzing questions of identity, of power, of manipulation, and for communicating persuasively' (2021: 5).

It is beyond the scope of this book to delve any further into Shakespeare's use of rhetoric but many others have. For those interested: Sam Leith's *You Taking to Me?* (2012) provides a highly accessible and witty overview. Benet Brandreth's *Shakespearean Rhetoric* (2021) focuses especially on ways to understand and inhabit Shakespeare's use of rhetoric from a performance perspective. Raphael Lyne's *Shakespeare, Rhetoric and Cognition* (2011) offers a deeper textual exploration of how rhetorical devices can reflect ways of thinking.

Shakespeare for oracy

In promoting the pedagogy of the spoken word, Alexander tells us: 'Of all the tools for cultural and pedagogical intervention in human development and learning, talk is the most pervasive in its use and powerful in its possibilities' (2008: 92); yet the value of talk (including sign language) and the pedagogy needed to develop the skills of oracy are currently largely unrecognized in our school systems. Hattie's meta-analysis of education research (2009) found discussion between students remains important throughout learning whether structured by the teacher or not, because before we read and write, we speak and listen. The tools of writing have enabled more precise passing on of knowledge, but our social brains need the basis of talk to build understanding. Evidence is accumulating that being better able to express your own thoughts and feelings, actively listen to what others think and feel, and use those skills to engage creatively, critically and collaboratively in discussion with others, is valuable not just for academic and career success but also for personal and societal well-being.

In the UK, a recent report from an All Party Parliamentary Group (APPG) enquiry into oracy recognizes talk as 'the currency of learning' (2021: 4). The report calls for 'high-quality oracy education as a consistent and comprehensive entitlement' but notes that the 'status and provision of oracy education in England today falls significantly short of this vision' (2021: 34). It finds that most teachers recognize the value of oracy but do not always feel they have the training or the time to effectively embed it into their practice; particularly when government policies and guidelines prioritize reading and writing. Nearly 80 per cent of young people said they wanted oracy to be prioritized in schools to support their learning, but only a third felt it was (2021: 10). Reviewing a cumulation of evidence from experts, employers, teachers, parents and young people, the report concludes 'There is a powerful cross-sector consensus on the importance of oracy supported by a robust evidence base', and from all stakeholders a 'demand for a stronger emphasis on oracy in education' (2021: 33).

Many of the arguments for the value of oracy development and the pedagogies to do it will be familiar to drama teachers. In their influential book with the self-explanatory title *Asking Better Questions*, Norah Morgan and Juliana Saxton (1994) use their expertise in drama education to offer tools for cross-disciplinary oracy approaches, which they claim as essential to fostering democracy. Speaking to the APPG, Alexander also claims 'Talk is a fundamental prerequisite for democratic engagement' (APPG 2021:24). Alexander defines dialogue as requiring 'willingness and skill to engage with minds, ideas and ways of thinking other than our own' and provides a useful list of the skills such dialogue involves: 'the ability to question, listen, reflect, reason, explain, speculate and explore ideas; to analyze problems, frame hypotheses and develop solutions; to discuss, argue, examine evidence, defend, probe and assess arguments' (2008: 122); skills inherent in theatre-based study of Shakespeare. Gary Taylor provocatively proposed: 'We find in Shakespeare only what we bring to him or what others have left behind; he gives us back our own values' (1989: 411). The dialogic approach Alexander itemizes allows us to explore those values in the light of others'. Everyone has their own model of the world and may see something we don't. Unless we engage in dialogue, we will never know what they see or understand the possibilities and pluralities of perspectives available. Shakespeare's use of language helps us understand how words illuminate rather than define meaning. Wittgenstein offers an analogy that thinking the ambiguity of language is a defect 'would be like saying that the light of my reading lamp is no real light at all because it has no sharp boundary' (1958: 27).

Throughout this book, we have argued for active speaking and listening as the very fabric of theatre-based practice. Working with Shakespeare brings a *language-rich* environment, and theatre-based practice puts that rich language into young people's ears and mouths and bodies. Active and critical close reading of the texts provides material for investigating forms and structures and introduces new vocabulary. This in turn stimulates investigative talk about meanings from within and without the texts. Traditional so-called knowledge-rich approaches to Shakespeare that treat the plays as texts for examination of reading, measured through writing, may involve some discursive approaches but miss out on the drama activities that support young people to feel the embodied affect of his prosody. Rather than being easier, a relatively more passive reading often simplifies how young people are able to respond, robbing them of complex responses to the complexity of the texts.

Talking back to Shakespeare

In this chapter, we have proposed how theatre-based practice can support young people to learn *through* Shakespeare the communication skills that many suggest will positively impact their lives. In thinking about how Shakespeare can support young people in developing their skills, it can be interesting to consider how he developed his own. Although we cannot be certain that Shakespeare attended the King Edward VI School in Stratford, and while acknowledging that an Elizabethan schooling is not unproblematic from a modern perspective, it seems highly likely that he profited from an education influenced by the traditions of medieval scholasticism which provided grounding in the dialogically focused trivium of grammar, logic and rhetoric. Shakespeare and his school friends were most probably brought up on a diet of Ovid, Plutarch, Seneca and Cicero, digesting classical texts that blend history and literature and exposed them to philosophical arguments about the place and purpose of humanity. The boys were taught to engage with the ideas classical thinkers presented through absorbing their styles and learned how to debate from either side of a complex question. Colin Burrow suggests this training 'had the secondary and unintended consequences of developing students' ability to engage in what would now be called imagining a different point of view' (2013: 42). Lynn Enterline describes how 'Schoolmasters required young orators to learn how to use and refine the chief tools of their trade: eyes, ears, hands, tongues' (2012: 3). She argues that through the process of *imitatio*, grammar school boys were trained to imitate 'the physical as well as verbal techniques that would touch the "hearts" of those who heard and saw them' (2012: 4).

It seems that Shakespeare and his peers learned not only to write, but perform as they translated and analysed speeches attributed to lovers and warriors, slaves and politicians. Shakespeare went on, not just to appreciate the literary authority figures preferenced by his schooling, but to creatively and critically interact with them, developing their perspectives, arguments, rhetorical techniques, poetic devices, narrative structures, allusions, and analogies to offer his own ideas. Much of this parallels our relationship to Shakespeare as the literary authority figure of our own time and echoes the notion of teaching to develop learner author/ity as discussed in Chapter 1. Creative contemporary theatre and literature across the world is in dialogue with Shakespeare, considering what he can mean for us now and how he can be used to make us think and reflect on our own world, just as he drew from classical examples. In the pragmatic and collaborative world of theatre, Shakespeare would have brought his scripts but worked with his company to adapt, explore, solve problems and review since, as Brook points out, 'Shakespeare was not a poet living on an island, he was writing for a community with a precarious way of life' (2013: 11).

Shakespeare as a working artist exploited theatre as a medium not just to appreciate 'the best that has been thought and said' according to the dominant culture of his time, but also to turn 'a stream of fresh and free thought upon' his sources and challenge his actors and audiences to consider other perspectives. Theatre-based practice invites today's young people to do the same with him.

Across Part One of this book, we have aimed to draw together diverse thinking and scholarship underpinning and evidencing the value of theatre-based Shakespeare teaching practice. We have drawn from across disciplinary concepts to build a wide-ranging theoretical framework for the pedagogical study of Shakespeare which might be seen as an ecosystem of approaches, principles and practice. This framework rests on the three principles, set out in the introduction, that any theatre-based classroom study of Shakespeare should: (1) invite prior knowledge, ideas and values to bear on a shared experience of understanding a literary text; (2) combine intellectual, social and emotional learning through embodying the text; and (3) develop criticality in questioning a cultural inheritance and how that canon can in turn raise questions about today's world. It is our strongly held belief, shared with many, that Shakespeare still has much to offer young people everywhere as a resource providing a moral and linguistic playground in which to explore, discuss and learn. We are also, however, too well aware that many young people leave school indifferent to, or alienated from, Shakespeare because of how his work is imposed in their lives. As established in our introduction, teaching and learning Shakespeare cannot solve the problems young people face today, but through the principles of theatre-based practice, we have explored and discussed in these chapters, perhaps playfully active and critical engagement with his works and the knotty cultural incrustations they carry can support young people into becoming, as Bruner describes, 'more effective, less alienated, and better human beings'.

PART TWO

Perspectives from organizations and practitioners

5

Perspectives from organizations and practitioners

Introduction

In this Part Two, we collate and present extracts from ten interviews carried out with freelance practitioners and leaders from a range of organizations involved in theatre-based Shakespeare education practice. You can find details on the ten interviewees in the list of contributors on pp. 8-9.

During her research into the place of Shakespeare in education around the world (Irish 2012), Tracy encountered many creative projects, ranging from the small scale of Aimara Resende's (2019) 'Shakespeare e as Crianças' (Shakespeare and the Children) which uses the vehicle of Shakespeare performance to develop the social and communication skills of the young people in Resende's local rural community in Brazil, to the larger scale of 'Shakespeare4All' (2023) in Hong Kong, whose programmes develop English language competencies in partnership with a wide range of schools. In *Reimagining Shakespeare Education*, Liam Semler, Claire Hansen and Jacqueline Manuel showcase twenty-one such projects to celebrate the range and scope of innovative work continually emerging from the global field of Shakespeare education. They describe their collection as 'suggestive, rather than representative' since, 'There are infinite, unique Shakespeare projects that flourish around the world and deliver significant experiences and insights to participants, yet never become widely known as published case studies' (2023: 6). All over the world there are pockets of pedagogical disruption where young people are encouraged to find ownership of Shakespeare for themselves and to treat him as a living artist. All over the world there are theatre companies that have Shakespeare in their repertory of both performance and educational offer. We would love to have interviewed more of them, but in the limited space of this second part of the book, we present a range of voices that can also be thought of as 'suggestive, rather than representative', in this case of the views and values of organizations and practitioners promoting active, theatre-based Shakespeare. You will find voices from organizations with substantial offers for teachers and young people (RSC, Globe, Folger, SSF) alongside a suggestive sample of theatre education practitioners and smaller youth organizations.

Approach

The interviews cited here all took place between the summer of 2022 and the spring of 2023. The majority were conducted online, though some occurred face to face. All the interviews were recorded, transcribed and edited in order to make them more accessible for someone reading rather than hearing them. This meant, for example, removing discourse markers and repetitions but not changing words. Where a word has been added, this is represented in [square brackets]. Our interviewees then had the option to amend the excerpts we selected for use. We have collated the interview extracts under three chapter headings, which broadly represent a summary of the range of questions the interviewees were asked and also offer a continued development of the core questions explored in Part One. Responses are collated in this way in order to give a parity of voices across our interviewees and a sense of both converging and diverging areas of discourse across the theatre-based Shakespeare education community. Within this structure, we have therefore made the editorial and curatorial decision to place extracts from multiple individual interviews 'in conversation' with each other under these different headings. It is important to note, however, that while contributors are aware of each other, these extracts do not represent a live conversation.

In Chapter 6, we draw together responses dealing with the overall aims and scope of the different organizations covered, as well as particular current areas of focus. We recognize that for some of the larger organizations interviewed in particular, it is not possible to accurately represent the full range of current, past and upcoming projects, but we have aimed to give a suggestive sense of current areas of attention within Shakespeare education practice. In Chapter 7, we have collated responses that deal with the different external and cultural contexts our interviewees operate in. This includes their perspectives on working with schools and young people, and their responses to current public debates on Shakespeare's cultural value and place within twenty-first-century life. Finally, in Chapter 8, we collect together the contributors' wide-ranging and reflexive responses to questions of why Shakespeare *has been* taught for so long and why *should we* continue to do so.

In curating these extracts across the following three chapters, we let contributors 'speak for themselves' as much as possible while recognizing transcripts are always co-constructed and mediated by the interviewer

(Mann 2011). As emphasized in Part One, we see the teaching, studying and performance of Shakespeare as part of a broad and eclectic community of practice. Through these extracts, our intention is to provide informal access to a range of experiences and perspectives within this community.

Funding

Organizations' different priorities and approaches are inevitably affected by how their work is funded. In the UK, the Arts Council is a major source of government funding from which some organizations are lucky enough to benefit. In both the United States and the United Kingdom, endowments, corporate funding, private donations and so forth are crucial alongside any charge to participants in maintaining the sustainability and scope of the work. Our interviewees are from a range that gives a sample of funding models. The work of the RSC is funded through a 'mixed economy' of Arts Council grants, donations from charitable foundations, corporate sponsors and charges for various workshops. Funding allows an organization space and resources to grow, develop, reflect on their practice and gain further funding. In the case of the RSC, historic access to public funding through Creative Partnerships, alongside a partnership with the University of Warwick, began a research journey that has resulted in the company being awarded Independent Research Organization status and that means they can apply for further funding from the UK Research and Innovation Council.

Shakespeare's Globe does not receive Arts Council funding and without that foundation, as Lucy Cuthbertson describes: 'You're either doing things because they're commercially worth it or you're doing it because somebody has funded you to work there.' Freelance practitioner Emma Manton describes an outcome of this: 'With the Globe, the space earns its keep. So often you're going and doing those tours and there's a rehearsal on stage with the actors, or a voice class, or a tech, or a changeover – but they [students] get so much out of just watching the space in action and hearing what notes are being given and what's changing, and just being in the space.' Shakespeare North does receive funding from the Arts Council, although as Head of Engagement Evonne Bixter explains 'that's not all of the funding that we need. It's from a lot of different areas: commercial activity but also from fundraising and from funding applications. It's a complex jigsaw.' Coram Shakespeare Schools Foundation similarly operates on a jigsaw of funding with their core work supported by, as Francesca Ellis describes, a combination of 'Earned income through school registration fees, theatre festival box office, sale of workshops and training (to schools and businesses) and merchandise sales [and] voluntary income from trusts and foundations, individual donors and some corporate support'.

Smaller theatre organizations in the UK can apply for Arts Council grants for particular projects. Karl Falconer from Purple Door, for example, told us of an Arts Council grant for their Shakespeare-focused youth theatre project but adds that justifying such funding can bring a tension around the purpose of youth theatre. He explained how two of the group went on to drama school and says 'those are the kinds of things we would quote in the Arts Council evaluation form, because that sounds better than the kid who just said "Yeah, I had a good time", but is one experience more valuable than the other?'

Online

More and more resources for teaching Shakespeare can now be found online. The Folger, the Globe and the RSC all offer a wide variety of resources that can be accessed by teachers and students to support their study of Shakespeare. As across so many sectors, the 2020–22 Covid pandemic pushed these organizations into exploring new technologies and thinking about how they could move more sessional work online. Faced with how best to support a community of teachers across the expanse of the United States, the Folger had begun holding regular professional development sessions online before lockdowns but found uptake for those meetings increased considerably. Peggy O'Brien probably speaks for everyone creating online sessions at that time when she says: 'We needed to figure this out, you know, it's like teaching the class where you're one page ahead of the students – we had to figure out how to do all this stuff on zoom'. The Folger led regular sessions for teachers, hosted online study meetings and invited speakers, and released the rights to audio and filmed recordings of popular productions for students to watch. Other examples of digital offers developed at that time include the RSC's series of videos called 'Homework Help' with actors offering advice on aspects of Shakespeare study and Shakespeare's Globe live-streamed online professional development for teachers offering bespoke sessions using interactive workshop approaches. All companies continue to review how best to take their learning from that time forward.

As mentioned in the introduction, within the limited scope of this book. digital offers are not our main focus. There are many interesting avenues to explore in the relationship between a practice that so fundamentally depends on the interaction of ideas, experiences, voices and bodies in a four-dimensional space together and what can be communicated through screens. We can only limit ourselves here to echoing our arguments in Chapter 4 that ever-expanding technologies bring massive advantages in how they can democratize communication and make connections across cultures, but they also make us more aware than ever of what we miss through not sharing real space in real time with our fellow humans.

Common values and themes

While there are many nuances and differences in specific focus on the nature of the work and targeted audience, our interviewees and the organizations they represent share many approaches and values. As Lucy Cuthbertson of Shakespeare's Globe observed: 'I think you see quite a lot of the practices spread amongst lots of companies, which is great. I don't think there needs to be this sense of: "We do something that other people don't." I think if we do something that's really great, I think we should want to share it and therefore it's being done more.' Such sharing of practice seems inevitable when practitioners share rehearsal and project experiences while working across different organizations. The work of individual practitioners is framed to a certain extent by the aims of the organizations they work for, just as the work teachers do in the classroom is framed by the policies of their school. Like teachers, however, theatre practitioners bring their own knowledge, their own experiences and their own style. Freelance practitioner Emma Manton sums this up beautifully by saying: 'I mean, kids are kids and Shakespeare is Shakespeare at the end of the day. And I am me. So my practice is only ever going to be what I can bring to it.'

There is an overwhelming sense arising from these interviews of a diverse and dynamic ecology of theatre-based Shakespeare education practice, overlapping and diverging in fruitful ways. Jacqui O'Hanlon, Director of Learning and National Partnerships at the RSC, places this in an international arts context: 'We're part of an arts ecology – we're part of a national and global community around Shakespeare's work and we're part of a national and international arts ecology. Our collective endeavour is the democratizing of arts and culture.' This shared commitment to Shakespeare as a resource for cultural democracy – acknowledging his complexity while taking him off any 'pedestal' and inviting learners to meet and explore his texts on their own terms – echoes throughout the extracts presented in further chapters. The following chapters are therefore a suggestive configuration of the rich discourses and experiences present in this evolving ecology of practice.

6

Aims, scope and areas of focus

In this opening chapter, our interview contributors discuss the overall aims, scope and specific areas of focus of their Shakespeare education work. The responses here arose from a range of questions we posed covering the practicalities and realities of working as a theatre-based Shakespeare education institution or practitioner. As would be expected from this diverse international group, there is a wide range of work covered. This is grounded in the variety of organizations represented: from theatres and charities with an international profile, through regional community and youth companies, to the Folger which, as Peggy O'Brien emphasizes, 'is not just one thing. It's a rare book library. It's a theatre. It's a museum.' The scope of particular projects is wide-ranging in age, scale and focus. From family work, continuing professional development (CPD) for teachers, one-off workshops, youth theatres, young companies, large-scale performances and curriculum-focused projects, the range is inspirationally broad, demonstrating the malleability of theatre-based Shakespeare practice in diverse contexts.

The overall aims are diverse, though share a common thread in charting connections between social and theatrical experience, as in Evonne Bixter's commitment to 'partnership working' at Shakespeare North Playhouse; Jaqui O'Hanlon's focus on the RSC as 'a place of possibilities' or Darren Raymond's discussion of developing 'life skills' through the work of Intermission Youth. In this, the organizations and practitioners echo some of the key themes we draw out in Part One around the deep but contested interconnections between Shakespeare and social justice, and the rich possibilities for exploring this within theatre-based practice.

Aims

The overall aims of our contributing organizations and individuals presented here reflect recurring themes of *accessibility* and *ownership* for learners and young people, and the commitment to the progressive pedagogy of meeting them 'where they're at' in order to construct a live and contextualized connection with the texts.

EVONNE BIXTER, SHAKESPEARE NORTH PLAYHOUSE: What I talk about a lot is partnership working and socially engaged practice and then obviously what underpins everything we're doing which is creativity and thinking about how we explore creativity and the creative process. We're really keen to engage with young people who perhaps would have initially felt that this wasn't something they'd be interested in.

PEGGY O'BRIEN, THE FOLGER SHAKESPEARE LIBRARY: The Folger is not just one thing. It's a rare book library. It's a theatre. It's a museum. And we are also the publisher of the Folger editions of Shakespeare's plays. And also, besides the Folger editions in print, we also have the Folger Shakespeare, which is online and free to everybody. So we're all of those things and education grew as the institution grew. We have local programmes for kids, and performance festivals and we have workshops for teachers – but our education work has really grown a lot on a national level because it was made clear that there was a national need. And that's about teaching and it's teaching primarily in middle and high school, because that's where Shakespeare shows up in the curriculum. We work with those teachers because we figure that if we give everything we have to a teacher, then their students from then on are the beneficiaries of that. And so that is the strategy in a country that's as big as this.

JACQUI O'HANLON, ROYAL SHAKESPEARE COMPANY: My favourite thing that an actor said about the rehearsal room is: 'It's a place of possibilities' and I've loved it because that speaks to me as an educator. It's what I think a classroom can be and what learning can be about. So that was what beautifully encapsulated it for me – about why we talk so much about the classroom as a rehearsal room.

EMMA MANTON, FREELANCE PRACTITIONER: I absolutely approach it as an actor. My ethos, my appeal to my students is always, 'I am an actor and this is what helps me. Maybe it'll help you' or 'This is what I've seen help other people, maybe it'll help you'. I think being in plays is the main training, or the training we have in observing each other and skill sharing.

KARL FALCONER, PURPLE DOOR: Our primary focus is Shakespeare and community – those are the two words that I hold up. This wasn't necessarily part of the artistic plan that we had when we started but the thing that clicked into place was a realization that there were other people in my shoes. I didn't enjoy Shakespeare at school, it didn't seem relevant. But then also, being from the North West as an emerging creative, there's not the opportunities, so you feel like you need to go to London and then that comes with a financial barrier. With those two things together, our work is focused on: can we do something different with Shakespeare that speaks to the community that we've got in terms of the artists that we work with and the audiences that we want to reach? That's taken loads of forms – we've had an Arts Council-funded youth theatre, which looked at Shakespeare and his contemporaries as a season of work. We've got our main company and now we're moving into the venue stage of our life, and what that might mean in terms of how we bring all those things together – to reimagine what a theatre could look like. The idea of Purple Door is what happens if culture is free at the point of entry, so that you don't pay for a ticket? What happens if you remove the delineation between the social space of a theatre and the performance space – and what does that do in terms of what the work looks like, who can engage with the work? I think it's a broad question about any theatre engagement generally, which is what is the ultimate aim of it? And I suppose for me at this point the ultimate aim is that if somebody feels they could take a risk coming into our space, because it feels less risky, because it's cheaper, because it's closer to them, because there's other people there like them. If that means that six months later they feel that they can take another risk in going to the Everyman; or they saw five minutes of some Shakespeare and it wasn't as scary as they thought, I think that's our aim.

FRANCESCA ELLIS, CORAM SHAKESPEARE SCHOOLS FESTIVAL: Our mission [is to] transform lives through the unique power of Shakespeare. The world's largest youth drama festival lies at the heart of CSSF's work. Every year, we work with thousands of pupils from every community, background and school type across the UK. Months of preparation culminate in exhilarating performance evenings in professional theatres nationwide, a night which gives confidence and self-esteem to last a lifetime.

DARREN RAYMOND, INTERMISSION YOUTH: We work through the medium of theatre. So it's about learning together what it takes to be an actor. We also work predominantly with Shakespeare's text. But it's not just about acting, I've got to be clear about that. And it's not just about Shakespeare. It's about life skills and preparing our young people to become better versions of themselves so they can be equipped better for life and make better-informed choices.

LUCY CUTHBERTSON, SHAKESPEARE'S GLOBE: I see our aim as trying to keep Shakespeare relevant and exciting and very broadly accessible. So that everyone just feels that it's nothing to be frightened of. That's the thing about it that those of us who work with Shakespeare really love and really feel excited about. The normal thing you hear from young people is: Shakespeare, it's long and boring. The challenge there for me is to try and help them to appreciate bits of it and to feel like they could own it. That's really another of the big things we're trying to do here in education – to genuinely pass over ownership. Because I think if you care about relevance and you care about the aspects of decolonization, which have to happen with Shakespeare, what it was and what its history is, you have to be also pedagogically really interested in ownership.

I'm interested in where we are meeting young people – where they're at and what they're bringing. I want to know what they think of stuff and what ideas they have and what they see. The only way this kind of work will continue into the future is if we stop thinking there's a body of expertise around it and you need to understand that – an elitism around that I suppose – and look at the stories, what's interesting in these stories? Why should we still be telling these stories? The Globe was set up for a particular reason initially in terms of this idea of original practice – and there are some people who hold on to that idea as a guiding principle, that this is about original practice, it's about a radical experiment – but where do those things move with the times? How many times do you need to see whatever an original practice version of *King Lear* is? You might as well just film it and put it out there. At what point have we discovered everything this building is going to throw up regarding the experiment and then what are we doing? If people think that we're a heritage place and a museum for Shakespeare, that's horrific. If that's still the perception out there, it couldn't be more wrong.

Scope

It would be impossible to enumerate here the full range of work and specific projects offered by these different organizations and individuals. In the next set of collated responses, however, we hope to give a taste of their scope. From large-scale organizations such as Shakespeare's Globe and the RSC we hear of the diverse offer between their everyday workshop-led work, and more focused and strategic projects as well as longer term partnerships. Francesca Ellis for CSSF discusses how their flagship festival project functions alongside more focused work. Peggy O'Brien speaks of actors and teachers finding points of connection across their practice with Shakespeare's language at the Folger, while Darren Raymond's work at Intermission Youth begins with explorations of themes and story and then weaves into Shakespeare's text the phrases spoken by young people in their improvisations. Darren speaks of allowing participants to find points of salience with their own lives and argues for a dynamic co-existence of participants' everyday discourse and Early Modern text that brings out the playful expressiveness of both. This diversity of projects and approaches demonstrates the malleability of theatre-based Shakespeare practice depending on the scope and focus of the work and positionality of the participants. Yet, as Lucy Cuthbertson from the Globe emphasizes, 'It always comes back to you using the scripts and putting it on its feet'.

DARREN RAYMOND: Initially when a young person comes into a workshop and discovers that we're doing Shakespeare, they're not interested – and I don't blame them because I'd be the same at that age because I had a negative experience with Shakespeare. So what we do is we don't mention Shakespeare at all. The first six, seven, eight weeks of workshops, it's just improvising conversations and looking at themes and issues that may be taken from a Shakespeare play. If I take you back to when we first started in 2008, we were looking at Shakespeare's *Julius Caesar* because for me, that was the ultimate knife crime and in 2008, knife crime was pretty rife in the capital, and it still is today sadly. So for me it was about drawing situations from Shakespeare's *Caesar*, and putting that into a workshop and saying: 'What would you do if you knew one of your friends in your circle was becoming too powerful, or taking advantage and abusing power? How would that make you feel? How would you react?' And then what we'll do is, probably about two-three months down the line, I would say to the group: 'Okay, we're gonna do a play' and they're like, 'Yeah, cool, what are we doing?' 'We're gonna do a Shakespeare play'. 'Ohhh, come on, Darren man. We don't wanna do no Shakespeare play. Forget that'. And I'd be like, 'Well, you've just invested in one of Shakespeare's plays in the last three months in the work you've been doing'. 'What are you talking about?' 'Well, you see that improvisation that you did three weeks ago? There's a similar situation in Shakespeare's *Caesar*, where I've drawn inspiration from to bring into our workshops'. And then it gives them a reason to ask questions about Shakespeare – and they do. And that curiosity, because it's coming from them, carries much more weight – they go with it and they enjoy it because they've invested into it already. They've created their own characters: they've created their Caesar, they've created their Brutus, their Mark Antony, their Calpurnia. So there's a reason for them to want to do that work. Because they've invested in this work with their own ideas, their own lives, they bring that into the room with their own experiences. People tend to say: 'Oh, you're dumbing down Shakespeare. Why can't the young people just do Shakespeare's text as it is written?' Because that's where the magic is, in the words that he created; in those lovely imaginative words that he came up with. But our young people are doing the same thing today – they invent new words, they have their own form of expression through words. Language evolves, and it's about us appreciating that language evolves and appreciating the creativity of our young people in their use of words. So I would suggest the opposite. I would say that what they're doing isn't dumbing down Shakespeare, it's ensuring that he has a legacy. If we all did Shakespeare the same, I mean, what would be the point?

LUCY CUTHBERTSON: In Learning [our offer includes], the 'lively action package' which is a tour inside the theatre and an hour's practical workshop on a play. Also GCSE or A level study days. [Another] huge thing that we do here is the Playing Shakespeare project. So that's a funded production, a full-scale production, funded by Deutsche Bank. [We] put a whole production on and give away about 26,000 free tickets during the course of March every year to young people from state schools in London and Birmingham. We're trying to get those young people into the Globe who are statistically probably less likely to be coming to the theatre outside of their school. This is a huge project, takes a lot of time, a lot of staff time, loads of free CPD for teachers, loads of workshops free in school if schools ask for it. We do CPD for teachers – standard ones and ones through particular social justice angles. Teaching anti-racist Shakespeare is one that is really popular; Shakespeare and Women – looking at various famous characters from a feminist angle; and we've just launched Shakespeare and Sexuality – a queer-focused look at the plays. We have launched a youth theatre, to show people that young people can create work and be artists in their own right. We do other one-off projects and all of this work is under an umbrella of practical activities around the plays. I think it always comes back to that. It always comes back to you using the scripts and putting it on its feet. I'd say that is the main aim of everything we do.

JACQUI O'HANLON: We have a learning programme which we think of as our universal offer – the work that is available to any young person or lifelong learner or teacher or school that wants to access the RSC's work. That might be through conferences or online resources – for example, the Shakespeare Learning Zone. Or it might be through our teacher professional development programme – we have a large number of different touch points that anybody can access. Then we also have a team called National Partnerships and that is our targeted programme of long-term partnership with schools, regional theatres and adult communities across England. We are funded by Arts Council England, and so the focus for that partnership work is England. Typically, we work with over a thousand schools a year, and a quarter of those schools, 250, are ones we work with in long-term partnership through the Associate Schools Programme. These are partnerships in areas of the country we've made a long-term commitment to. They are typically in areas of structural disadvantage, where doing one off projects or even doing something for three years isn't going to make a long-term difference. What we need to do, and what we have done, is say we are here for ten, fifteen, twenty years as part of an integrated, co-created programme to help address the systemic kinds of disadvantage these schools experience. We know that talent and potential are everywhere, but opportunity isn't yet. Our partnership programmes are designed to address that basic inequity.

PEGGY O'BRIEN: In that little hothouse with scholars and actors – and it turned out that what the actors had to share was not a lot about acting, but they were also brilliant teachers – it [the Folger Method] developed and grew and got refined. For a long time, we talked about it as performance-based teaching until I went away from it for twenty years and then came back and I thought, this isn't performance-based teaching really – this is all about language. It's all about language. [For example] in the early days [1980s] I sat in the back of a class and watched an actor with a group of maybe fifteen or eighteen high school teachers and he had the first Mechanicals' scene from *A Midsummer Night's Dream*. Everybody had a script, they didn't have a book. They had pages, no notes, no nothing just the text. And so they went around, they read it in parts around the circle. They read it to the end of lines, to the punctuation. They read it in a bunch of different ways, and the actor would say: 'Don't worry about how you're pronouncing it, don't worry about any of that stuff, just read it.' And then he said: 'Who are these guys? How do you know? What makes you say that? Where is it in the text? What do they want?' It's like very basic questions, which I guess are questions that actors ask themselves. And so what these teachers realized after an hour or so is that they could figure out everything that was going on in the scene: 'What do they want? What are they doing? What are they worried about?' And then you would read it again a few times. And then, 'Did you learn anything else?' 'Oh, yeah, actually, I noticed *that*, I noticed *that*'. What they came away with at the end of an hour or so is that they could figure out what was going on in this piece of text together: 'Not only did we realize we could figure that out ourselves, but also the way that he was doing this, we thought, oh, I could do that. This is not fancy acting stuff.' It's focusing on the right thing, which is what are the words on that page. It was really obvious how it would help them get to the language, and also help their students get to the language. You set that up as a teacher, and then you get out of the way.

FRANCESCA ELLIS: We run the Shakespeare Schools Film Festival for a growing number of schools for whom the project is more accessible than the theatre festival (because of location or student need), or because they are interested in film-making as an alternative process. We also run shorter-term standalone workshops in schools across the UK, and sometimes residencies, especially in SEND settings. We train teachers of all disciplines to lead our projects in school, but predominantly English and Drama specialists (secondary schools) and class teachers (primary schools).

Particular areas of focus and interest

Again there is great diversity of approach in the work described here; however, some key themes emerge. First is a focus on intertextuality – for example in the Folger's use of text pairing activities or Shakespeare North Playhouse's Hip Hop project. Alongside this is a focus on contemporary salience – repeatedly respondents mention the legacy and impact of ongoing cultural crises such as Black Lives Matter (BLM) and #MeToo for their educational work. In this we can see the principles of constructivism and progressivism we argued in Part One as being the genesis of theatre-based education work in practice. Freelance practitioners Chris Nayak and Emma Manton meanwhile draw attention to the role of a shared sense of embodied *space* in theatre-based Shakespeare through their reflections on working in the Globe's reproduction playhouse; discussing how this connects to a shared past as well as a shared present through the interpersonal connections possible in that performance space. Karl Falconer of Purple Door also comments on the increased possibilities for understanding and connection possible from exploring the historical and cultural contexts of the plays.

CASSANDRA NWOKAH, FREELANCE PRACTITIONER: The work of Ayanna Thompson, and this idea of decolonizing Shakespeare, and really challenging the lens with which we are viewing Shakespeare with students – that's the part that really is inspiring me and keeping me connected to the work. The way that TFANA [Theatre for a New Audience] and the Folger has been doing it, and the way that they engage schools in New York, I think it's so rich, and that it enriches not just literary study, but the culture of the school itself – allowing these kinds of conversations to exist, using Shakespeare as the vehicle.

PEGGY O'BRIEN: We're doing a lot with paired texts. We define it in a different way, which is two texts that are both very strong – there's no primary and supplementary text there. Two really strong texts that if you look at them together they really illuminate one another. Pair Shakespeare with a writer of a different gender, century, religion, a different everything – and then what it illuminates, often, is what the differences and what the similarities are – and that is very exciting. We have found that to be incredibly exciting to students and also the teachers. I was just editing this chapter that's going to go in the Folger guide to teaching *Romeo and Juliet*, which is in the paired text chapter there. The high school teacher who wrote it compares Lord Capulet's speech: 'Hang thee young baggage, disobedient wretch . . .' to Troy's speech in Fences where he is completely irate with his son because his son has just told him that he's going to quit his job at the grocery store and play football. And when you look at these side by side they are the same father. It's the same father wanting to protect their children – and one of them was written by a white guy in 1595, and one of them was written by a black guy in 1995. There's something about that that I think is very valuable in all this.

LUCY CUTHBERTSON: I work closely with my co-director Farah Karim-Cooper. She's been working on Shakespeare and race for quite a number of years now as a specific focus and the Shakespeare and race academic community has grown hugely over the last five years. 'Black Lives Matter' was a big emphasis for people to start looking at things which hadn't been looked at or challenged in a way that they could have been. It was like an extra kick. We are interested in when the plays were written, what was going on at the time and we try to put that into context for young people, and for actors who come in the building, and for directors who come to direct, regarding the material they're working with. I think we do that social justice work really well. Teachers can feel worried that they don't know how to tackle those big subjects, and yet they have to – why else are you teaching this? If you're not, it's just a dead piece of work, isn't it? Also I think our family work is great – everything that makes the Globe different is what we're trying to get into the family work. It's cheap enough to be accessible and it's very much about inviting comments and involvement. I suppose it all comes back to this idea of allowing young people to feel they can own this. We're just trying to allow these things to breathe and to go where they want to go.

EVONNE BIXTER: Looking at how we make Shakespeare relevant to new audiences, one of the ways we are doing this is through a Hip Hop project. This year, 2023, is the fiftieth anniversary of hip-hop, but it's also the 400th anniversary of Shakespeare's First Folio. So we're looking at how the two things relate to each other and how we can explore self-expression, storytelling and rhythm through five elements of Hip Hop – MCing, DJing, Beatboxing, Breaking and Graffiti. By working with different partner organizations such as schools, Knowsley Council and Merseyside Police, we hope to reach young people who might not have otherwise engaged with Shakespeare North. They may not have an interest in Shakespeare, but they are looking for ways to express themselves and this project could give them a voice to do this creatively and constructively. Giving children and young people the chance to share their voice is something that I feel really passionately about. When we first opened, we did see instances where young people were unsure how to engage with the venue. They didn't understand the opportunities that a venue like ours presents to them, be that as audience members, participants or a future career. Coming up with a project that will appeal to a variety of interests is important, and Hip Hop is all about different artforms, knowledge and moving forward with that knowledge.

KARL FALCONER: I think what theatre can shine a light on – for me, the thing that made Shakespeare really interesting, which school did not do at all, – was, I know it sounds ridiculous, but I had no concept when I was in school that Shakespeare was a human being writing in a real world. Shakespeare and the context that he existed in I find fascinating now – the fact that *Macbeth* is so heavily linked to the gunpowder plot, that's really interesting to me and I'm sure it's really interesting to young people as well.

But I think teaching any artist in a vacuum – it's so much more representative when seen in the context that produced their work. That's the link to now, because any artist is producing work within a specific context. And for me that's what pushes the distance between Shakespeare and us that often there's those contextual reasons – things that he was going through in his own life that's relatable to me right now because that hasn't changed. The world outside has changed but those human things are really interesting.

JACQUI O'HANLON: This year we're doing either a very foolish or a very brave, or a bit of both, thing, which is we are undertaking a randomized control trial (RCT). We've recruited a set of schools all across the country that have never worked with the RSC before and have no experience of the pedagogy. They are all in areas of structural disadvantage; they have high levels of pupil eligibility for free school meals – and we've divided them into control and target groups. It's important to say that we will be working with all the schools over a two-year period. There are important ethical considerations in applying RCTs and we have therefore constructed a programme that means we work directly with target schools in the formal research year and then with both control and target schools the following year. We are using a combination of pre-existing validated tools and a new validation measure in order to see whether at the end of this academic year, through a rigorous RCT process, we will have any statistically significant movement in the language acquisition and development of children in our target schools compared to our control schools.

FRANCESCA ELLIS: 'Off Grid Shakespeare' is a project targeting hyper-rural primary schools, engaging with the whole staff base over fifteen months as well as delivering two performance projects with pupils. Within the Festival models, we specifically target 'Mission Priority' schools, located in the top three deciles on the Index of Multiple Deprivation – these make up between a third and a half of our schools annually: SEND schools, whose teachers receive additional training and support; and Pupil Referral Units, who receive additional training, student workshops and support.

CHRIS NAYAK, FREELANCE PRACTITIONER: [Working with the architecture of Shakespeare's Globe theatre space] the fact that there's a shared light, I think, is a huge revelation for students because we've all grown up in a proscenium arch culture. It's really hard for us to get that idea that there's no fourth wall, that you're being talked to directly, that those questions are directly for you. The second thing, I suppose, would be the way that Shakespeare writes different lines for different parts of the audience. That bit in *Macbeth*, where they talk about the blood on their hands: 'The multitudinous seas incarnadine', which feels very much a line for the educated people in the gentlemen's boxes, is immediately followed by: 'Making the green one red.' That inclusivity across different classes that the architecture gives. And then also the vertical morality of it, the idea that you have slightly poorer people at your feet, and slightly richer people above you, and the idea of heaven above and hell below. I think [exploring this historical sense of what the Globe stage was like] is really useful, but you can do it in the classroom really easily. There's all sorts of exercises that you can do, and, in fact, exercises that can take you past the Globe into the world that Shakespeare lived in. 'Sense exercises' about what the streets might have been like, and what life might have been like, physicalizing that space, thinking about what were those different roles for these people. Shakespeare gives us so much in the text that we can do that. At the end of *Macbeth*, where Macbeth says: 'They have tied me to a stake. I cannot fly. / But bear-like I must fight the course', there is a little bear baiting picture. If we wanted to build Shakespeare's Southwark, we could do that using quotes from his plays to flesh out that world for us. So I think if you have the building that does lots for you, but even if you don't there's lots of other ways of making that connection. We have taken Shakespeare out of the mud and off the South Bank and put him in this very velvet space done in this very particular way. I'm not saying any particular theatre company is guilty of that, in fact theatre companies seem to be the ones fighting against that. But we've placed Shakespeare on a quite unhelpful pedestal and revisiting his world is what we need to do to dismantle that.

EMMA MANTON: [At the Globe] we talk about the shared light, we talk about the circle and talk about the heavens and the trapdoor, and literally looking up at the signs of the Zodiac. You can see to the other side of the river and so we tend to do an introduction on the Bank side, so you can look over and say the puritans were over there, things were different over here. It gives it massive context and they get to come through the double doors onto the stage and we get them to say something. There's a lovely spirituality being in a beautiful place and being surrounded by wood and hearing your voice come back to you, but there's also just the practicality of knowing that if somebody's standing in the yard, you can see them and they can see you. It feels somehow much more visceral – all of those things just ping out to me now in Shakespeare's text that you're talking to the audience. And it's being able to see the three levels. I'm either talking to you down in the yard, I'm talking to you in the middle in my headspace or I'm talking to you up there when I'm up in the ethereal space. An extended thought has to extend physically through the whole space, so it feels very muscular and it's beautiful. And you sort of feel you hear the whispers of the days gone by.

7

On teaching, schools, and culture

In this section, we collate responses from our interviewees on how they see their relationships with the teachers, schools, young people and partner organizations they work with and also how they see their work, as well as Shakespeare more broadly, fitting into contemporary cultural contexts. The responses to this are broad and dynamic, speaking towards a lively international community working with and through theatre-based Shakespeare practice towards artistic, educational and social justice ends. Many responses reflect the competencies we propose in Chapter 1 that effective teachers of theatre-based practice: understand students as individuals within a social learning ecosystem; continuously develop their pedagogical practice; and create conditions for creative and critical interaction with received knowledge.

On teaching and schools

The overwhelming theme of these responses is an acknowledgement of the scale and range of challenges faced by twenty-first-century schools. As we alluded to in the introductory chapter of this book, and explored more deeply across Part One, literature, theatre and the arts and creativity more broadly hold an increasingly contested role in mainstream school education globally. Even as organizations such as the OECD (2022) are highlighting the value of creativity in education, reductive models of the cultural value of literature and the arts are problematizing the engagement with this sector for teachers, practitioners and organizations alike. Peggy O'Brien, from direct experience of high school teaching in the United States, Evonne Bixter, from her long-standing experience of supporting the arts in school contexts, and Chris Nayak, as a practitioner actively listening to teachers, all speak of the pressures in mainstream schools and of the space needed for playful experimentation. Karl Falconer, Jacqui O'Hanlon and Lucy Cuthbertson, meanwhile, all take different routes into the question of limitations of access for specific schools and individuals. This includes seeking proportionate representation of private and state schools accessing RSC educational offers; identifying the 'mental blocks' some working-class young people can feel when first encountering Shakespeare; exploring the courage it demands to be an 'arts rich' school and problematizing the issues of diverse and sustainable 'pipelines' into cultural professions. As Lucy Cuthbertson summarizes 'who's aspiring to my job and who feels that's for them?' In this, there is the acknowledgement of theatre-based Shakespeare as an interdisciplinary ecology of practice: working alongside schools to deliver what is needed within the current frameworks, but also offering space for creativity and criticality to explore how things could be otherwise.

PEGGY O'BRIEN, THE FOLGER LIBRARY: [The Folger Method] came from – and this is a difference, I think, with other programs like this – it didn't come from a theatre. It came from a high school classroom. It came from an urban high school classroom in Washington, DC, starting with a teacher who was a second-year teacher – and that teacher was me. I was teaching Shakespeare and I had a class of really bright kids, really bright kids. And so we started to read, and I realized I knew how to teach, but I had no idea how to teach Shakespeare. I thought, God, you know, here's this guy who has had something to say to audiences for a long time and here are these kids who really, really want to get it and the person in between those two things is the teacher, is me. I've got to figure out how to do it. I knew nothing about theatre, but I thought, well, this guy wrote plays, and he knew what he was doing. And so the idea of chunking scenes together, the idea of cutting stuff, the idea of getting kids up on their feet and just giving them a chance to get breath around all this stuff. It was like necessity as the mother of invention, that's where it came from. And they were very enlivened by that. They absolutely asked fantastic questions.

CHRIS NAYAK, FREELANCE PRACTITIONER: Most of my understanding of how schools work is from having gone into schools as a visiting practitioner, and got an idea of their processes, and from having talked to teachers. I feel like I've been so lucky that I've led so many CPDs [professional training days] because every time I do one, teachers come with all of the successes and obstacles that they are up against. They share. So, for example, the fact that time and space are massive issues in the classroom, and how we, as practitioners, need to adapt our practice to make sure it can fit that. Teachers have this massive passion for [Shakespeare] and this huge desire to want to share their love of it. And then there are all the restrictions that are put upon teachers, all the different things that they have to deal with that mean they need different routes into it. I feel that as practitioners, that's something we can give. We can go: 'Here's six different ways of getting into *King Lear*. You choose the one that's best for you and save the other five for another day'.

JACQUI O'HANLON, RSC: Who believes that a company called the Royal Shakespeare Company, with Shakespeare as its house playwright, has a relationship to their life or to the lives of the children they teach? In my early days in this department, it was very clear that certain schools felt that Shakespeare really did have a relationship to them, and another set of schools didn't and there was a state and independent school divide in that. So, for example, in the mid-late 2000s, if you looked at the data of what kinds of schools were accessing RSC learning, 60 per cent of the schools that worked with us were from the state sector, and 40 per cent were from the independent sector, whereas the demographics of our school population are 93 per cent of schools are state-maintained, and only 7 per cent are independent. And therefore we had a disproportionate number of independent schools working with us. I've been in my post for fifteen years and now the data overall is 89 per cent of the schools that access the totality of the RSC's work are from the state maintained sector.

What we hear increasingly and very worryingly in the English education system is that teachers and headteachers say it takes a level of bravery to work in a way that brings all of these things into the classroom – we might describe it now as 'arts rich'. School leaders tell us that being in an arts rich school feels like an act of bravery. There's a lot of rhetoric about a broad and balanced curriculum, but we actually have a system that narrows choice. That's because we have reduced the experience of being at school to a set of subjects defined as 'core'. What is wonderful is that we do have lots of teachers and headteachers who really believe in arts learning as a key entitlement for young people. They believe there needs to be a broad base of experiences, and they understand that Shakespeare's work and making theatre are part of a rich tapestry of experiences, not just an end result in the GCSE exam.

KARL FALCONER, PURPLE DOOR: I think that's the world of difference between a theatre mindset and an education mindset, that education is about outcomes, and the process is deemed to be less important and individuality within that process is almost seen as being not relevant, whereas theatre is about the process. When young people have made the transition to working with us, they always say 'Oh I didn't know Shakespeare was like this' – that's almost become an unremarkable thing because that's what most people who work with us say – and I don't think that's because we are doing anything revolutionary but because school is so rigid. And the idea that you can kind of say, yeah, I, as the director, don't know what this line means either, so let's figure it out; or that didn't work, let's try again. There is no weight given to failure in schools, failure is a negative thing. I think if you've got a productive rehearsal process, you know that you're going to go up ten roads that lead nowhere but you need to go up them to find the road that goes somewhere.

Confidence is a huge part of this whole process, I think. We've worked a lot with working-class kids who overwhelmingly come from state comprehensive schools and 'I can't do it' is the mental block. Seeing that from the teaching perspective as well I'm not surprised they say that because Shakespeare is something they either get right or get wrong. And it's really not a case of within twenty minutes of being in a workshop with us will change your whole perspective. It's a real long process of going, 'You don't know me. This is not as stable, or recognized as school which you are programmed to trust and to think as being right, but maybe there's a better way of doing things'. That is a long process. I do think the issue, and therefore the solution, with a lot of young people is the confidence thing. I would increasingly like to go in, spotting the kids who've got talent, because they are less likely to be able to capitalize on that talent. I think some of the successes that we've had speak to that. But whether or not they'd say that when they've finished drama school and not had a job for six months – and they were really good at maths and I put them off doing maths! But I think if you help to open the door that might not have been opened, then fab.

EVONNE BIXTER, SHAKESPEARE NORTH PLAYHOUSE: What's amazing is talking to schools about how they may have been struggling to talk about PSHE [Personal, Social and Health Education] topics in a way that is engaging. I know from work I've done in secondary schools, it's often a bit of a side-line, but showing that actually when they're in their English lesson and they're studying this play, they are looking at PSHE, and they're looking at citizenship and they're looking at well-being – it's just showing that everything is connected. It's more about the whole person and how you can explore that really in a rounded way. We know the challenges that schools and teachers face. What we want to do is give them a space to experiment and play that helps them to be more creative within school, because I know that they don't have the time and the space to do that all the time at school. So if we can be that experimental environment for them [and] the children, that's great.

FRANCESCA ELLIS, CSSF: We develop teachers of all disciplines. We run CPD that challenges, supports and inspires, inviting teachers to move out of their comfort zone, to learn new skills – how to direct; making Shakespeare accessible – but always to have fun. Our training rooms are places of play, delight and laughter. In student workshops, we work alongside teachers to rehearse their scenes, acting as a 'side-coach', developing their practice and championing their skills in front of students. We develop close and long-term relationships with teachers – some have worked with us for well over a decade.

LUCY CUTHBERTSON, SHAKESPEARE'S GLOBE: I guess we're really interested in the pipeline and how we change the pipeline into the profession of Shakespeare. That could include acting, but also the Shakespeare business – who's aspiring to my job and who feels that's for them? Unless you change who is choosing A-level English and who is going on to do English at university and beyond, then that will never look any different. It's trying to look at what is happening in teacher training and how is Shakespeare being taught? In universities the teachers, who may have had a really uninspiring time with Shakespeare themselves at school, are they just perpetuating the long and boring 'we have to do this' message, or are they able to find excitement in it and pass it on?

On culture

The language of using Shakespeare as a vehicle for enquiry about our own times is common across active theatre-based Shakespeare: organizations and practitioners appear in many cases to be embracing the potential of interculturally democratic models of Shakespeare's cultural value. Our interviewees spoke of different lenses to focus this line of enquiry in their own contexts, from their own knowledges and experiences. For some, this was about the urgency of climate change or injustices raised through the MeToo and Black Lives Matter movements. For others, it was about placing their work in a broader tradition of social activism. Being led by Gen Z and Gen Alpha's hunger for social change and social justice is discussed, referencing the arguments of Thompson and Turchi (2016). Freelance practitioner Cassandra Nwokah in particular talks about how exploring explicitly decolonializing approaches to theatre-based practice allowed her to re-engage in the Shakespeare conversation on her own terms and pass on that sense of inclusion and belonging to her students; how theatre-based practice opened up the discovery of the salience, rather than assumed relevance of Shakespeare (Dadabhoy and Mehdizadeh 2023). Cassandra's reflections on her need to find a purpose and resonance with Shakespeare for her physical and socially contextualized self speaks to the potential of embodied theatre-based practice to discover and build this sense of purpose; a purpose which narrow 'bardolatry' or cultural 'incrustation' around Shakespeare can sometimes seek to deny.

Across all of this, as exemplified in Peggy O'Brien's discussions of bringing Shakespearean academics and teachers together to explore issues, there is a sense of a live, dynamic and discursive approach to Shakespeare's cultural meaning and significance. While being driven by a passion and fascination for Shakespeare's works, there is nothing in these responses which seeks to essentialize or universalize what learners might discover in them.

CHRIS NAYAK: Suddenly the lens of the world changes and the life of the play changes. And for these plays to be able to do that speaks to their strength but also speaks to our need to keep interrogating them, because otherwise you're not building any new facets to Shakespeare you're just stuck with what you had for the last hundred years.

LUCY CUTHBERTSON: This idea of universality I think we reject anyway. In education it does get used all the time but I don't think [the plays] are universal. However, if young people in the future want to pick this stuff up and they want to keep it alive, it's there. It's going to be their decision, it's not our decision, but how well we pass that on is going to be the measure of whether places like the RSC and the Globe and Shakespeare North have a future.

A-level English and the IB [International Baccalaureate] are moving in terms of lenses – how do you look at the play through an ecocritical lens, or a race lens, or feminist lens? I suppose Farah and I – because we both come from a social justice activist background – we're very interested in that. I'd say we think it's just there in the plays anyway, but then how do you not ignore it? How do you bring it to the forefront? This is really genuinely exciting because this is then a 400-year connection with stuff that you can relate to. I think we have to remember with Shakespeare a lot of the [cultural] weight is eighteenth century onwards. What was happening in his time was putting on popular plays. If people didn't like it they didn't do it again. All that kind of Bardology Shakespeare's happened since the 1800s onwards and how it is linked to colonialism, slavery and the sense that his work is part of what made the UK superior and better. It all came later.

EVONNE BIXTER: It's how we're using Shakespeare as the key to unlock loads of different discussions about different things – and that it's not just about the analysing it academically, or the language, or the performance, but it's actually about the wider context. To show that the value isn't just something for people to come to as theatre, it's something to be discussed and performed in a classroom and not just read. One of the main things I think about when we do sessions with young people is that I want to give them the opportunity to interpret it however they want and that I'm not going to tell them exactly what something is about without giving them the opportunity to discuss it and share their thoughts. I want young people to have that opportunity to do that, to interpret it themselves, and to think of it through their eyes now, which is quite different to even a few years ago, before the pandemic; before MeToo, and Black Lives Matter, and environmental crises were so much in our shared consciousness. All of these things have changed how we interpret Shakespeare. We need to look at it again. I want that to be an ongoing thing. I don't ever want to be complacent that 'this is what it means' because it doesn't always mean that. It can mean new things each time you read it.

JACQUI O'HANLON: What we see with Gen Z and Gen Alpha is this very socially conscious generation where issues of social justice and equity are incredibly live and there is an urgency for them about how their explorations of any classroom subject, including Shakespeare, help them make sense of this very different kind of world that they are living in and wanting to shape.

So what role does Shakespeare's work have in young people being their own agents of change – making sense of what they're going through, making sense of a curriculum that isn't mirroring their experience, and making sense of theatre that isn't mirroring their experience. For example, around gender identity – for the young people that we're working with, there is a disconnect at the moment between their experience of gender identity and what they are seeing reflected on main stages. For example, they're still seeing predominantly binary relationships in Shakespeare plays. Now those questions are hugely important ones for the RSC to think about.

CASSANDRA NWOKAH, FREELANCE PRACTITIONER: The work of decolonizing Shakespeare came to me really almost out of the blue, and at a moment where I was really seriously questioning why am I doing this? Why am I convincing kids to care about this? Do I even care about it? I'm not sure I do. Then, one of my first zoom experiences was a lecture with Folger talking about the work of Shakespeare and race. [I read] the book that Ayanna [Thompson and Laura Turchi] wrote: *Teaching Shakespeare with Purpose*, and after reading that and listening to a few lectures, I was like, 'Oh, I'm on board'. The connection that I felt like I had lost with Shakespeare was immediately like a lifeline thrown. It felt like this is something that tethers me to this thing that I love in more of a purposeful way, that I've been searching for. It's not that it needs purpose, but for me, in this body I exist in, within the context of this timeline I exist in, I needed purpose for why I was giving so much of myself to this work when there are other authors that I love. Because of the way Shakespeare exists as this canonical figure that is revered, and the pedestal that was built in the echelon of literary masters, there is very little space for anyone else, any other work to exist at the same level when we're in classrooms, and that was very frustrating for me. When Shakespeare was given to me, I felt very much like it was forced on me, but it didn't need to be. If I had been invited to it in the right way, I think I would have loved it without that battle of 'No, this is not for me'. So when the idea of the decolonial work came up, my leg, that was outside of the boat ready to swim away, lifted a little bit out of the water. With all of these stories I grew up with – Jane Austen and all of these English stories – I didn't feel there was space for me to exist, but that in order to pass as a good student I needed to try to lift these up like, 'Oh, I get it. I get it'. The rehearsal room practices are just so intrinsically open to new ideas and play, and to the commotion of what it is to try, and throw out, and to grapple with it in such a beautiful, playful, healthy way. For the decolonial approach to work, I think you need a space like that, you need a container that allows that kind of grappling without danger or without really being able to harm somebody – you need that container that rehearsal room techniques offer.

PEGGY O'BRIEN: If we knew how to talk to each other about differences like race and religion and gender, everybody would be a lot better off. So one of the things that Shakespeare does is throw it all out there – and that's of interest. We would talk to teachers, for example, about 'the rich jewel in the Ethiope's ear'. Teachers would just glide right over that. I glided right over that as a teacher, and we can't glide over that, we have to talk about what that is. It's putting differences right in front of teachers and saying, here's what it is. If you put Claudius's 'My offence is rank' speech in front of kids and teachers, he uses white and black imagery in the same speech to talk about devilishness and virtue. And so all you have to do is show them that and they're like: 'Oh, oh my gosh!' And then you can go on from there in terms of, 'Well, how do *we* describe virtue?' It's a starting point and you can go on from there – there's so many examples. The Folger Institute did a whole series of critical race conversations in 2020 and 21. Folger Education did an invited symposium in September of 2019 and invited twelve scholars – all of whom are probably names that you would know – and then twelve middle school and high school teachers, all talking together. The first thing we did was bring the scholars up to speed on what a day was like for one of these middle school and high school teachers, and how much time they had to teach a play. It was tremendous, and that has informed a lot about what we did going forward, because we knew we wanted to lead in this for middle school and high school teachers, but we wanted to make sure that we knew what we were talking about.

KARL FALCONER: Especially working on Shakespeare in a traditionally working-class area, there's all sorts of questions that come up in terms of, is Shakespeare the right person to look at? What are we trying to achieve? Are we trying to make people better at performing Shakespeare? Are we trying to appropriate people into feeling that they can have Shakespeare in their life, or that they've achieved something, and that they're better if they get Shakespeare than they were beforehand? I feel that when you properly interrogate Shakespeare's work – and I think this is where our focus on Shakespeare has come from – that really, when we started to look at it on our own terms, away from the way that we were taught it in school, we kind of realized that, oh, actually, there's a lot more to Shakespeare than we realized. There's a lot of things that you assume about Shakespeare that are not entirely correct, they've been filtered through a lens. So, therefore, especially with our youth theatre work, I always start from an enquiry of 'we're going to uncover this play together'. I do feel like people are more aware of and keen to bring up issues in rehearsals than they were even a few years ago. When we've done *Merchant of Venice* for example, we're not going to start from a point of view of going, let's put on this racist play or let's put on this non-racist play, we're going to discover this play for ourselves, and then we're going to make those judgements in the context of where we are. I've increasingly moved towards, rather than having a big idea and a concept that I'm going to impose on the actors, that we collectively discover what this play means to what's in this moment. And I think the only times that I've felt kind of culturally like we're not doing it, that something is a lie, is when we've revisited the play that we did last year and we've tried to put it back on again – because it's very much a result of those people at that moment in that time, in that space with that audience.

DARREN RAYMOND, INTERMISSION YOUTH: Look, we're all different, and we work with a certain demographic of young people and maybe our approach is not going to work with everybody, but it certainly works with the young people we work with – and that is be really *free* with Shakespeare. Use what you want to use in Shakespeare – you don't have to be reverent with the text; we don't have to hold Shakespeare on a pedestal. Yes, he was great – he was a fantastic, brilliant writer, but he wrote stories, right? We all have stories to tell, and our stories are just as important as Shakespeare's stories. So why can't we bring our stories to his work? Why can't we lend our experiences and see how that plays out in his stories? So I would say don't feel pinned down by the text. Don't be afraid to change the language. I think it is important that our young people feel an ownership over it, so we have to be innovative, just like Shakespeare was.

8

Why Shakespeare?

Our question about 'Why Shakespeare?' asked our interviewees to reflect on why they felt Shakespeare is such a significant part of the school curriculum, what they personally felt about that position and how their organization made sense of this position through their work. As across responses elsewhere, there is a range of nuanced reflections and discussions. Some commonalities emerging include a shared drive to remove Shakespeare from any pedestal he has been placed on, a desire to support young people to meet the challenge of Shakespearean texts from their own starting points and to engender a sense of agency in their work. Specific themes include exploration and reflection on Shakespeare's language in particular, and the challenges, ambiguities, richness and beauty this can present. Our contributors promote engagement with the texts as *language in action*, as we explored in Chapter 4, and reflect on how the storytelling, theatricality and heightened poetic language of the plays stimulate creative and critical interactions with what the texts can mean now, because as Cassandra Nwokah says, 'We are our stories – and how you live your story can be impacted on by how you were given story, or how you encountered story before'. Contributors continue to reflect on the questions posed by studying a specific set of English Early Modern texts in global twenty-first-century contexts and also consider how such work might be represented in evaluation, research and impact assessments.

EVONNE BIXTER, SHAKESPEARE NORTH PLAYHOUSE: It's beautiful, for a start, and it's fascinating. It's rooted in so much humanity right the way [through] 400 years, how could it not be relevant?

CASSANDRA NWOKAH, FREELANCE PRACTITIONER: If you ask why students in the United States are required to read Shakespeare, I think the requirement mostly goes back to the origins of colonialism and imperialism and how Shakespeare was one of the vehicles of anglicizing the countries that were being taken over – and this is a vestige of that. But also it's beautiful work. Not to devalue the way it's beautiful work, however, the way that we come to the text can be shifted. It doesn't have to be like: 'Meet me at this pedestal, and if you are worthy, then you will get through this class.' I believe it's required because of systemic reasons outside of our control, but the decolonial approach for me gives it purpose – it allows for that requirement to make sense in the time that we're in.

FRANCESCA ELLIS, CSSF: He is widely considered England's foremost writer, because of the scope and variety of his canon of work, because his stories and characters have captured imaginations through the centuries, and because of the beauty of the language. He is Britain's most successful export and a keystone of English literature. The cultural capital of Shakespeare surpasses any other author – if you know Shakespeare's stories, characters and quotes you will find their influence everywhere in English and international culture. Our approach to Shakespeare has much in common with other theatre-centric organizations, in that we take an active approach, believing the texts should be performed rather than read. All our work is participatory, we do not produce performances for young people, young people *are* the performers. For us, Shakespeare is the vehicle, not the point. We take an irreverent, child-centred approach which uses the playwright rather than serving him.

LUCY CUTHBERTSON, SHAKESPEARE'S GLOBE: [The plays] are famous for a reason. They have remained out there because people want to do them, want to read them, want to perform them. When children get taught Shakespeare really well and they find a way into it and then they own it, something very empowering happens. Now, this thing about empowering – I don't like the connections with this idea of missionary kind of improvements: it'll do you good. So I find I'm always questioning myself about what I mean by that. But there is a challenge to interpreting a text which is not easy, it's not given to you on a plate. Like a foreign language, it's not easy. And I think there's something inherently pedagogically exciting about a challenge like that.

JACQUI O'HANLON, RSC: Our objective is not that 'everybody has to love Shakespeare'. I'm interested in what difference it makes to a child we've been working with throughout primary when they go into secondary school and have such a strong sense of ownership of a complex part of the curriculum, one that now holds no fear for them? What we hear most often from the schools is how the work expands the children's horizons and how that in turn compensates for an experience deficit. And that's the important thing about arts learning, about any partnership with any arts organization, that some children will automatically get access to certain kinds of experiences, and some absolutely won't. And that isn't equitable. We know that arts subjects and experiences create opportunities for children to discover new things about themselves. That the work gives children a sense of their own worth, their own ability. They begin to believe they can do different things. That's what the work's about: 'I've discovered a different potential. I didn't know this was who I could be. I didn't know this is what I could do.' Fundamentally, the work is about agency.

PEGGY O'BRIEN, THE FOLGER LIBRARY: I think if people want to say, 'Bag this guy' [Shakespeare], they should bag him. They should not teach him. Also, I think, if you teach in a high school, and kids read four Shakespeare plays, or three Shakespeare plays in four years, and they don't read James Baldwin and they don't read – you name it, then that's wrong. That's an imbalance, and you should sort that out. I do think kids ought to be exposed at those ages to the sweep of literature. In terms of studying Shakespeare, one of the things that we say about the Folger Method is get him, drag him off that pedestal, he doesn't belong there. The idea of getting kids to be able to see what's there, and what's not there – and talking back to Shakespeare. We do this great thing where we have Romeo's lines – where Romeo is talking about how beautiful Juliet is with all the fairness and doves and all that stuff – and then we match that up against a poem by Maya Angelou called *Ain't I bad* – it's like extolling the beauties of blackness, it's just wonderful. And then kids mash those up. It's awesome. We've done a lot of exploring because we think it's important – but if people think, 'I'm done with this guy', I mean that's okay.

KARL FALCONER, PURPLE DOOR: Thinking specifically about Shakespeare, those moments of tension are there – you can almost open it up as a shared moment between us to think about what Shakespeare might be saying, or, in fact, to critique what Shakespeare's done. And I think you need to be able to treat the play, not through a lens that everything Shakespeare did was perfect, and you can't criticize it, but equally not to go in, you know, we're going to trash Shakespeare because we want to find something edgy. I think if you treat him like it was a play that was written yesterday, and that you're in a conversation with him, and there's a dialogue, that's where the interesting things can happen.

Challenging language

Typically the work of organizations and practitioners is playful and explores Shakespeare through the voices and accents in the room. Peggy O'Brien from the Folger discusses the confidence that can come with fruitfully grappling with Shakespeare's language; Darren Raymond at Intermission describes the value he places on breaking down barriers between the language that young people use in their everyday lives and the language of Shakespeare. Other contributors take alternative routes into the texts, but consistently they acknowledge the challenges the language can sometimes pose, as well as the value to be found in its richness and complexity. As Francesca Ellis from CSSF states, 'By reputation his plays are difficult, his language challenging, understanding them is something to be proud of'. The contributors reference how there is a sense of agency or authority – author/ity (Povey et al. 1999) – to be found in meeting the complexity of this language. Cassandra Nwokah defines the experience of seeing students 'self-authorize to get down and dirty with literature in a way that hasn't been presented'. Contributors value both this experience in itself, and the potential they see it holding for their learners to carry on and tackle other complex educational and social challenges.

PEGGY O'BRIEN: Teachers and kids universally, in this country anyway, think that the language is the stumbling block, right? That the language is the problem. That for one thing, it's complicated and on the other hand, I will never be able to understand it, it's way beyond me. I think some of the versions, the kind of dumbed-down versions I mean, I don't think they're any easier to understand than the real language. The fact that people have thought that it's the barrier and it's insurmountable – so we're just going to have to figure another way around it – I think it sells students short, and it sells teachers short. What happens on the other end is teaching this way [the Folger Method] totally enlivens teachers because it brings kids' interpretations into the game, and that's so exciting for them. They have power over deciding how they're going to play certain things and that's liberating, but it's also incredibly confidence inspiring. We do not have a ton of studies on this stuff, but one that we do have talks about kids' levels of confidence before and after, and it's very significant. They think: 'I did this hard thing. I figured this out. I know how to do this now, and so turn me on to the next hard thing', which could be trig or whatever, organic chemistry.

KARL FALCONER: I think I'm always asking whether or not Shakespeare itself is relevant. The best answer I've got in terms of 'why Shakespeare?' is that I think if you embrace the depth between where I am and Shakespeare's language is, then it becomes like a mask. I've found it's been really beneficial for developing people's acting skills, but also for developing their personal confidence – the catharsis of seeing Shakespeare as a mask – and that for me is what distinguishes our work from another youth theatre. The same group of people might produce a play about knife crime or something but you can play *Macbeth* and you can deal with those same issues and you can go to heights – the complexity, and the height of his language forces you to meet it. When you do that, when you get kids out of just staring at the words on a page and mumbling, when you start to perform it, that's where everything comes alive, and it unlocks something.

FRANCESCA ELLIS: By reputation his plays are difficult, his language challenging, understanding them is something to be proud of. But the stories are bold, thrilling, jam-packed with action – young people love them. They contain a kaleidoscopic spectrum of characters, who are both bold archetypes and familiar, resonant to us today. They deal with themes which are big and important and which echo through the centuries – grief, separation, home, leadership, love, death, families.

DARREN RAYMOND, INTERMISSION YOUTH: All the young people that we work with have similar experiences to what I went through, I would say, as a kid. Certainly, when it comes to Shakespeare, there doesn't seem to be an enthusiasm for that work and I suppose I've been interrogating that question as to why for many years. Partly, one of the main reasons is because, I feel, they don't feel it's a part of their history, so they can't connect with it. Partly the language or the words are very unfamiliar to them, and partly because of the way it's taught. So for me, it's about really breaking down all those barriers, letting them know that actually this is very much part of their history and their heritage and they have a right to this work. That the words that Shakespeare invented and the words that are used in his plays are English and it's just a way that Shakespeare expressed himself, similar to what we do when we use words today – so there's no reason to be afraid of those words. And to play – not to sit down behind a desk and be scared of what we're presented with, but actually to get Shakespeare on his feet and play with it.

CASSANDRA NWOKAH: If you tell kids 'Shakespeare', and they have any kind of inclination about it, they'll immediately put on this silly caricature of a British accent, and you know, their posture changes. That idea didn't come from nowhere but that doesn't have to be what it is. Let's take that away, and break it apart, and dive into it, and figure out: 'What are these stories, and what are these words and what is it saying to me? Where do I exist in here? Do I exist in here?' And then ask kids: 'Is it necessary to continue engaging people in this work?' They should have a voice. I had to pass my Shakespeare unit and recite a monologue by rote with this very, like *Shakespeare* voice, you know? To show: 'Oh, yes, you understand Shakespeare now. You've done it'. I didn't understand a thing! I didn't know what I was saying, I just knew I had to memorize it and say it in a particular way to get my check mark. And I just think that doesn't pass muster anymore. These students are whip smart, and they are hungry for honesty, and they don't put up with the lack of truth. So when you present them with an opportunity to honestly ask questions and to investigate in a truthful way and give them the lead, I think you are giving them the keys to unlock Shakespeare. But it shouldn't stop at Shakespeare – use Shakespeare as the vehicle, but then they can unlock anything after that. They can grapple with any writer from any century and feel like, 'Okay, I can take ownership of how I interpret this work, how this work affects me, and how this work affects how I am in the world'. And I think that is, for me the goal – if I can leave a classroom, and even one student feels like they have the authority they can give themself – self-authorize to get down and dirty with literature in a way that hasn't been presented, then that's winning.

EMMA MANTON, FREELANCE PRACTITIONER: All there is, is the words. There are the words you're saying and the person you're saying them to and the words that they say back. And I find that really liberating. I love those light bulb moments that young people have, when suddenly something that they didn't understand five minutes earlier suddenly seems clear. And I love the moments when I have those light bulb moments when they say something and suddenly I see the text differently. I think because we're all exploring with it, because there is nothing straightforward, that it's open to so many interpretations and so many possibilities, that we're all on a journey together.

CHRIS NAYAK, FREELANCE PRACTITIONER: I think if [Shakespeare] is going to be a compulsory part of the curriculum, you need to justify that. I don't think that we should simply assume that Shakespeare should always be put on a curriculum. I would very much make the case for him for three reasons. First, because I think he's great. I think he's really good because he's a poet turned dramatist, and so not only does he understand the stagecraft, but he's able to give all of his characters this phenomenal language that, as teachers, allows us to springboard off into so many different directions. The idea of using poetry actively – the shared sonnet of *Romeo and Juliet* being a great example – it's an active use of poetry. It's not just poetry for poetry's sake, it's poetry to tell us something about character and situation and feelings and emotions and I don't know anybody who does that as well as he does. I think his genius is in that characterization. Second, I think he's really relevant. I think the reason he's so relevant is because he writes human beings so well and the way that we talk to each other. I remember doing *Romeo and Juliet* with some students – we talked about how Mercutio behaves to Romeo when he's met Juliet, and how Mercutio is a little bit off with him, a little bit like: 'Oh, why are you hanging out with the girls now? Don't you want to play with us anymore?' And every lad, lots of the eighteen- to nineteen-year-olds were like, 'Yeah, that's so true. I can totally relate to that'. And the third reason is because I think he's really accessible. I've done *Winter's Tale* with six-year-olds; *Antony and Cleopatra* with a company that ranged from nine to eighty-nine. He knows what he's doing, and I think the reason he is like that is because he was playing to audiences who, if they got bored, would just walk out. That attitude that we have to television, I believe, is the same attitude that Shakespeare's audiences would have had to his plays: 'I'm not really engaged – there's loads of other cool stuff happening around here – bit of bear baiting, bit of cock fighting. I'm just going to go and do that instead'. So the idea of putting the audience at the forefront means that he has to be engaging.

Having an emotional engagement first [through theatre-based activities] – and that's all actors do is put themselves in the character's shoes, emotionally connect and pretend – by doing that first, it allows us to feel that that's what Shakespeare's doing with these characters. So it immediately feels relevant. Then when you have six lines of poetry, rather than thinking: 'Oh, God! Six lines of poetry! I don't know what any of that means.' You think: 'Ah, great! I don't know what any of that means, but maybe I can use it to make him do what I want him to do.' So it makes the text an active weapon with which you try and achieve your objective, rather than poetry that's totally removed from your sense of understanding. Because if you read it on the page, it's somebody else saying it. If you're reading it on the page, Lady Macbeth is saying it, but if you stand up and face off with a Macbeth, and think: 'I want you to go and do that thing and these are the words I have to get you to do it.' It's not somebody else, it's you. It's your words. It's your intention. It's your action. And that means that you have such an emotional investment in it the words become your friends rather than your enemies.

Raising questions

In this section, we have collated responses which explore the questions Shakespeare raises for our interview contributors, and the conversations these prompt in their working lives. Common threads here include acknowledging the complexities and ambiguities that come with working with Shakespeare's texts, and the way this prompts an ongoing, dynamic relationality to Shakespeare through their work. Emma Manton speaks of the conversations that can happen through Shakespeare; Jacqui O'Hanlon describes one such conversation through a large-scale consultation process; and Evonne Bixter and Francesca Ellis highlight the breadth of curricular and extracurricular areas these conversational experiences with Shakespeare can benefit. Many focus on the advantages of theatre-based practice, and its embodied, discursive approaches for these rich and sometimes challenging conversations with Shakespeare. As Cassandra Nwokah states, 'There's something about drama play that just explodes open our senses and our ability to take in and exist within the story in a more tangible way'.

JACQUI O'HANLON: Earlier this year the RSC undertook the largest consultation process it has ever undertaken to ask what kind of RSC should we be by 2030? In those wide-ranging consultation sessions, what came through loud and clear from young people and from teachers was a huge belief in the power of Shakespeare to ignite the kinds of conversations we want to be having in our classrooms – conversations about identity, conversations about politics, about religious intolerance, about ableism, about embedded whiteness. Shakespeare gives us the opportunity to ask those questions in our conversation across time as we encounter 400-year-old cultural attitudes. And that's the exciting opportunity that Shakespeare plays give us. It doesn't give us any answers – it gives us a whole load of brilliant questions to ask in classrooms and in rehearsal rooms – and it's this same interrogation that we're doing, whether we're a professional actor that's been working for thirty years, or just come into the profession, or we're ten or eleven or fifteen or seventeen and we're meeting the plays for the first time.

At the heart of our partnerships is shared exploration. We've always started with questions about 'Why Shakespeare?' We are interested in what the combination of Shakespeare's language and a pedagogy rooted in rehearsal room practice brings to the classroom A pedagogy that stems from the fact that these plays are hard, and you need a way of accessing them in a rehearsal room for professional artists that acknowledges this is deeply complex literature – and the way you approach a new play won't cut it – you've got to have different ways of accessing these plays. We've never taken for granted Shakespeare's place in the curriculum. It hasn't felt enough to say, well, Shakespeare is a compulsory part of all children's learning experiences in England and Wales, and in a very significant proportion of curricula internationally. What we've been interested in is why. We have commissioned different forms of research all trying to help us understand the relevance of Shakespeare's work in a contemporary twenty-first-century curriculum. What role does it play in the learning and development of children and young people? And we're thinking there about elementary school, primary school children, as well as into secondary and high school and, of course, beyond. So the partnerships that we've developed have been about answering that because we have to.

EMMA MANTON: I think there are lots of big conversations about the big issues facing our world we can look at through the lens of Shakespeare – it sort of acts as a filter that we can be talking about something quite triggering or quite controversial. That isn't always welcome in the classroom, but because it's through Shakespeare it feels like we have a distance between us and the subject that can be quite useful. I love working with primary school students with this because they haven't got to a point yet where they have to understand everything and they are still always piecing together the world from what they do understand. I think the longer we keep that openness the better and Shakespeare helps us keep that in our classrooms, that sense of discovery and not having to have the right answer.

CASSANDRA NWOKAH: I appreciate that all writers write, whether intentionally or not, in the constructs of the time they're in, the societies that they inhabit and the identities that they also inhabit as they weave through the space and time that they exist in – and because of their work we have a historical record, but also a commentary on humanity and society at a particular time. I think it's always worthy to investigate how humanity existed or does exist, and I think part of examining how we currently exist is taking in how we existed in different points of time. And so referencing that, I think particularly with students in middle school and high school – where they are forming their worldview, and coming to an idea of their outlook on the world and what it means to them and what their place is in the world, and starting to figure out how they want to interact with the world and leave their mark – I think having them encounter artists who have left their mark is useful. There is something about the way we hold stories, and how stories help us navigate our then and now that is so integral to how we show up in the world. We are our stories. I really believe that. We are our stories – and how you live your story can be impacted on by how you were given story or how you encountered story before, as you were growing and forming your perspective. I think we stand more of a chance when we allow students to meet story in a way that they have ownership of their examination of it, and they are given the space of honesty to really sit with it and take it apart and put it back together to decide: 'How do *you* want to be a storyteller?' Because, whether you like it or not, your living this existence is a story, and it is adding to our collective story, and somebody will write it. When I see somebody who looks like me as Hamlet, that is a different story than the Hamlet I was told, or the only kind of Hamlet that was allowed to be, when I was in school. It's the same story, but it's a little different, and it allows for a little different engagement and outlook on what the world is, and how I want to see the world, or what I don't see in the world. And it asks: 'Why is that? And who decided? And can it change, or does it need to change?'

There's something about drama play that just explodes open our senses and our ability to take in and exist within the story in a more tangible way. Your imagination can be at play when you're reading a novel, but when you are standing up and stepping into the shoes of whoever, you're engaging your entire being into existing within the story in a way that is just irreplaceable and more intentional, I think, than simply reading. I don't want to take away from the incredible gift that being able to sit with and read a novel is, but people respond to embodied storytelling for a reason. We go see plays, we go to cinema, we go to performance art for a reason. We are impacted differently. It goes like oral storytelling – it's a very communal experience. The collective energy of everybody in that room, there is something about sharing that kinetic energy of being in a story together.

EVONNE BIXTER: The way that we use Shakespeare is as the key to unlocking the curriculum in loads of so many different ways. We're not just exploring Shakespeare in a solely literary or performance capacity. We use Shakespeare's work to explore performance or English, but also to explore nature and the environment, or using it to explore lots of social issues such as for PSHE sessions or to think about careers in the arts. Shakespeare is absolutely at the heart of everything that we do, and in our work we seek to show how it is still relevant today, that beyond the language is the fact that he had such an amazing understanding of people and of behaviour and also of place and history, his knowledge of people and the environment is fascinating. There's a lot of different ways that we use Shakespeare and I think a lot of our productions have surprised people with how we have interpreted and presented Shakespeare.

FRANCESCA ELLIS: Children take part in our projects from all walks of life. At the beginning, they may think Shakespeare is 'not for them'. It's too clever or too posh or for children who are different to them. Then, taking part in our theatre festival for example, they play Hamlet, or Lady Macbeth, or King Lear, or a messenger who brings vital news. It's a challenge, but they work with their teacher and their friends and it's fun, and the words start to make sense. Then on the performance day they step out into the lights at that theatre down the road – the one they knew about but had never been to. Their parents are there, their friends are watching, and they absolutely smash it. And at the end, they take a bow and the theatre erupts in applause. Afterwards, they think 'Hey, I thought Shakespeare wasn't for me. But look what I did! Maybe there are other things I thought weren't for me that could be maths, or getting a good job, or going to university even though no one in my family has before'.

PEGGY O'BRIEN: I think we read him and we should talk back to him. I think for some people it's a lot easier to say: 'He's the dead white guy, let's get rid of him'. Except that that's the kind of thinking that got us where we are right now – we don't want any writers of this kind. If you lay out the sweep and you teach kids to read resistantly and to talk back to authors, then we're in a much better place, I think.

DARREN RAYMOND: I first encountered Shakespeare at secondary school and it was *Macbeth* and I hated it. And the reason being is because we were sat behind the desk and expected to analyse act one, scene two without seeing a version of the play or reading the play in its entirety. And as we all know, the language or the words are very unfamiliar to some of us, quite dense, and were written hundreds of years ago. So I didn't really understand why I needed to learn this work and for that reason I shied away from it – but also I didn't feel connected to that history and that was a problem for me. My second encounter with Shakespeare was a little bit later in life and I was in a difficult place in my life. I suppose I was searching for something, searching to belong. I had an identity crisis. And I was introduced to a story, a play, a character who was going through similar things to me – a character that I could relate to, and that was Othello. The practitioner that was working with us at the time had this brilliant skill of making the text meet us halfway and vice versa. You know, we brought our lives to that text as well, and it was at that moment that I really kind of appreciated

Shakespeare's words and his skill as a writer and actually his storytelling which helped me to learn more about myself in the world that I was living in – and that was cool.

Impact

Impact assessment is on the one hand part of the strategic dance of arts education organizations and practitioners: funders, stakeholders and participants are interested in evidence, often preferably in the form of 'hard' data. Impact assessment can also, however, be a space for reflection, for consolidation, a process from which to draw hope and to chart the next steps forward. In these responses, our contributors share the range of ways they gather and respond to impact assessment, from large-scale consolidation of existing evidence to reflexive engagement with daily moments demonstrating engagement.

JACQUI O'HANLON: We've been so astounded by how rich and diverse the impacts are. When we started these partnerships, at its core was Shakespeare's work and a belief that exposure to that work through this pedagogy made a significant difference to learning outcomes for children, particularly in terms of language acquisition and development. Recently, we did a kind of temperature test with all of the representatives of our 250 Associate Schools network. And what was extraordinary was those are still the important things for those schools. It's about Shakespeare's work, and it's about the learning that work enables for children and young people who are entering the school system having had less access to literature in their lives, to words in their lives, than more advantaged peers.

What we've learned over fifteen years of asking that question [Why Shakespeare?] with teachers and with young people is we have different forms of research telling us similar things. I have a chart that aggregates the five themes that are most common across all of those fifteen years of different forms of research. One common theme is overall progress and experiences. That encapsulates reports from teachers of progress in grades, improvement in inclusion, engagement, ownership of the work, changes in aspirations. So there's a bucket there that is about progress and experiences. A second bucket is about specific improvements in oracy and literacy, so language acquisition and development, improvements in vocabulary, sentence construction, language choices, etc. A third bucket is improvements in attitudes, empathy, agency – agency hugely important – so that is about the self-concept of the student – and we see significant and consistent report of that positively changing. A fourth bucket is around the impact for teachers – and what we see most often reported there is improved teacher-pupil relationships, raised expectations of the teacher for the students, positive changes in the learning environment, greater trust, collaboration, etc. The fifth bucket is about wider community impact – increased parental engagement, support for the child, a greater interest in the child's learning, in theatre, in Shakespeare, in the local community, a greater engagement around the school, a greater sense of togetherness, belonging. They are hard things to quantify and measure but they are things that we see most often reported.

EVONNE BIXTER: It's already had a huge impact – even just in the town of Prescot you can see Shakespeare everywhere. The fact that a huge proportion of our audience is local, that's been brilliant because that's exactly what we wanted, to be relevant to this community. Anecdotal evidence is seeing people's reactions when they come and actually it's just a huge amount of pride that this has been built in their town, that this has been built 'up north'; this is an investment. It really is beautiful to see people come and look at the cockpit for the first time and become emotional when they see it. There are other things to do with sessions that we're offering, the schools saying how great it is that they normally would have to do a trip to Stratford or London to see a theatre like this and the fact that they can come and see it on their doorstep, it's really exciting. So I think it's already had this huge impact. It's just now we're beginning to gather evidence of that impact, and it will take us a few years to have a really good picture of what that is.

PEGGY O'BRIEN: The study that I really want to do is show what the improvement is with reading, kids' ability to read and to put this stuff together. We did a study of this – it's a teacher report of students, and that is not as strong as direct student data, but it breaks down with the specifics of reading fluency and comprehension, the five specifics, and the kinds of improvements teachers saw in their classes. We talked for a long time about how we could put some kind of study together and we figured it would be too hard – there were so many things that you couldn't control in terms of reading – what other input students were getting, and all, unless you like, put them in a cave somewhere.

FRANCESCA ELLIS: We carry out detailed evaluation of all our programmes. Predominantly through teacher surveys [although in] the past we have also evaluated impact on students with baseline and endline evaluation, and surveyed the audience members attending performance nights. In our most recent evaluation of the theatre festival, for example: 98 per cent of teachers reported their students were more confident as a result of taking part; 97 per cent of teachers reported their students worked better as a team as a result of taking part; 96 per cent of teachers reported their students were more ambitious as a result of taking part; and 96 per cent of teachers said they now have a stronger relationship with their students.

CHRIS NAYAK: [Working with students on Shakespeare] is something that my passion for has grown the more I've done it because I feel like having that experience with students of watching them get passionate about something they initially thought was boring – or watching them have a revelation about Shakespeare that they haven't had before – and often that I've not had before – spotting things in the text or in the character that were totally new to me – makes me realize how hugely rich these plays are. A group of actors getting excited about Shakespeare is fine and wonderful but is nothing compared to a group of teenagers, who previously might have hated it, finding it exhilarating. I think it's also a little bit like discovering that you've been using a laptop as a coaster for most of your life. There's this thing that is capable of all this incredible stuff and you've just been using it in one boring way – and wanting to go to everybody else, 'Oh, my God, you know what guys? If we take our plate off this coaster and open it up, you can get on the Internet!' That's a bit of a crass metaphor, but you know what I mean.

PART THREE

Perspectives from the classroom

9

Perspectives from the classroom

Introduction

In Part Three, you will find the voices of teachers using theatre-based practice with Shakespeare in their classrooms. Our aim in this last part of the book is to offer examples of the scope of possibilities in how theatre-based approaches are being used to benefit the learning of young people of different ages, backgrounds and abilities. With the collection of chapters that follow, five teachers of Shakespeare, working with very different constituencies of young people, open a direct window onto their research, experiences and reflections. Each of these chapters has been written by teachers who have engaged in postgraduate study through the MA in Shakespeare and education at the University of Birmingham or through the (no longer available) MA in the advanced teaching of Shakespeare at the University of Warwick. Two further chapters by early career researchers open two different windows: one looking at how government policies affect the ways early career teachers can teach and the other exploring the place of Shakespeare on the South African curriculum. We introduce these chapters further, alongside additional reflections (see text boxes) from a range of other Shakespeare teachers who have had opportunities to reflect on their practice. Once again we are offering this collection as suggestive rather than representative, this time of the many amazing teachers of Shakespeare across the world.

The teachers in this collection value Shakespeare and have engaged with and reflected on the possibilities and practicalities of theatre-based practice in their classrooms. They have found the practice professionally satisfying but not an easy option. Teachers who value Shakespeare in systems where he is compulsory are often battling preconceived ideas about him as boring, difficult and irrelevant. Teachers who choose Shakespeare in systems where he is not compulsory may need to justify why they value him even more. A view persists among many commentators that Shakespeare is too difficult for those considered less academically able and second-language English speakers. Alongside this is often a presumption that active approaches are ways to make Shakespeare less painful rather than being a theatre-based pedagogy that can open up the understanding, engagement and salience that can lead to well-rooted and thoughtful analysis. Professional passion drives our teachers, and many more like them, to seek out the most effective ways to develop the learning of their students both about and through Shakespeare and you will find many echoes of the passion of practitioners from the last section. This includes witnessing the extent to which students' academic and social skills and competencies increase alongside their enjoyment and engagement, and the common outcome that when students discover they have something to say and are listened to, they seek out better ways to listen and be heard.

The chapters that follow are roughly in order of ages taught, and so we begin with Mary Carey. Mary is the headteacher of a rural primary school in the Channel Islands, working with a small mixed group of primary-aged children. Her chapter is evocatively titled 'Dirty Shakespeare', a title which immediately implies a playful and subversive approach but which most directly derives from getting outside into the elements. Mary describes how the sensory input from the outdoor environment enhances not just enjoyment but also the development of literacy skills. The term Mary and her colleagues coin of 'acting for writing' underscores how the experiential learning of theatre-based practice can give students something to speak, and then write, about. In the box that follows, Jan Anderson offers further thoughts on the literacy benefits of working with Shakespeare at primary level. Jan is a lead teacher in the RSC's Associate Schools programme. She has tracked the benefits of working with primary-aged pupils using the RSC's 'rehearsal room pedagogy' since 2013. Jan, like Mary, has noted improvements in her pupils' behaviour, self-esteem, attendance, confidence, well-being, resilience and cooperation through using theatre-based practice but has been especially interested in how the pedagogy, in conjunction with Shakespeare's texts, has fed into measurably better writing skills.

TEACHING SHAKESPEARE IN PRIMARY SCHOOLS

Children's writing resulting from work with Shakespeare's text and this pedagogy shows improvements with cohesion, vocabulary choices, tone, characterization, awareness of audience and purpose. The experiential nature of the work enables children to visualize, imagine and internalize elements of plot, setting and character. The archaic nature of the language gives children permission and models for ambitious vocabulary choices. The ambiguous form of the play, where so much is implied rather than told, helps children to replicate implication within their own writing. The learning is carefully layered and designed to engage learners physically, mentally and emotionally, which leads to the knowledge being remembered and truly learned. The social nature of the pedagogy where children learn as an ensemble, means that they are not limited to their own knowledge and understanding but have access to everyone's. The performance element of the pedagogy gives children a strong awareness of audience which is transferred to their awareness of a reader when writing, enabling them to make far more controlled and deliberate choices in order to affect the reader. All of the elements of the pedagogy combine to lessen the cognitive load which children face when writing, giving them the capacity to focus on making effective choices.

Jan Anderson

Using spaces beyond the classroom, whether indoor or outdoor, is not an easy option for teachers. Risk assessments, timetabling and a host of practical and administrative obstacles are deterrents, perhaps particularly at secondary level. In the next box, Chloe Chelsea talks of the benefits of outdoor learning with her high school students. Chloe teaches English in a European international school and took advantage of some flexibility in her school's timetable to take her Year 9s to the beach for a lesson on *The Tempest*. Like Mary, Chloe found the benefits went well beyond greater engagement with Shakespeare.

OUTDOOR SHAKESPEARE WITH HIGH SCHOOL STUDENTS

Teaching 'through' Shakespeare will ensure passion for literature in all its forms is nurtured and safeguard the canon for future generations. 'Gen Z' students seem more inclined to look for ways to explore social inequalities than previous generations were, perhaps in response to living in a more globalized society. Drawing on the theme of the environment offers parallels that appeal to the sensibilities of today's young people. Specifically, the plays are vehicles for debates concerning contested environmental realities.

An enrichment activity which allows students to practice Shakespeare in an outdoor setting, such as a park or beach, is an inexpensive and practical option to increase engagement in the work. The interdisciplinary approach I adopted for the eco-Shakespeare enrichment day (fieldwork and drama) aimed to engage students in a setting which required them to interact with nature and members of the public. The sensory stimulation provided by nature is a way in which students could relate the world of the play to the ecosystem they inhabit. Ecological issues are something

> which interest and concern young people as proven by the evaluation of the beach day. Providing contexts for students to navigate the play, as well as the world beyond the school gates make for memorable experiences.
>
> Chloe Chelsea

Shakespeare's global currency is nowhere more apparent than in international schools. Current estimates put the number of schools with international status above 12,000. The majority are fee-paying, English medium and based on a British or American curriculum. Even more schools around the world include some provision for learning about texts of global cultural influence and for English language learning; areas where Shakespeare often features (Irish 2012). International Baccalaureate (IB) programmes are offered across over 5,600 schools in 160 countries and while IB schools are not required to study Shakespeare, many do (IBO 2022). Judith Berends O'Brien has taught in schools in the UK and internationally and her chapter offers a perspective on Shakespeare's value as a unifying force in the multilingual and multicultural environments of European IB schools. Her chapter reviews her experiences of cross-phase projects that play with the material Shakespeare offers to re-story his work and support young people in finding connection and belonging with each other and global culture.

Kirsty Emmerson is a teacher in the multilingual and multicultural environment of a state secondary in London. Although in a very different socio-economic environment to Judith's, in her chapter Kirsty also explores Shakespeare through a version of re-storying. Her particular focus is on the efficacy of playfulness with language that invites in the rich diversity of cultural and linguistic knowledge and experiences her students can bring. She carefully structures activities to develop understanding and appreciation of *Macbeth* through active, dialogic methods, which provide plenty of space for independent discoveries. The resulting work leads to genuine playful engagement with language where Kirsty learns alongside her students about what *Macbeth* can mean refracted through the diverse lenses of London teenage cultures.

Shakespeare is globally owned across many different cultures, in many translations and in many different schools. An attitude persists, however, that since Shakespeare's language is difficult for native English speakers, it should be avoided with learners of English as an Additional Language (EAL). Teachers like Kirsty, along with Sam Lane in the box that follows, and Nobulali Dangazele in the last chapter of this collection challenge this assumption. Translating as complex a text as Shakespeare can seem daunting and is indeed highly skilled if working towards a professional outcome. In conversation with Tracy Professor Martin Hilský gave an illuminating example of the need to consider ambiguities and how rhythms and imagery are linked to cultural expression. He explained how the musicality of 'womb' and 'tomb' in line four of Sonnet 86 is lost in a direct translation to the Czech words *lůno* and *hrob*. Instead he used the words *kolébka* and *lebka*, where *kolébka* means cradle but contains the word *lebka* meaning skull (Hilský 2009). This example also illuminates the playfulness of language and how nuance, as explored in Chapter 4, is not just an aesthetic or academic aside, but a core aspect of how words work in our everyday interactions, whatever the language we speak. Encouraging EAL students to explore this playfulness can build confidence, and working with their EAL peers can perhaps support monolingual students to better appreciate language at play. In the next box we hear from Sam Lane, an English teacher working in an international school in China. Sam is interested in how using theatre-based practice with his students can support them, not just in knowing more about a global cultural icon but in developing their English language proficiency.

SHAKESPEARE IN THE EAL CLASSROOM

There are two stand out reasons for including Shakespeare in the EAL classroom. First, too often EAL texts are one-dimensional and transactional in nature; they do not invite an emotional response from the student. But human emotions do not require translation. Shakespeare can be taught in such a way so as to invite in the thoughts and experiences of students' lives from beyond the curriculum. Second, Shakespeare's characters frequently 'play' with language and can encourage students to want to do the same. By exploring and experimenting with the multiple connotative possibilities of Shakespeare's language, students gain proficiency in expressing themselves effectively in English. They also practice negotiating meanings with others and I have witnessed first-hand how quickly students realize the importance of context and intention during these negotiations. Ultimately, the study of literature may free an EAL student to think for themselves in English as they do in their native language. This relies heavily on spoken discourse that is not limited by the concept of finding the right answer or indeed the answer that the teacher expects to achieve.

Sam Lane

Many of the teachers we have worked with over the years have used theatre-based Shakespeare with young people with various Special Educational Needs and/or Disabilities (SEN/D), sometimes with students in mainstream classes, sometimes in special schools or units. There is so much valuable work happening in this field in classrooms, with theatre organizations and through applied theatre that it would take another book to properly represent it. To offer just a few examples: Sue Jennings's use of Shakespeare in her innovative practice of Neuro-Dramatic Play (2021); Flute Theatre's work with young people with autism, following Kelly Hunter's Shakespeare-focused theatre-based techniques (2015); 'Signing Shakespeare' with resources on *Macbeth* for use with young people who are deaf or hard of hearing (Irish and Rokison-Woodall 2023). In the limited space we have here to explore diverse areas of practice, we include a chapter by Eleni Kmiec, a teacher in a special school in the US for young people with autism. Eleni's inspiring study looks at the value of working with theatre-based practice to support her neurodivergent students in their study of *The Tempest*. She picks up particularly on how the texts are incomplete until realized in performance where the performative environment and the semiotics of stagecraft allow an audience to, in her word, 'context' their way to understanding. Eleni develops theatre-based project approaches that invite in the students' personal interests, knowledge and experiences.

In the following box Hannah Young, a drama teacher at an SEN school in the UK, describes working with young people with autism (ASD), attention deficit hyperactivity disorder (ADHD), global developmental delay (GDD), emotional and behavioural disorder (EBD), moderate learning difficulties (MLD) and profound and multiple learning difficulties (PMLD). Hannah brings her skills as an experienced actor and theatre-education practitioner into how she uses Shakespeare with her students to help broaden and enrich their thinking and develop healthy mindsets.

SHAKESPEARE IN THE SEN CLASSROOM

I am continually inspired by the deep emotional response my students experience in their journey through Shakespeare's work. In our setting, we reimagine the texts to provide our students with an accessible way into the world of the plays: sensory stories for our PMLD students; attention autism 'bucket stories' for our learners with autism (an intervention model designed by Gina Davies, Specialist Speech and Language Therapist); and as immersive sequenced drama lessons for our students with MLD, GDD and EBD. The scope of Shakespeare's plays introduces students to complex theatrical worlds beyond anyone's lived experience and exposes in sharper contrast the tangled webs of human interaction. The plays offer them the opportunity to live other lives and therefore interpret the world around them in more complex ways. The moments when students are able to connect their learning of the endless, shifting sea that is the human condition to their own lives are the best moments of teaching. When a student can see themselves in a character, or feel a dilemma, or can argue a different way of seeing or feeling, it means that there is deep experiential learning at work. The fact that the plays were written over 400 years ago and in a poetic language gives the plays a distance and an otherness that is essential to the journey of self-discovery, because it means we travel further to get to the truth and the journey is everything.

Hannah Young

Teachers of English and language arts generally understand the value of literature as both a door to other worlds and a way to better understand language. Teachers who studied literature at university, however, can feel more comfortable with the skills of literary analysis than of composing an effective piece of writing. They may also have a level of affinity with writing that makes them less aware of the components of their competency and why others struggle. Carol Parker is a teacher of both literature and composition at a Community College in the United States. Her chapter addresses an aim of all teachers of older teenagers: the need to develop personal, informed opinions, gained through critical thinking, that can also be coherently expressed in written form. Carol explores how literary analysis and composition skills are different but complementary, and how that complementarity not only deepens skills in both areas but also provides important transferable skills for other subject areas and for the realities of life outside the academy. Carol proposes the skills that go into building a good thesis statement can be time efficient, productive and engaging as the foundations for effective writing, literary analysis, informed discussion and better understanding of different perspectives in the world in general and finds theatre-based practice useful in achieving those goals.

Our contributors are not impartial. For a book advocating theatre-based practice, we have invited contributions from authors who have something to say on that topic. They are invested in using the practice with their students and have challenged perceived obstacles such as time, space and governmental or school policies that relegate active, drama work. In this way, they are perhaps not representative members of their profession. For her master's dissertation research, English teacher Rosalind Faulkner (2020) carried out an indicative survey, recruiting respondents via Twitter. Her 250 respondents may not constitute a representative sample but did cover a wide range of experience. She found that 19 per cent felt only 'somewhat confident' at most in teaching Shakespeare to fourteen- to sixteen-year-olds for whom that study is compulsory. In a follow-up survey, Rosalind found that half her respondents did not feel confident in using active approaches in their Shakespeare teaching and that the majority of the other half felt only 'somewhat confident'. This resulted in 60 per cent of respondents saying they did not use active approaches at all. If we accept Rosalind's findings as even somewhat representative, we find support for anecdotal evidence that most English teachers are not comfortable with using active or theatre-based approaches with Shakespeare in their classrooms.

The confidence and commitment to take the risks theatre-based practice entails often inhibits teachers (Irish 2011) and there remains limited understanding from many policymakers and commentators about the potential of the practice to provide structured opportunities for creative and critical interaction with the cultural inheritance of Shakespeare texts. For newly qualified teachers entering the profession, facing these barriers can understandably lead them away from trying out any active approaches in their classrooms. Karen McGivern's chapter looks at the absence of support for active approaches to Shakespeare in current government policy documents in the UK. As an experienced teacher, now early career researcher and tutor of trainee teachers, Karen considers the school environments new teachers are going into and reviews the key policies that determine what successful teaching is considered to be in the current climate. She finds enthusiasm for theatre-based approaches from her trainees but increasing structural hostility. Karen's chapter highlights the continuing top-down perspective that preferences pedagogical approaches concerned with reading Shakespeare as a cultural inheritance of received knowledge over theatre-based practice that interacts with and disrupts that knowledge.

This collection concludes with a chapter by Nobulali Dangazele, actor, academic and artistic director of ShakeXperience (2023), a theatre company based in Johannesburg with a strong education offer. As we have discussed, Shakespeare is a global resource reinterpreted daily across the world as young people encounter him through the lenses of their own cultures and languages. However, he carries with him a weight of historical baggage that can present obstacles for anyone wanting to use his work as a vehicle to question and challenge the assumptions that baggage can entail. In 'Much ado about decolonized Shakespeare', Nobulali describes the controversy around the place of Shakespeare on South Africa's curriculum. She recognizes the colonial baggage he brings but suggests that it is *how* the plays are studied that is the problem. Nobulali offers the work of her colleague Marvelous Jore as the solution. Mr Jore is a teacher dedicated to the progress and success of his students in a globalized world and for this reason, he makes space in his teaching for theatre-based practice with Shakespeare that encourages creative, critical and collaborative competencies.

In the box that ends this chapter, Anjana Saha offers a perspective from India on the flavour she believes Shakespeare can add to a curriculum. Anjana Saha is the principal of a co-educational school in Kolkata run by India's Central Board of Secondary Education (CBSE). Except for a few excerpts from plays and poems in grades 6–12, Shakespeare is not part of the CSBE syllabus. Just like Nobulali and Mr Jore in South Africa, however, Anjana Saha and the English department of her school decided that Shakespeare had more to offer their students. She proposes, as Nobulali does, that young people find stimulating connections between Shakespeare's eurocentric world and their own *if* the plays are treated as living art to explore in a spirit of intercultural democracy.

TEACHING SHAKESPEARE IN INDIA

We include abridged versions of Shakespeare plays in grades 6–8 and a full text in grade 9. We want our young readers to fall in love with the nuances and cadence of the language and to find a taste for Shakespearean themes that will spice their palate and leave them hungry for more. 'Masala Shakespeare' has become an essential part of our curriculum and students are surprised to find innumerable connections between Shakespeare's works like *Macbeth*, *Othello*, *Hamlet* and *A Comedy of Errors* and our Bollywood films. The characters they study come alive right before their eyes as they find interesting parallels and doppelgangers with their favourite Indian movie stars.

Then comes another process of discovery and exploration as part of the experiential learning pedagogy we follow here, resulting in the revelation for students that there is a world of similarity between the oft-repeated themes by the Bard of Avon and the Bard of Bengal, Rabindranath Tagore. Both speak of inclusion in a world divided by differences and students are enthralled to perceive the deep connection between Tagore's song *Krishnakali* dedicated to a dark beauty and Shakespeare's Sonnet 127: 'In the old age black was not counted fair'. It is a theme that touches their hearts as many grapple with issues like body shaming and obsession with fair skin as the only acceptable definition of beauty in a country often divided by caste, community class and colour. 'That every tongue says beauty should look so' was a line that lent itself to rich debates, discussions and exchange of ideas at an assembly held on Shakespeare's birthday. Students arrived at the conclusion that black is beautiful and so is yellow, orange, red – all colours, all castes and genders are equal and deserving of empathy and respect in society. What a brilliant lesson on inclusion with conclusions drawn through a personal journey of reflection and introspection by our young ones.

Thus, Shakespeare remains topical and contemporary for our students as we blend the teaching of texts with art integration, role plays, site specific journeys, and the creation of contemporary issue-based plays derived from themes explored in prescribed texts. We follow a physical process of kinaesthetic learning wherein students often adapt portions from their texts to create 'street plays' which raise awareness about issues such as gender equality and respect for women in society. Students are inspired by female leads like Portia and Rosalind, while characters such as Shylock often touch a raw nerve with students from marginalized sections of society as they identify with his plight. What often follows is an argument for his cause thus giving vent to their feelings in the safe space that we create in our classrooms. *Macbeth* is often used as a leitmotif in our leadership training sessions for student council members for them to realize the tricky balance between personal aspiration and common welfare.

The magic of romance, the thrill of the supernatural, the tragedy of loss, the lack of self-knowledge and the resolution of conflict in a comedy, are universal themes that our young learners discover and identify with as we create an appetite for gourmet Shakespeare in the years to come.

Anjana Saha

10

Dirty Shakespeare

Outdoor learning with primary pupils

Mary Carey

Be not afeard. The isle is full of noises,
Sounds and sweet airs that give delight and hurt not.
(*TEM* 3.2.135–136)

The term *Dirty Shakespeare* is one I devised to refer to the teaching of Shakespeare using active techniques in an outdoor space. It does not follow Forest School pedagogy, with its prescribed programme using specially trained teachers (Knight 2013) but does use outdoor learning in a more general sense, using the outdoor space, sights, sounds and environment to explore Shakespeare using ensemble approaches. The word 'dirty' captures the element of the outdoors with its connotations of being messy, collaborative, adaptable and fun.

Both Louv (2021) and Palmer (2007), outdoor learning protagonists, have claimed the practice not only heightens self-esteem and the senses but also particularly calms neurodivergent children, raises self-confidence, increases mood and fitness and generally enhances understanding and engagement. I have found similar advantages working with active Shakespeare pedagogy, where I have observed increases in self-confidence, speaking and listening skills, empathy, enjoyment and engagement in four- to eleven-year-olds. The techniques have proven particularly useful with Special Educational Needs and Disabilities (SEND) pupils who seem to find a voice and a freedom. *Dirty Shakespeare* embodies the coalescence of active Shakespeare and outdoor learning in nurturing attributes such as self-confidence, creativity, empathy and engagement that many, including Claxton and Lucas (2015), claim schools need to teach to prepare their students for the future.

I am the sole teacher in a school on a small island in the English Channel. The island has no cars and a population of under a hundred people. It has white, sandy beaches, and a wide variety of fauna and flora. There is a pub, an eleventh-century chapel, self-catering cottages, a hotel, a shop and my school. My pupils range from four to eleven years old. I commute twenty minutes by a small boat in all weathers and teach in a rectangular, uninspiring, flat-roofed room, with an interior in desperate need of refurbishment. I try, where possible, to use the outdoor spaces around the island, and use literature as the gateway to engagement.

My own introduction to active Shakespeare was back in 2008, when I attended a course run by Andy Kempe of Reading University. At the time I had no experience or training in Shakespeare and was told by a colleague that Shakespeare was 'too hard' for primary pupils. The versatility of active Shakespeare pedagogy, however, soon became apparent. I built on my early successes by carrying out action research in 2015 which involved integrating story and text from *Richard II*, *Henry VI* and *Henry V* into our study of the Middle Ages. Making use of our outdoor spaces, a castle was designed and built out of pallets on a hilltop as our setting to explore the initial jousting scene in *Richard II*. We constructed tents in the woods for Henry Bolingbroke's camp when he returns from exile and found a rocky outcrop for the castle scene of Richard's abdication. We found other open spaces for Henry V's camp on the eve of Agincourt. The children's subsequent writing showed noticeable improvements as they incorporated their experiences of the outdoor environment. One child, for example, used the phrase, 'Richard's words lost their power in the wind' when describing the feelings of Richard confronted at the castle by Bolingbroke. Further class-based active lessons showed deeper understanding of the emotions and situations of the characters, once they had experienced the sensations in the outdoor sessions. For example, two collaboratively created soliloquies to be spoken by Henry Bolingbroke, the first after being banished from his homeland and the second on his return to claim his title following the death of his father, were greatly enhanced by having acted the scenes on a beach and feeling the sensation of the 'homeland' sand in their hands.

Fiona Banks, writing about teaching styles at the Globe, describes active Shakespeare pedagogy as 'physical activity; students discovering and exploring language through action – the type of exercise that can require an empty space where students move more freely' (2014: 5). Surely the outdoor space would give even more freedom? Cathy Bache, the founder of an outdoor nursery school in Fife, Scotland, claims that being outdoors does not just give a sense of freedom, but heightens pupils' senses: 'We become aware of the forest smells: dark and dank, light and ferny, gentle and sweet, each smell transporting us into a different scene: a battle with pirates, a meeting with the fairy queen, a hunt for a tiger, a sleep of a hundred years' (2021). While interviewing Jon Cree (founding chair of the Forest School Association UK) in June 2015, I asked him of the benefits of learning in outdoor spaces. He replied, 'The outdoors offers adventure and curiosity as it is not predictable. The main benefit for me is the outdoors gives children and learners a sense of place and connection with the world. There are loads of other benefits, for example, it stimulates the senses, offers opportunities for all types of learners, is truly holistic and can enhance any area of the curriculum.'

Encouraged by my own experience, I wanted to discover whether the incidences of deeper understanding by my pupils could be commutable to other pupils and teachers. I approached schools on the neighbouring larger island to take part in further research and worked with two primary teachers: one studying *The Tempest* with a Year 3 class and the other studying *Macbeth* with a Year 6 class. With the participating teachers, I shared techniques and strategies I had learnt, and we jointly devised a programme of study using the RSC's *Toolkit for Teachers* (2010) as a scaffold. The ensemble-based learning, with 'its stress on interpretative choices, discovery, risk and struggle' (Neelands and O'Hanlon 2011: 7) was embraced and welcomed by the educators. In each case study, Shakespeare's text was used and made accessible to the pupils by taking part in activities designed to create empathy with characters by using what we called 'script scraps' (small extracts). The Year 6 teachers planned an outdoor session on a heath-like common to introduce *Macbeth*, with the teachers-in-role as the weird sisters. Initially, pupils re-enacted backstory scenes of a lively skirmish in the Scottish countryside against invaders from Ireland and Norway before any mention of Shakespeare or the play.

The Year 3 class were lucky enough to be able to walk to a beach for their sessions. Pupils had to shout lines above the wind, improvise with natural items such as sand, shells, seaweed, stones and sticks, and were free to use nature's scenery as a backdrop. Playing the shipwreck scene in *The Tempest* was evocative on the beach as the pupils could see, hear and smell the sea and shoreline. Their participation in delivering lines was enthusiastic, loud and atmospheric. Their writing included references to the senses enlivened in the outdoor experience: 'I step out of the boat and my feet touch bright, warm golden sand. I can feel ice cold water making my feet freeze. Above my head I can see and hear loud, crazy creatures.' It became evident to me that stimulation of the senses was integral to a more comprehensive learning experience. The practice of studying *The Tempest* on an actual beach, or *Macbeth* on a foggy common, enhanced sensory abilities which gave a more holistic exploration of the plays resulting in deeper understanding.

We also used a teacher-in-role strategy successfully, taking advantage of the outdoor space for effects and atmosphere. As Prospero, I emerged from the sand dunes, using a piece of driftwood for a staff and shouting above the wind. Apart from a magic cloak for Prospero, we took little or no props with us, instead either taking props from nature or simply imagining objects. Collaborative storytelling techniques also worked well outdoors with the children becoming totally focused and attentive as the story unfolded and they played the parts as the teacher read the plot. The texture of the sand and shells as a carpet added a reality to the experience, with children using seaweed and shells as props and vigorously repeating words from the text. Another technique used was where one child acted as a character while the other children went up individually to put their hand on the character's shoulder to give them advice or thoughts. One pupil was standing at the shoreline, holding his staff to the sky while dressed in Prospero's magic cloak, the wind billowing it behind him. The other pupils took turns as Miranda, voicing her thoughts about his actions that had caused the tempest and wrecked the ship. Their reproaches were made more powerful by having to shout against the wind and fight against his cloak. The experience seemed to be beneficial for SEND pupils who seemed to engage more with the language, remembering lines and acting with more commitment than usual.

The teachers spoke about the importance of the outdoor space in playing a role in pupils' understanding alongside physicalizing the words and coined the term: 'acting for writing' to describe how bringing the words to life supported subsequent writing activities. The pupils said they felt more able to express themselves, being in an open space and appreciated their teachers modelling 'doing' as a way of understanding before writing. Their writing reflected the stimulation to their imagination the sensory outdoor experience gave them with many descriptive references to smells, sights, sounds and textures that they had experienced first-hand.

In subsequent interviews, the teachers repeated their surprise that active outdoor work had had such an effect on the whole class. They ascertained that most pupils had improved and learnt from *Dirty Shakespeare* and said they would definitely endeavour to include it in future practice, perhaps adapting active techniques to other areas of literature; for example *Dirty Brontës*, with Heathcliff and Cathy on the moor, or even *Dirty Wordsworth* in a field of daffodils. Although there had initially been a fear of the process taking more time than a class-based lesson, the time walking to and from the beach was seen as valuable reflection time for the pupils to talk about what had happened and what they had experienced. Dunn and Stinson (2011) state a direct impact on learning outcomes in these unrehearsed experiences. One pupil said enthusiastically, 'We got to get air instead of just being stuck in a room ... fresh air, not like normal air, fresh air!' The benefits the outdoor space can bring to learning seem even more important in the post-Covid-19 world. Louv, who claims a deficiency of nature can be detrimental, argues:

> Outdoor learning is *better learning*. A growing body of research points to improved critical thinking, problem solving, teamwork, leadership and

personal resilience; as well as longer attention span, better motor skills, a stronger sense of independence, better impulse control and increased environmental literacy. . . . Not incidentally, the research suggests that teachers who take their classes outside suffer lower rates of burnout. What's good for the student is good for the educator. (Louv 2011)

And surely pedagogy which benefits both teacher and learner is worth embracing.

11

How relevant is Shakespeare in an international school context?

Judith Berends O'Brien

The international school context

I am an English and Drama teacher with fifteen years of teaching experience in secondary schools. Eight of these years have been in international schools (Gran Canaria in Spain, Stavanger in Norway and Utrecht in the Netherlands). I consider myself to be an International Baccalaureate (IB) educator, as it is a system of education that actively prepares students for an increasingly complex world and prioritizes student agency, helping them to think for themselves and respect the beliefs of others (Bullock ND).

International schools are multicultural, multilingual and transient in nature, making them complex environments, where having a sense of community can be difficult (Murphy 2004). For many teachers, parents and students, the school community may be their main source of social interaction in their new country of residence. Unfortunately, one of the challenges that these schools face is dissonance. Walker (2000) argues that schools have a responsibility to acknowledge and deal with dissonance, to avoid issues of student isolation, feeling undervalued, having resentment, and even conflicts. Osterman (2000) observes that in a school community where students feel cared for and recognized, there is less likelihood of dissonance. As international school educators we can all do our part by providing inclusive and nurturing spaces for students to thrive and feel they belong.

Through the active exploration of Shakespeare texts with young people, there are opportunities to create inclusive, nurturing and stimulating classroom and rehearsal room spaces with students. Kitchen (2021) explores this through the notion of a 'third space' – a nurturing, dialectical space, where ensemble exploration happens. Applying this to an international school context, the third space can mean many 'in-between' states: a space that allows for student's differing values; a space between the world of the play and the world of the students; a space between the differing cultural influences that sit within the students themselves (which can be a complex mixture); and finally, a space between the language of Shakespeare and the languages of often multilingual students. For this reason, I strongly believe that working with Shakespeare can be a powerful way of tackling dissonance with groups of students, as these polarities can co-exist in the nurturing, dialectical space (Neelands 2002, 2009a; Kitchen 2022). In this chapter, I will reflect upon how active work with Shakespeare's texts can meaningfully impact the community of an international school, drawing on academic literature, my teaching experiences in English and drama classrooms, and my experience of planning and delivering a Shakespeare festival in an international school.

Shakespeare in an international classroom

On the prescribed reading list for the IB diploma programme (for ages sixteen to eighteen), Shakespeare is one of the approved authors for teachers to choose in designing their curriculum for the Language and Literature course. However, in my experience, many international teachers are nervous about exploring a Shakespeare text with multilingual students at varied levels of English language acquisition. Another concern teachers may hold is that British texts can carry a disproportionate weight, perpetuating imperialism (McGregor 2021). These valid concerns require the international schoolteacher to work sensitively and collaboratively with colleagues, ensuring that if you decide to include Shakespeare, you also ensure exposure to a range of texts from other cultures and time periods, inclusive of works in translation which will be meaningful for the students' multicultural context. This selection of texts also needs to support the exploration of a range of relevant 'global issues', which are transnational and significant in nature (IB Language and Literature curriculum subject brief, 2021).

Miazga, an experienced IB educator, working alongside Folger Education, posits that Shakespeare's texts lend themselves to the exploration of a range of global issues. He also asserts that using a range of creative collaboration tasks can help students prepare for IB oral exams (Miazga 2014). I have experienced this in my own practice. As part of a collaborative English teaching project in Norway in 2015, I worked with American and Australian colleagues to create a six-week project, focusing on Shakespeare's *Macbeth*. We used a combination of workshops, post-workshop class discussions and close textual analysis tasks, using extracts from *Macbeth* alongside a range of modern texts. This approach led into more advanced exploration of global issues such as gender representation, corruption, violence and conflict. We found students actively engaged and they showed increased confidence in expressing their own interpretations of the text. The collaborative context, along with the focus on contemporary global issues, provided a foundation for a diversity of independent thought with regard to Shakespeare.

This relates to the concepts of 'counterstorying' or 're-storying' that have come from critical race education, a process whereby students examine and reshape stories, establishing their own meaningful connections to the original texts (Kitchen 2022). In the aforementioned example, the students' oral responses to the play, which were framed around their own choice of global issue, could be seen as an empowering act of 'counterstorying' or 'restorying'. Many of these students revisited their experience with *Macbeth* in the months following, sharing that it had been a positive experience for them, which had helped develop their confidence in actively interpreting other texts on the course.

The impact of a Shakespeare festival

When I was teaching at the International School Stavanger in Norway, I noticed that the school sections had limited interaction with each other, an observation confirmed by other teachers. This was partly due to the physical separation of the buildings of the primary, middle and high schools. Literature on international school contexts suggests one of the ways to strengthen a community is through creating shared goals, and that larger artistic events can 'inspire a feeling of togetherness' (Willis 1992: 26). I decided to plan a Shakespeare festival at my school, hoping it would be an opportunity to show members of the school community how they could collaborate more regularly.

The festival was an evening event with performances in the school theatre, followed by a selection of Shakespeare-related workshops and an exhibition of projects related to Shakespeare in a communal exhibition space. In 2015, I was also engaged in postgraduate study and conducted an ethnographic study of the festival, to examine its impact on the school community. My conclusion was that the festive spirit it created led to greater interaction across different ages and groups, and this generated a sense of celebration and belonging for those involved.

Within the festival 'core' were three ensemble groups with whom I worked over a few weeks of rehearsals. A primary ensemble performed a shortened *Macbeth*; a middle school ensemble performed an adaptation of the mechanicals scene from *A Midsummer Night's Dream*; and a high school ensemble performed a selection of short comic adaptations of Shakespearean comedy scenes. As part of my ethnographic study, the students from all three ensemble groups gave feedback. I gathered this feedback through a series of unstructured interviews with each group, followed by an individual reflection task.

The feedback from these three ensembles gave a cohesive message: most students felt they had improved their confidence, their communication, and their conflict resolution. There was also a general sense of pride in having performed something from Shakespeare, which was seen as very challenging. The most striking impact that I identified was for two students from the middle school group, a French boy aged fourteen, and a Texan girl aged fifteen. Both had previously expressed feelings of dissonance from the community as they struggled to adjust to their recent move to Norway as well as their new school environment. After the festival, both expressed a strong sense of pride. They also expressed an eagerness to perform again and to have more opportunities of this kind in the school. They said they would audition for the school musical the following year, which would have been unthinkable for them before. The example of these two students could be relatable for other professionals working in a social context where there is a need to develop a sense of belonging, as the creation of the 'third space' (Kitchen 2022) supported these students in navigating their earlier feelings of conflict within their group, as well as their sense of dissonance from the wider school community.

I also discovered how the atmosphere of festivity had encouraged laughter and fun, which led to a playful connection between the festival goers and the performers. This festive spirit and how it helps to develop bonds is something that was also noted in some of the international Globe-to-Globe festival performances in London in 2012 (Yon Li Lan 2013). The secondary school students' adaptations of the short comic scenes, which were drawn from a selection of plays, were irreverent and playful in nature, and this drew the audience into a playful 'restorying' process, leading to a warm community spirit, which was evident in the feedback from the performers, as well as the photographic evidence from the event.

On reflection, a practical piece of advice for planning a festival is to form a strong team of professionals and students at least six months before the event and not to take too much on your own shoulders. I tried to do it in four months and I did too much on my own, leading to unnecessary stress. Adequate preparation and trust are the essential factors in making a festival committee come to life. When you trust that it will all come together in the end and you have a strong festival committee of colleagues, students and parents, it is most likely that it will.

Of course, it is a lot of work, so why would you bother? Well, one thing to consider is how the impact can linger with the participants after the event in ways that are difficult to measure, which is a phenomenon that is often examined by other drama practitioners (Somers 2008; Gallagher and Wessels 2013; Gallagher 2014). In terms of what lingers after the Shakespeare festival, I can confirm that some students were still talking about their experience months later. I left the school in 2016, and I was encouraged to hear from my former colleague, a visual arts teacher who had worked with me on the festival, that she had been inspired by her experience to create a cross-curricular and cross-stage arts festival the next year. From my point of view, this was a sign that the positive school response of the school community had created the inspiration for more events of that kind.

Final reflection

Being part of an international school community reminds us that we are not all the same, and we come from so many diverse cultural backgrounds and life experiences. In this complex environment, being open to including dissonant voices can be described as 'redressive action', which can forge bonds and address conflict or dissonance in a positive way (Neelands 2009a). Students need these spaces to talk about their ideas and concerns considering the social and mental health impact of long periods of Covid isolation, anxiety about climate change, concerns that have come out of the aftermath of the MeToo and the Black Lives Matter movements, the ongoing discrimination felt by many members of the LGBTQ+ community and finally, the disparate, and sometimes extreme, views that exist in our increasingly polarized societies. With so many pressing concerns, it is more likely that dissonance would exist in international school communities in 2022. Providing opportunities for bringing people closer together in active engagement and dialogue, certainly carries a lot of value in these times, and engaging with Shakespeare's texts in a nurturing and engaging way can open a door to shared understanding or at least, greater respect for differences.

12

Macbeth, ماكبث -, *Макбет*

Utilizing students' code-switching as a tool for engaging with Shakespeare at secondary level

Kirsty Emmerson

My students regularly question the value of studying Shakespeare in modern society. 'He speaks a foreign language, miss', they tell me. Such students often speak second languages alongside Multicultural London English (MLE) outside of the classroom. Kerswill describes MLE as 'a dialect of London English which has emerged since the early 1980s in parts of London where there has been a relatively high level of immigration. MLE is based on the traditional East End Cockney dialect.' Borrowings into MLE originate from a range of sources, including, but not limited to, Jamaican slang, Punjabi, Arabic and Turkish (Kerswill n.d.). This leads to students code-switching between their home language, MLE and what the National Curriculum calls 'Standard English' (DfE 2014), with the codes and conventions of each creating a form of Cultural Literacy, allowing students to navigate different societal groups (Hirsch 1987: xiii). The requirement that students use 'Standard English' (DfE 2014) implicitly ranks students' languages, often relegating home languages to the hinterland of the classroom. Shakespeare's language, however, is not standard and I wondered whether students' already-extant code-switching skills could act as a learning tool in their understanding of Shakespeare. I designed a set of workshops to investigate this question (Emmerson 2022).

My research was inspired by a group of Year 9 students who requested a gloss for line 7 of *Sonnet 116*, 'It is the star to every wandering bark' (*Son* 116.7) as they struggled to understand why Shakespeare was talking about trees. Suggesting that 'bark' had a sixteenth-century meaning of 'boat' (OED 2022), I was met with revelations from students whose home language was Romanian, as the word translates similarly: *barcă*. Unlocking the metaphor this way allowed them to engage more independently with the text, connecting Shakespeare's language with their own. Wittgenstein's suggestion that 'the meaning of a word is its use' (1967: 20) became clear: once students had a context created by their bilingualism, they could understand the meanings surrounding the unknown word and its images. By linking their identities to their studies, students felt more confident exploring the texts with less facilitation from their teacher.

My workshops encouraged students to utilize their sociolects and home languages to explore *Macbeth*. These workshops borrowed the ideals of Intermission Youth Theatre, who 'mix [Shakespeare's] 400-year-old language with . . . street slang' in productions using text adapted with input from their cast to create a sense of ownership and engagement (Hurrell 2018). Given that 90 per cent of my participants were classed as having EAL, and felt alienated from Shakespeare, I believed such ownership could begin to break down barriers in accessing Shakespeare. Jami Rogers notes that in Britain, Shakespeare performance has been 'dominant[ly] white theatre', with 'citizens of colour' portrayed as 'foreigners' and therefore lacking belonging (2022: 199). My workshops hoped to expose that dissonance, highlighting that my participants' readings of Shakespeare's text did not have to originate from preconceived stereotypes but could be rooted in their own experiences. I intended to decentralize my position as the 'explainer' (Thompson and Turchi 2016: 43) and instead encourage students to 'make meaning themselves' (Young 2021: 254).

The workshops built upon skills practised over the course, engaging with different forms of code-switching, and while there were four in total, only two will be explored here. The first, 'Shakespeare Translate', directly borrowed from Intermission's work to focus on my participants' interaction with Shakespeare in their own sociolects. The other, 'Global Shakespeare', explored the idea that Shakespeare's work could be transposed into any language of my participants' choosing, interacting with Dinda L. Gorlée's concept of semio-translation (2004: 25). This is the concept that implicit meanings are conveyed through signs or ideas in a text, and those meanings must remain throughout the course of translation. As the workshops encouraged students to utilize their own language and cultures to take Shakespeare's text and make it their own, the result was a range of student-led, socio-culturally driven interpretations blending modern language and Shakespeare's original text.

'Shakespeare Translate' asked participants to take an extract from *Macbeth* and translate it from Early Modern English into 'the way they speak', justifying their choices in discussion. I directed students to Act 1, Scene 5, where Lady Macbeth instructs Macbeth to 'look like the innocent flower / but be the serpent under't' (*Mac* 1.5.65-6), and several students concluded that Lady Macbeth was more powerful, suggesting that 'she doesn't see her husband as her equal even in a patriarchal society'.

To facilitate such interpretations, I created a worksheet modelled on the Google Translate interface. To support students, I translated the first two lines: 'My dearest love / Duncan comes here tonight' (*Mac* 1.5.58–9) into: 'Babe, Duncan's on his way', however, I emphasized that they could alter or discard this as they saw fit. Within minutes students were asking, 'Are we allowed to use . . .?' as, in a usual classroom, non-standard English would be prohibited. By permitting them to translate as they pleased – including using expletive language – interpretations became more personal. Some focused on how the scene drove the plot: 'When is he [Duncan] coming?'; 'He should die before tomorrow, or you will never be king' while others prioritized the central images of the text. This reflected Gorlee's semio-translation in action, as rather than having a face 'as a book', or looking 'like the innocent flower', Macbeth was told, 'not to get caught lacking by the opps'; to 'act two-faced', and asked, 'why do you look like you're going to shit yourself?' before being told to 'stop being a little bitch'. Their interpretations retained the idea but adapted the image used to convey it. When asked to explain their decisions, students suggested that Shakespeare wanted to show Lady Macbeth's power over Macbeth, and the demand not to get 'caught lacking by the opps' – not to get caught out by the enemy – suggested Lady Macbeth's distrust of Macbeth, interpreting the line in which 'men may read strange matters' (*Mac* 1.5.63) as one of concern. While this task supported students to work with Shakespeare's language independently, it might raise comments as to the legitimacy of the translation, as per Bannet's reading of Wittgenstein's analogy theory (1997: 655). Yet such paraphrasing in such a way is commonly used to make meaningful connections between the text and reader. The use of expletive language and colloquialisms might seem undesirable in the classroom, but I found they created a mirror to the original text which 'puts the language into words [students] would say in everyday life' (Gonsalves and Irish 2021: 89), creating a bridge between the distant language and their own experiences. The act of cultural translation developed students' analytical and collaborative skills as they engaged with explaining and discussing the choices they made while paraphrasing the text. Although we were not analysing the imagery in a traditional academic sense, the students demonstrated skills of adaptation and creation of analogues, which showed significant understanding as they were able to recreate the intent of an image into a more familiar cultural context. As an introductory activity for students new to working with Shakespeare's language, 'Shakespeare

Translate' worked to effectively build not only confidence but re-creative skills.

These skills were developed in 'Global Shakespeare'. Participants took extracts from *Macbeth* and transposed the lines into their home languages. While 'Shakespeare Translate' utilized MLE, 'Global Shakespeare' reached more expansively. Most of my participants were bilingual – speaking Arabic, Romanian, Somali, and Pashto – with several having migrated from abroad. Many of them felt disconnected from Shakespeare because their view of his plays was one which had its roots in a perceived tradition of white British actors producing something by a 'Posh Englishman': they simply did not see themselves as fitting the imagined target audience.

The introduction to 'Global Shakespeare' borrowed images from Shakespeare's Globe's 2012 Globe to Globe Festival. The aim was to encourage students to see how Shakespeare's texts had been appropriated into other languages and tied into the cultures of the performers. These images showed actors from across the globe, highlighting how productions of Shakespeare can utilize any cultural heritage and remain valid interpretations of his work.

Students then worked to adapt key scenes from *Macbeth* into their home languages. This was to be done in three steps: first, to read and familiarize themselves with the scene; second, to paraphrase it into their sociolect; and finally, to translate it into their home languages. To prevent discomfort and maximize engagement, I allowed them to choose the language that they performed in. Students were also permitted to choose the groups in which they worked, meaning that many of the groups became multilingual.

One group, with four participants speaking four separate languages, performed as Macbeth and the three witches in Act 4, Scene 1. Choosing to translate lines into Somali and Arabic, they created phonetic scripts which provided pronunciations for those who did not speak the languages. In their adaptation, the witches became Islamic spirits, or *djinn*. The group collectively identified as Muslim, and it made sense to them to change this aspect; if they were speaking their own languages, they wanted to include their beliefs too. Also notable was that while in their modern English version, they retained the concept of 'sow's blood' (*Mac* 4.1.64), in performance they altered this to simply 'blood', due to their religious beliefs. In discussion, they stated that they simply felt that blood of any kind was enough to create the horror of the scene, it did not matter where it came from. This raised a factor of cultural collaboration that I had not previously considered: I had been working from the perspective of linguistic translation, yet students had found common religious-cultural ground to include in their text. While, technically, they did not understand each other's language, their beliefs were common among them.

A second pair, who also spoke Somali and Arabic, worked with Act 5 Scene 8, where Macbeth and Macduff come face to face. They kept their lines and translations separate, to convey that Macbeth and Macduff were on different sides of the war but blended their home languages with their modern paraphrasing. Here, Macduff used the diminutive 'doggy dog' rather than 'hellhound' (*Mac* 5.8.3) and in a mirror of the previous group, suggested that Macbeth should go back to *Jahannam*, an Islamic idea of hell. The student playing an Arabic-speaking Macbeth included further links to their religious beliefs, repeating *Wallahi* in their modern English transcription. Roughly translating to 'Swear to God', this underscored the frustration that Macbeth felt, but possibly undermined Shakespeare's emphasis that Macbeth was no longer able to say 'amen'. When questioned, students asserted that this was more a colloquialism than blasphemy. They argued that this emphasized the differences in cultural understanding between us. This challenges Rogers' concerns that a facilitator's input might skew interpretations through 'problematically rooted . . . portrayals' of cultures, (2022: 157). Instead, my facilitation invited in my students' cultural experiences and adapted Shakespeare's text around them. Where students were engaged through their opportunity to make connections between their own cultural and religious experiences and those of Shakespeare, participants agreed that their understanding was amplified by their ability to relate it to their own experiences. For instance, giving participants information about seventeenth-century socio-cultural values allowed them to explore how those values manifest in the text and interpret them through the lens of their own contemporary beliefs. This interaction allowed them to understand Shakespeare's language far beyond reading for comprehension.

These workshops allowed for the creation of diverse interpretations of Shakespeare's work and celebrated identities which are frequently distanced from Shakespeare's plays by the boundaries of cultural and historical perception. Where a conventional approach designed to adhere to the skills required for exam success did not appeal to participants, they explicitly stated that this exploration was more enjoyable because it deviated from the ways they had encountered Shakespeare before. By approaching *Macbeth* without significant teacher guidance, students gained confidence to experiment with personal interpretations which were grounded in Shakespeare's text.

13

Salvaging the bard

A success story of theatre-based practice for neurodiverse learners

Eleni Kmiec

In *The Taming of the Shrew*, Tranio compares the value of educational studies to satiating hunger: 'Fall to them as you find your stomach serves you. / No profit grows where is no pleasure ta'en: / In brief, sir, study what you most affect' (*TS*, 1.1.38-40). As both a Shakespearephile and literature teacher within a special education classroom, I fantasize that my course will delight students with unravelling meaning in Shakespeare's language labyrinth. Be assured that my hopes are dashed on an annual basis by dismayed student utterances. While Tranio would seemingly support the removal of Shakespeare from the malcontented students' studies, I believe that he reminds educators, particularly those teaching in neurodiverse classrooms, that there must be pleasure in the process of learning. Achievement of that pleasure may require a path unique to the neurodiversity of each learner, but it is important to move against the stereotype that Shakespeare's work is not accessible for all learners. At times, salvaging the bard seems impossible, particularly for teachers of neurodiverse learners. Even up against a wave of student disappointment and anxiety, however, teachers are in a place to capitalize on the strength inherent to Shakespeare's work: theatricality.

But what are the benefits of teaching Shakespeare as theatre-based practice specifically for neurodiverse high schoolers? The answer requires a basic understanding of neuropsychology within the student body. Although I like to describe my students as delightfully quirky, inquisitive and highly intellectual, rather than by their diagnostic labels, it is important to make room for neurodiverse learners by acknowledging how best to feed their learning styles. While almost no two students in my community share the exact same neuropsychological framework, there are trends within their profiles. Among the most common language used to describe their learning needs and social-emotional challenges are ASD, ADHD, and non-verbal learning disability (NLD). These diagnoses are often accompanied by anxiety.

The following descriptions include only the traits of the diagnoses that apply to the students I currently serve; their learning profiles are discussed only as they specifically pertain to teaching Shakespeare for both academic purpose and social practice, and it is critical to note the following definitions are across a spectrum that is too nuanced to define in this essay. ASD is defined by 'social communication deficits' and 'restricted/repetitive patterns of behaviour, interests, and activities and their absence in social (pragmatic) communication disorder' (American Psychiatric Association 2013: 53). An ASD diagnosis hardly takes on the exact same attributes in any individual, creating a myriad of cognitive abilities for which teachers should academically plan. Oftentimes, ASD will be concurrent with ADHD, by which 'inattention and disorganization entail inability to stay on task' as well as the student's hyperactivity and impulsivity (American Psychiatric Association 2013: 32). Students with NLD tend to have superior verbal abilities, but 'shortages in psychomotor coordination, in exploring behaviour and in perception' (Molenaar-Klumper 2002: 25). This can manifest in challenges with physical coordination and reading or verbal comprehension. Additionally, these students may find non-verbal self-expression challenging. This includes misinterpretation or limited ability to express with and decipher meaning from body language, facial expressions and intonation.

In 2019, I collected data over a two-month period from students ages sixteen to eighteen with the aforementioned learning profiles (Kmiec 2020). This theatre-based literature study of Shakespeare's *The Tempest* followed the Royal Shakespeare Company's educational resources. Among my conclusions, I discovered that this approach positively played to my students' learning styles in three primary areas: (1) activeness improved attentiveness; (2) growth in social and creative confidence; and (3) collaborative learning through ensemble practice.

Activeness improved attentiveness

According to Tranio's insight, there is no educational profit, unless pleasure is taken in the process. For students with language-based challenges, it might be difficult to imagine a context where reading Shakespeare is productive, let alone palatable. Although Shakespeare is synonymous with both theatre and literature, there was significant diversity in his audience's literacy. Additionally, Shakespeare invented words fairly consistently, and the audience was expected to 'context' their way through it. Audiences relied on semiotics in stagecraft: gesture, lighting and stage properties that were interwoven with their language-based comprehension.

Like Shakespeare's audiences, many students rely on semiotic cues to increase their reading and verbal comprehension. Every ASD student has a different learning profile, but the majority of my students have high verbal comprehension scores (measured through standardized neuropsychological evaluations). Among these same students, however, verbal comprehension scores are accompanied by diagnostically lower processing speeds, resulting in slower verbal comprehension. This means that while 'the ability to understand spoken language' is very high (McDuffie 2013: 3241), the part of the brain that 'integrates new information, retrieves information from memory, and performs certain tasks' processes slower than average or compared to the student's abilities (Braaten and Willoughby 2014: 42). This makes it challenging for these students to infer, decode and interpret while reading.

The students with ADHD most enjoyed the activeness of a theatre-based approach to Shakespeare's language. For students with attentional difficulties, the chance to learn kinaesthetically was more engaging than learning solely from behind a desk. For others, theatre-based practice allowed an opportunity to decode what they did not aurally comprehend by putting the language in their bodies. Permitting students with ADHD to move made for improved 'on task' engagement. Those that chose not to actively participate were better able to 'context' through the pieces they could not decode strictly with language by watching their peers display and embody it in a performative context. One student, who I had taught for two consecutive years prior to my study said: 'I was entertained. I realized that I could understand the words we had just read while watching the scenes. Usually my mind goes somewhere else, but I was interested and able to remember the plot points and differentiate the characters moving forward. This is not something I can usually do when reading in class or independently.' In this way, Shakespeare's plays offer more than access to traditional literature capstones and create a more appetizing way for students with alternative learning preferences to digest language and better understand the plot, structure, and character development.

Growth in social and creative confidence

Part of the pleasure of learning is feeling confident about the content. Shakespeare's plays are reconceptualized in theatre and film regularly, proving their transpositional timelessness. In addition to performativity, the plays lend themselves to students thinking like designers, directors and creatives. Creative design projects are particularly useful for students with circumscribed interests. Circumscribed interests (CI) are often characteristic with ASD. CI are described as 'a restricted range of interests to the exclusion of other activities. This can result in detailed knowledge of specific subjects but very limited awareness of others' (Cobb et al. 2002: 11). Additionally, theory of mind (ToM) is challenging for students with ASD. This includes 'the ability to understand one's own and others' minds', perspective taking and interest in conversations that do not pertain to the individual's CI (Bogdashina 2005: 12).

Assignments that allow for creative transposition of Shakespeare's plays empower students' special interests. As Tranio encourages, students are 'studying what they most affect'. For example, one student produced a design in Minecraft for *The Tempest* to be set on *Star Wars'* Dagobah Island. Another student illustrated costume concepts for Prospero, Miranda, Caliban, and Ariel in traditional Peruvian Festival style. Within my class, the use of independent areas of knowledge and CI deepened the students' overall connection with plot and characters. The students showed more confidence in presenting *The Tempest* content under the guise of their area of knowledge. This resulted in more easily being able to relate their choices directly back to text. For example, the student with a long-standing interest in Peruvian folklore created a vision board using descriptors of Caliban from the text such as 'demi-devil', 'Poor credulous monster', 'puppy-headed' and so forth. She tied Shakespeare's words to images of Maricoxi, the South American equivalent to sasquatch, thereby justifying her design concept for the character.

Because many of my students have similar CI, the class was engaged and inquisitive about their peers' presentations. In a group where socialization is challenged by ToM differences, this approach ultimately increased social-communication practice and even developed new friendships. Some discovered shared interests, which led to new social successes. Students who might not typically respond in an open discussion seemed more willing to participate. Overall, accommodating unique interests and knowledge created savoury conversations. This simultaneously strengthened students' understanding of the play, and nuanced their perspective-taking of character arcs by placing them in a context in which students could more easily relate.

Collaborative learning

Tranio speaks of scholars falling towards educational topics that best serve individual appetites. Just as all palates are sated differently, so are minds; therefore, having an appetite for learning must account for diversity in the learning process. This is particularly necessary for students who do not conform to traditional educational environments. Additionally, within neurodiverse communities, there will never be a one-size-fits-all for learning. Offering multimodal lessons due to the variety of learning styles and needs are essential. Fortunately, multimodal and ensemble learning are inherent in theatre-based practice of Shakespeare's plays.

Ensemble-based learning in the modern classroom is a prerequisite to success with Shakespeare's work. Not unlike the group efforts of the *King's Men*, every company member has an essential role within their area of expertise; a neurodiverse classroom is modelled similarly. Instead of mending learning deficiencies, theatre-based practice allows students to maximize their strengths. Within my classroom, highly verbal students with strong reading fluency and language decoding skills might be satisfied with re-reading the same passage several times and uncovering multiple meanings. A student with attentional or hyperactivity challenges might enjoy acting out passages. A student with NLD may prefer to illustrate a character's emotional state with pen and paper or digital design. More importantly, employing a variety of learning strengths illustrates that students' individual learning styles are resourceful to the entire community. Each individual's interpretation is part of the conversation, reinforcing the entire group's holistic understanding of the play.

Theatrical examination of Shakespeare's text grants responsibility to students to determine what roles are best suited to their strengths. This helps students evaluate their learning profiles, which is foundational to their overall life and learning trajectories. My students were assigned to stage one scene from *The Tempest* with costumes, lighting design, and scenic and prop elements for a live performance. In addition to the scene, the group was asked to create a presentation that addressed the concept and chosen setting (location, terrain, special qualities of the island, and portrayal of the characters) and analyse how the text supported their design and staging choices. The only participation requirement was that each group member must contribute in some way. This provided an opportunity for students to identify what they felt they could contribute. The student with the strongest organizational skills assumed the stage manager's position, a student with confidence in leadership jumped in as director, and it was no surprise that the majority of students who took on roles as actors were those with ADHD diagnoses who just wanted to stay active. Students who were anxious about being in the spotlight took up roles of researching and building concept-appropriate props, sourcing costumes, and creating lighting designs in collaboration with the director. All students took part in group conversations. Those who chose to curate the presentation component observed rehearsals and spoke with those on the creative and design teams. The multimodal elements of theatre-based assignments increased students' ability to work in an ensemble of very different learning styles and allowed them to positively contribute to that ensemble in ways that felt rewarding.

While Shakespeare's works were not intended to be didactic formats for neurodiverse learners, they fulfil so many of the requirements that teachers strive to employ for successful lesson planning and projected outcomes.

The summation of my experience uniting Shakespeare's texts with theatre-based practice colludes against the stigma that Shakespeare is exclusive and inaccessible. This structure proved particularly instrumental for those students whose strengths and interests do not always parallel conventional learning systems. The opportunity to satisfy individual appetites for learning served as inspirational.

14

Transference and Integration

Using Shakespeare to teach composition

Carol Parker

In the United States, there are approximately 1,500 community colleges, mostly serving seventeen- to twenty-year-olds. In my role as Literature Department Chair and Assessment Lead at a community college in Colorado, I have noticed an alarming lack of skills transference from the composition courses taken as part of the two-year programme of study, resulting in a host of writing deficiencies across the academy. I wondered if this could be addressed through pairing 'Advanced Composition' with 'Introduction to Shakespeare'. R. M. Mueller asserts the value of 'including literature in two-year college curricula so that students, rather than being assigned exercises in writing, can be taught to respond to a unified method of reading and making meaning of what they read' (1986: 1). In the current climate, however, the disciplines have become unhelpfully separated.

For decades, literature and composition were inseparable. Students learned to write well by reading and studying masters like Shakespeare, Thoreau and Aristotle. Ivy League schools on the east coast to newly established universities in the west relied on a classic liberal arts model of education in which English meant both reading and writing as co-dependent parts of the whole. However, in the 1960s, composition as a discipline separate from literature began to emerge on college campuses across America, following two significant theories: first, that students don't consume non-fiction to the same degree as fiction; second, that fictional texts create a disconnect between students' lived experiences and their writing. Many prominent scholars argue that because writing is a process of exploration that allows students to discover who they are and what they have to say (Shafer 2013: 34), students find self-discovery difficult when they are constricted by confusing texts, predominantly classics.

The move away from literature resulted in a move towards texts seen as conducive to this social-theoretic model that claims writing as an act of social communication necessitating real-world connections for students. When Common Core emerged as a nation-wide curriculum in 2010, K–12 language arts and literacy instruction responded by aiming for an equal split between fiction and non-fiction texts. Many college composition courses over-corrected, with first-year courses either banning or significantly limiting fiction, and focusing almost myopically on contemporary cultural, social and political issues, often opinion pieces or personal narratives. This denies composition students the opportunity to explore political, social and cultural values from centuries past because those ideas have been banned as racist, insensitive, misogynistic or culturally irrelevant. Shakespeare, especially, falls into the banned list: 'punished for being mainstream and famous, a repository for the "bad" values of earlier generations' (Stern 2005: 123).

Composition pedagogy over the last several decades has been designed for students to learn the component parts of writing and equip them to produce reasoned arguments using credible, scholarly sources. They find it hard, however, to adapt writing from one situation and set of criteria to another and don't make intuitive leaps when asked to write in other disciplines. Jeffrey Wilson explains that many students 'try to write the paper that [they] think they should write – detached, scholarly, objective, perspectiveless – as opposed to the paper that [they] can write – invested, situated, personal, perspectival all while being fundamentally argumentative' (2021). They learn the process, but the product is often disconnected from the needs and also the content of other courses. Carol Poston argues that composition texts are often reflective of 'the instructor, her themes, her interest, her topics' and fail to teach research writing because the process is 'non-collaborative' and 'rarely asks for the student's voice' (2003: 69). This leads to students regurgitating ideas gleaned from curated materials without developing confidence in themselves as critical thinkers capable of constructing and expressing meaning. They often lack adequate skills to culturally contextualize content because they are not reading critically or widely and, too often, are writing for an audience of one: their composition instructor.

Formal and informal assessments of our students identify the most frequent deficiencies: weak thesis statements, poor organization of ideas, insufficient connections between evidence and analysis, and sophisticated summaries. Thesis statements are either too simplistic or too broad. Students struggle to develop ideas in response to prompts worded as commands. For example, when encountering prompts such as 'Shakespeare uses music throughout *The Tempest*. Explore the possible purposes of music as a plot device and as a theatrical tool', the word 'explore' confounds many students because it is too abstract or ambiguous.

Poor organization and insufficient connections between evidence and analysis stem from failure to link ideas across texts. Students break the paper into sections that move through the texts chronologically rather than conceptually. They organize by characters or, if using multiple texts, they address the prompt in one text at a time rather than showing how concepts are at work across texts. For example, students may be asked to use any two or three of Shakespeare's plays to demonstrate how female characters defy traditional gender roles and what effect their defiance has. Students will go through one play, summarize rather than analyse the effects and then move on to the next. They struggle to organize by types of defiance, such as failing to submit to male authority, exhibiting agency, defying parents or disguising as male. The essays are disjointed, and the analysis is weak because of the disconnect.

The 'sophisticated summary' is the most common problem we encounter. Students submit essays with flawless writing conventions but offer only a few droplets of analysis that are washed away in the deluge of summary. Ironically, many of these students verbally express insights, synthesize ideas and ask probing questions. When asked to formalize their ideas, however, the lack of skills transference becomes a barrier to effective expression.

So how can a model that pairs programmes in Composition and Shakespeare address these problems? Some of the techniques of a professional rehearsal room that engage with how and why Shakespeare is relevant today can be highly useful in reintegrating the process and product of writing that we are currently missing. Shakespeare's texts afford a unique focalizing element. In addition to students encountering complex language and superior craftsmanship, which offer both a challenge and a model, his work supplies students with a rich trove of historical contexts for exploration of subjects of continuing relevance that traverse disciplinary boundaries. In my paired model, students read fiction texts imbricated with non-fiction pieces related to the plays that explore race, gender, identity, feminism, power, money and social class. This allows them to research ideas and discuss connections in a similar way to the reading and experiences that directors, designers and actors bring into a rehearsal process. Performers do not simply project language on a stage, the work begins in the rehearsal room where actors and directors must 'feed in social and historical knowledge to root the work in a real-world context' while also considering 'the world in which a story is taking place' (RSC n.d.)

Shakespeare's work transfers across so many curricular divides that students feel empowered by their knowledge and their ability to apply that knowledge broadly. Studying the historical context of the author helps students interpret the text, especially at a minimum of 400 years removed. Sean McEvoy identifies 'the necessity of reading texts inside history, and not in some idealized nowhere-place. This means we read texts as products both of their time and place, and within a discourse which has been created by the historical circumstances in which we find ourselves now' (2005: 102). Planning and delivering such a broad range of contextual content is difficult but can be resolved by collaborating with instructors from other disciplines: a biologist can explain practical uses of plants used in plays; a religious studies professor can address the tensions between Christians, Jews and Muslims, both past and present; a psychologist can describe trauma. Community college professor Dora Tippens, for example, explains how studying psychopathic behaviours and conduct disorders in their psychology class led her students to insightful discussions about Richard III and Iago that allowed them to 'appreciate the genius of an author who could make their villainy credible but who frustrated our attempts to reduce them to simple labels' (1984: 656).

In addition to the research into contemporary understanding of a play, getting Shakespeare's words into students' mouths rather than just their hands means using rehearsal methods to open up students to new ways of experiencing the texts. Drama interactions require more of the students and bring up discussions of character and circumstance, real conversations about situational ethics and diverse viewpoints that take place on a far more sophisticated level than discussions of rhetorical efficacy. Students have room to accomplish modes of analysis and response through reading, discussing, acting and writing because the academic tasks and individual responses happen alongside one another rather than privileging one mode over the other. When students discover they have something to say about Shakespeare, they are eager to engage in the process to express their discoveries. Understanding how the text transfers from page to stage adds an essential facet to students' ownership of their work.

Students recognize Shakespeare as a link between the past and the present that presents social dilemmas they can identify in their own lives. Shakespeare's canon provides examples that help students appreciate, 'what happens if two children, two adults, two households, two countries, two religions, two races, two ideologies cannot accommodate each other' (Gregory 2005: 21). Shakespeare portrays the other, the outcast and the non-conformist with complexity and depth. His tragedies allow students to question the nature of suffering and injustice. Using Shakespeare to connect students to their own and other cultures links the social-theoretic pedagogy predominant in composition classes with literary study. What students might perceive to be a clash between Early Modern culture and their own becomes an opportunity to find patterns and analyse enduring biases, and an opportunity for self-reflection and connection.

These approaches involve close reading and critical thinking, which can be modelled by the teachers and practised as integral parts of learning to consume and produce texts. The creativity of these processes then regains its place in the scope of knowledge students need to be successful readers and writers and leads to insights about themselves, their world and their place in that world. Understanding rhetoric is seen as valuable because it provides a framework for analysing language and arguments that can be applied to any speech or text in supporting thinking and understanding language in general.

Students' ability to develop strong thesis statements, organize their ideas and connect evidence and analysis proceeds from their ability to dissect a text, glean meaning from their dissection, and reassemble the disparate parts into an analysis of how they work together to create meaningful insights. When students cannot complete this process first, they are left with nothing to proclaim in a thesis statement. They are at the mercy of a blinking cursor or blank page and often attempt to fill the page with something or anything related to the topic. When students find multiple entry points into a text, they begin the invention process without a pen in hand. Engaging with Shakespeare through reading aloud, acting, discussing and challenging each other's ideas allows students to consider their purpose, audience and occasion for writing; all essential elements to constructing a persuasive thesis statement that presents a narrow, deep, original approach to their topic.

When students understand their thesis functions as a promise to readers, and the body of the essay delivers on that promise, they begin to formulate cogent and cohesive arguments. Shakespeare's plays provide excellent examples of arguments in dialogues, monologues and sonnets. Sonnets especially can be highly useful in recognizing the importance of structure to meaning. Students can break down the argument; recognize what happens at each stage, the importance of the volta and the function of the rhymed couplet; and work on understanding the sonnet to present it orally in a way that amplifies the meaning(s) for an audience.

Recognizing patterns and organizing ideas reduces students' reliance on summary. They understand that a good thesis and a strong organizational scheme minimize the urge to summarize, but the most important deterrent to summary is when students find they have a voice they are equipped to use. When the habits of mind developed in studying Shakespeare coalesce with the habits learned in composition, students can overcome the barriers that plague learners in disconnected courses. They see how reading and writing work together. They understand that the writing process is a step to creating finished products that transfer across disciplines. They understand the relevance of context to engaging with content and making critical cultural connections between themselves, the texts they consume, the writing they produce and the people they encounter in life. Students can break down the process to see how components work together to create a unified whole that becomes the vehicle of self-expression and find that their expression can be, like Shakespeare's, powerful and enduring. As Thompson and Turchi advise, when we teach Shakespeare with purpose, we provide 'a bridge for students from appreciation to analysis without disavowing the fun. After all, learning to analyze a complex text is pleasurable, like working through any difficult puzzle' (2016: 2).

15

Theatre-based pedagogy in a knowledge-rich curriculum

Perspectives from initial teacher training

Karen McGivern

While not uncontested by teaching associations and commentators (McAllum and Bleiman 2022), Ofsted's 'English Research Review' provides those involved in initial teacher training (ITT) with an unequivocal guide to what is considered best practice for English teaching in England. The review surveys existing research to identify factors that 'contribute to high-quality curriculums, pedagogy, assessment and systems for managing the subject'. The acquisition of knowledge is presented as central to these factors (2022a).

An expectation of a knowledge-based curriculum is compounded in Ofsted's inspection framework: schools must ensure that young people are provided with 'the knowledge and cultural capital they need to succeed in life' and that curricula deliver 'sufficient knowledge and skills for future learning and employment' (Ofsted 2022b). Together with the ITT Core Content Framework (CCF), which specifies the minimum curriculum entitlement for trainee teachers (DfE 2019b), and the Early Career Framework (ECF) (DfE 2019a), which sets out content for the training and support of teachers in the first two years of their career, these documents influence ITT providers, school leaders, teachers, mentors and, in turn, trainee and Early Career Teachers (ECTs), in the teaching of English including Shakespeare.

The documents provide a base from which to identify where, and indeed whether, theatre-based pedagogy is situated in the apparently ideal English curriculum and classroom.

The CCF describes learning as a 'lasting change in pupils' capabilities or understanding', explaining that 'prior knowledge plays an important role' in this learning and that 'committing some key facts to . . . long-term memory is likely to help pupils learn more complex ideas' (DfE 2019b: 11). Direct instruction and metacognitive strategies are foregrounded as the optimum ways of ensuring progression of learning (2019a: 13; 2019b: 14). There are no references to the potential of active drama or theatre-based pedagogies in this, or the other documents, but there is some inclusion of research that relates to oracy and to communication development (Ofsted 2022a). There is also an acknowledgement that 'high quality classroom talk' can be beneficial to the consolidation of understanding and that paired and group activities can increase success when carefully supported by teachers; however, it is implied that these pedagogies emerge from a starting point of conveyed and retained knowledge (DfE 2019b: 18; DfE 2019a: 16).

The research review gives an example from *Hamlet*: 'knowing that, in Shakespeare's time, a nunnery was also slang for a brothel means that Hamlet's command to Ophelia, "Get thee to a nunnery", is even more heart-breaking and emotionally charged. Enjoyment and knowledge can grow through text-based conversations, discussions and debates' (Ofsted 2022a). Here there is an acknowledgement that students might explore Shakespeare's language and works dialogically and even co-constructively, but the assumption is that this exploration must emerge from a taught knowledge base. Students speculating on or playing with meaning from the starting point of dialogue, action and scene does not appear to be a possibility; 'knowing' must come first. The orthodoxy presented here is that activity/dialogue/collaboration must grow from knowledge; knowledge cannot grow from activity/dialogue/collaboration. Indeed, educators are warned of the 'risk' of focusing on 'modalities' (of pedagogy) at the expense of identifying 'foundational' knowledge (Ofsted 2022a). With reference to the research on dialogic pedagogy, there is a warning: 'Using such a pedagogy to help pupils learn any objective across curriculum subjects should not be conflated with the prior teaching of the structures of language that would allow effective communication in the first place' (Ofsted 2022a).

Conspicuous by their absence, one wonders whether the active approaches that have formed part of many English teachers' toolkits would elicit similar or stronger warnings; whether, in the current pedagogical context, theatre-based approaches to Shakespeare would only be considered valid where students have been supplied with a full understanding of the dramaturgy of the Elizabethan stage. Moreover, the lack of reference in the Ofsted recommended research to key proponents of active approaches to Shakespeare, such as Gibson (1998), Stredder (2004) and Winston (2015), may signal that such approaches are no longer considered valuable in a classroom set up to maximize the retention of knowledge.

In the remainder of this chapter, I consider whether teacher educators and trainee teachers are able to find space to teach, champion and employ active, collaborative, theatre-based approaches to Shakespeare, considering the need to prepare for the knowledge-based curricula and practices dictated by policy. I draw on five perspectives from the field of ITT: my own from the last five years working as an English teacher trainer and mentor and those of four of my most recent trainees: Ciara, Caitlin, Bella and Elliott, all under the age of thirty (names are pseudonyms). The trainee perspectives were gathered via a survey, with questions focusing on their experience of learning, observing and employing active, drama and theatre-based approaches to Shakespeare teaching.

For most teachers, exposure to potential pedagogies starts with their initial teacher training. University providers are required to cover the content of the CCF as a minimum provision (DfE 2019b: 3). In my experience, a balance is sought to ensure that trainees are conversant with the cognition-based definition of learning that runs through the CCF together with other modes of learning that are not given prominence, for example, co-constructive learning. As a consequence, some active approaches have been taught as part of the university-based postgraduate certificate in education (PGCE) sessions on Shakespeare in the two universities at which I have been involved in English teacher training.

Based on my own involvement and observations of other tutors, I would say that there remains an intention to equip trainees with creative ideas for teaching the plays that will engage students. Though not necessarily defined by tutors as drama or theatre-based pedagogy, the activities draw upon techniques and approaches derived from drama and theatre. I recall a competition to employ costume or props to represent a Shakespeare character that was wholeheartedly embraced by trainees. I think of a session showing how sound effects and lighting can be used to establish setting and mood for a play and another signposting and modelling the RSC's active storytelling exercises.

The championing of creative approaches was recognized by the students in my survey. When asked to talk about their Shakespeare sessions at university, Caitlin remembers the teaching of 'Conscience Alley', an embodied approach that encourages students to consider the motivations of characters in the play. Ciara describes her university sessions on Shakespeare as involving 'a range of abstract activities'. Bella refers to encountering 'creative/practical/drama-based activities to try out with classes'. In spite of this, in answer to a specific question about whether they were taught active/theatre/drama-based approaches, three of the four respondents reported that they were not. The discrepancy here perhaps stems from terminology: if the activities were not described as drama or theatre-based, students may not have seen them as such.

University-based teaching days are limited, and tutors and lecturers can only give a snapshot of potential activities. Active work must sit alongside desk-based teaching approaches to language, form, structure, plot, character and theme analysis. Furthermore, as university ITT curricula are examined in the second stage of reaccreditation as part of the ITT market review (DfE 2021), it is possible that the need to show fidelity to current pedagogical orthodoxy will further decrease the space for the teaching of active and theatre-based approaches.

My wider experience of trainee English teachers is that they are generally keen to employ such approaches and the four who took part in my survey believe they are important. Elliott compares a desk reading of a Shakespeare play with reading song lyrics: 'half the experience is lost.' Caitlin believes that the plays need to be 'lived out'; she analogizes that reading a play is like trying to learn to drive by reading a book. All four trainees tried out theatre-based approaches in their own lessons during their PGCE. Caitlin taught *Macbeth* in what she described as an 'immersive' way: 'lights dimmed, blinds closed ... weather sounds ... [the] banquet scene ... taught around one long table, with food and pop music playing and costumes borrowed from the drama department.' Ciara had her class 'engage in a courtroom style session to try and defend the actions of Lady Macbeth'. Two of the survey participants talked of employing techniques that are likely to have come from a previous experience of drama. Caitlin described drawing on Stanislavsky's 'Magic If' and Bella employed 'tableaux, narration, levels, and proxemics' during a lesson in which she was specifically considering the impact of theatre-based approaches to Shakespeare.

Beyond those in the survey, my observations of trainees' lessons and planning suggest that the space and potential for employing active practices while on placement varies across and within schools. Though the principles of planning are taught initially on university-based training days, trainees usually work with the school or department's frameworks when planning their lessons. The opportunity to practise theatre-based activities is therefore additionally dependent on the *ethos*, approach and levels of autonomy in the school as well as on a teacher mentor's own experience and confidence in using theatre-based pedagogy.

Three out of four trainees in the survey reported being aware of active or theatre-based approaches employed in their wider department or of observing them in the lessons of other teachers. Bella would have liked to have seen more of this; though she spoke to some English teachers when preparing her reflective practice on active approaches to Shakespeare, she gained more information by speaking with drama teachers. Elliott worked with a teacher who 'liked to get students moving as much as possible', whereas most Shakespeare lessons that Ciara observed were reading based and centred on assessment strategies.

I have observed an increasing number of trainees working in schools where lessons are assessment and examination focused and tightly structured around metacognitive approaches: 'Do Now' starters; direct instruction; spaced practice; interleaving; modelling; retrieval practice. Such structures prioritize a transactional imparting of knowledge along with checks to ensure that knowledge has been retained. The outcomes of theatre-based pedagogies are not as easily verified and assessed; perhaps, as a consequence, they appear less frequently in lessons of this format. I have also observed trainees who have worked within a more organic planning approach. It is my impression that these situations have left a greater space for theatre-based pedagogies.

In terms of the perceived impact of theatre-based approaches, Elliott makes the point that the attitude and confidence levels of students are key to their success. He explains that some students 'held a lot of anxiety' when performing in front of the class, but that those with a drama background were more willing to take part. He does not comment on the outcome of the active approaches but does note that 'different dramatic adaptations' shown to the students made the text more accessible.

If space for drama pedagogies is diminished in the increasingly typical knowledge-focused classroom, it would be unsurprising that students, unaccustomed to drama activities, feel less comfortable when asked to take part in them. It may also be the case that distancing restrictions during the SARS-CoV-2 pandemic led to a more static classroom and that this norm has been maintained. 'Traditionalist' behaviour strategies that favour seating in rows (see, for example, Bennett 2017: 71) may have a further impact on the amount of movement and space for theatre-based approaches in the classroom. The use of filmed drama, via adapted forms, is perhaps a practical and non-threatening way that performance finds its way into Shakespeare teaching.

Bella and Ciara's views on impact are interesting, considering Ofsted's *Hamlet* example at the start of the chapter. In the example, prior instruction on vocabulary and context is required (of the word 'brothel') before students can profitably discuss the scene: imparted knowledge must come first. Conversely, Bella talks of how theatre-based pedagogies allow students to form knowledge for themselves. She believes that performing the plays is 'the best way to *inspire ideas* and understand complex language and themes' (italics mine). There is a suggestion, here, that knowledge *can* arise from modality, via the co-constructive processes of group scene creation. Ciara, on the other hand, appears more in step with the previously discussed documents in prioritizing teacher-conveyed knowledge. For her, theatre-based approaches 'create a stimulating atmosphere' and, in turn, '*consolidate students' knowledge* of the characters'. Bella's language ('inspire') is suggestive of a classroom where students are encouraged to form their own ideas about language and theme; Ciara's, ('consolidate') of one where the initial instruction of the teacher needs to be embedded.

Elliott, too, returns to the language of current policy in explaining how 'a nice, silly introduction to Macbeth' (where students could choose to perform the witches as football hooligans, children, or seductive ladies) led to the class having a 'vivid memory' of the opening scene and the ability to 'recall quotes with ease'. The assertion in the CCF and ECF that memory is a key factor in learning seems apparent in Elliott's success criteria (DfE 2019b: 11; DfE 2019a: 10).

It is clear that the participants are influenced by the policy that has informed their training, but the survey also shows that they have the training base, enthusiasm for, and space to employ theatre-based approaches to Shakespeare. However, there is a risk that this space will increasingly narrow, and even close, if teacher trainers, school leaders and teachers are pressured to prove ever-greater fidelity to the narrow definitions of effective pedagogy shown in the policy documents described.

16

Much ado about decolonized Shakespeare

Nobulali Dangazele

The values of collaboration versus individuality, the concept of identity as defined by relationships rather than self-absorption and the understanding that high status or true power are given by shared collective ambition instead of attained through individual personal ambition – these are at the core of both the South African decolonization project and authentic treatment of Shakespeare.

My company ShakeXperience was named in alignment with our main objective: to make Shakespeare experiential, shaking the paradigms of traditional study. Alas, the representative of the Department of Basic Education was not impressed with this name. I had just taken a seat in the freshly refurbished palatial office and accepted his offer of a cup of tea when he posed the perennial question: 'What business do you have with Shakespeare in schools when English is not your first language, and there are so many African scholars to choose from?' It is a question I have been asked on multiple occasions, such as when I chose to teach *Othello* in high schools as part of my Theatre in Education module; when I played Cordelia in Izingane Zobaba, a televised Zulu adaptation of *King Lear* on the South African Broadcasting Commission; and when I worked with schools in Limpopo as part of a British Council/RSC project (Dangazele and Mokuku 2013). The government official now sitting before me was one of the people who had played an integral role in proposing that Shakespeare be taken out of our public school syllabus; the question was thus apt for him.

At the dawn of the second term of the Democratic South African dispensation in 1999, the Department of Education embarked on a process of curriculum decolonization. Two decades later, Shakespeare's plays are no longer a compulsory text on the English Grade 12 syllabus but an optional set work chosen at the teacher's discretion. With Shakespeare being an option, there has been a steady decline in the teaching of his work. South Africa has eleven official languages, and all these languages are taught within a school, with each school being obliged to offer Grade 12 matriculants two compulsory languages and a third one when the resources are available. With this being the case, a school may fall into one of three language categories where English is taught as a home language (HL), first additional language (FAL) or third additional language (TAL). Shakespeare is an option on the English Paper Two exam, which includes the novel, drama, short stories or poetry. For the past seven years, Shakespeare is not offered to learners in most schools where English is taught as a first additional language.

In HL schools, this year's drama options are *Hamlet*, *Othello* and *The Crucible* by Arthur Miller. In most South African schools, English is taught as a first additional language. Within that curriculum, the only Shakespeare play offered is *Macbeth* with the alternative drama setwork being *My Children My Africa!* by Athol Fugard. Following multiple requests from FAL schools, ShakeXperience produced the Fugard play for schools to watch across the country in theatres, community and school halls. Prior to this, we used to offer Shakespeare-focused Drama in Education interventions. However, as the years progressed, we noted a decline in the uptake of Shakespeare as the drama of choice.

Most teachers choose not to teach Shakespeare due to the complexity of the language, the time it takes to read the plays, their complex themes and imagery and the challenges identified. Moreover, there are talks of the complete removal of Shakespeare from the curriculum across all South African schools, an opinion held firmly by Equal Education, a community membership-based organization advocating for quality and equality in the South African education system. This influential and highly recognized not-for-profit organization called for a curriculum review. In 2017, its former head Tshepo Motsepe said: 'We recognised the current curriculum as reinforcing colonial teaching and learning while neglecting African literature when looking at what is being taught in our schools' (Mance 2016). More recently, Troy Martens, a spokesperson for the minister of Basic Education, said: 'There is a discussion happening as part of our long-term goal for 2020-2030, to look at the relevance of some of our literature and make use of indigenous knowledge systems within our curriculum to look at more African, perhaps South African, literature' (Curré 2019). Many questions have been raised about Shakespeare's relevance in post-colonial South Africa.

It is clear then that not everyone shares my love for the bard. In South Africa, Shakespeare has been a fundamental aspect of the country's literary heritage and a vital part of the school curricula. His plays can also be seen as a tool of colonialism and cultural domination. They were used to promote the English language and culture during the colonial period, centralizing

European and specifically British culture and perspectives, and their continued study can come across as a perpetuation of this legacy. Shakespeare in schools is argued to be an erasure of other essential facets of education, such as promoting indigenous languages and cultures. In a context where decolonization is a priority, it is crucial to prioritize teaching South African history, literature, and culture rather than a 'foreign' playwright.

Nevertheless, my experience of Shakespeare counters this argument. I have found his work, the themes of his plays and an ensemble approach to them to embody a lot of African philosophies. The most important one is the principle of Ubuntu. Ubuntu is a Nguni term meaning 'humanity'. It is sometimes translated as: 'I am because we are'. Broadly, it is embodied in our culture through a collectivist approach to living with each other. In the classroom, it manifests in the qualities found in an ensemble approach to teaching and learning.

A key argument for Shakespeare's irrelevance in South African schools is that the works do not reflect South African students' experiences, cultural diversity and cultural backgrounds. With most of his characters written as white and from a European cultural background, that offers a murky mirror for many South African learners to see themselves reflected in the material. The wiping of this mirror is in the authentic treatment of Shakespeare – as a theatre text which can be discovered anew with each performance. The relevance of Shakespeare in South African schools is contingent upon the treatment of his works. A colonial approach, which reduces Shakespeare to mere Early Modern English linguistic difficulties and Elizabethan costume, fails to capture the central values and themes and deviates from the original intentions of his works. Shakespeare raises questions about love, diversity, class, inclusion, power, and justice that are still relevant today. Exploring those questions through drama means finding the values of collaboration, identity defined by relationships, and shared collective ambition, thus aligning with the goals of decolonization and providing a relevant and meaningful experience for South African students.

Shakespeare is, therefore, both irrelevant and relevant depending on the teaching style applied in the classroom. Shakespeare's plays are meant to be experiences on one's feet, not just read while sitting. All the classrooms are a stage, and all the learners are merely players. The mundane method of treating the plays as mere text to be read behind the desk mutes the curtain call, and learners may fail to experience the magic of the text in performance; thus, the text remains foreign. To truly capture its relevance in the age of decolonization, educators may adopt an approach that examines the values and themes present in his works rather than reducing his plays to mere linguistic and historical difficulties. Educators must employ creative and innovative teaching methods that allow students to engage with the material in meaningful ways which promote cultural diversity and representation.

One educator doing this very successfully is Marvellous Jore. Mr Jore is a teacher at a FAL rural school in Limpopo. He has explored the power of drama as an effective teaching tool in the classroom and conducted a study at his school on the impact of drama in teaching literature after identifying challenges presented by the students. Mr Jore interviewed students and teachers. He found that understanding figures of speech is difficult for learners whose mother tongue is not English and that they struggled to visualize a drama text. He concludes: 'Learners' attitudes towards drama become negative once the learners find drama difficult to understand' (2021: iv). Mr Jore developed an intervention where he worked with his colleagues to set up structures which would engage the learners in purposeful learning, encourage them to explore what they don't know rather than re-enact what is within their scope and allow for their spontaneity. This planning accounted for what W. Sawyer describes: 'A teacher needs to balance between his or her conscious self and ideal self, the motivation towards teaching and learning and the intensive, functional (operational) relationship with drama. These all give the ability to act in different situations, take risks and tolerate incompleteness in teaching' (Sawyer 2004).

The intervention Mr Jore and his colleagues devised focused on the following:

1. The adaptation of the text into the multiple languages represented in the class
2. The application of the core principles found in ensemble work
3. Adapting methods from Augusto Boal's *Theatre of the Oppressed* (1985) and the 'Whoosh' (RSC 2010: 300–1).

Adapting the text into multiple languages is crucial in giving learners ownership of Shakespeare. Chris Thurman describes how playful experimentation can 'invigorate Shakespeare's text by translating it into isiZulu, isiXhosa or Afrikaans and then back into contemporary/colloquial English'. He explains how 'Shakespeare always comes to us in translation. . . . Even if you are an English monolingual speaker, when you engage with Shakespeare's Early Modern English, you are already embarking on a process of translation. . . . There's no such thing as a kind of authentic, original Shakespeare' (Thurman 2016). Studying Shakespeare through drama in the linguistically diverse settings of South African schools offers opportunities to improve language abilities and cultural awareness. Various studies (Davies 2000; Matthias 2007; Lauer 2008) have explored the value of using drama in helping English as Additional Language learners develop their oral linguistic competence. They found that drama creates a purposeful and meaningful context that builds skills and confidence in the target language.

In teaching Shakespeare through drama, Mr Jore encourages a collaborative, ensemble approach alongside Image Theatre and 'Whoosh' techniques. I have found Boal's Image Theatre to be a powerful tool in teaching Shakespeare in South African schools, particularly in fostering critical thinking, creative expression and cultural awareness. Its political purpose is empowering individuals to challenge their circumstances and envision change (Dangazele 2010). In practice, it involves individuals creating visual representations of their thoughts, emotions and experiences to create a shared understanding and to work towards resolving conflicts or enacting positive change. This theatrical method helps to bridge the gap between the language and context of Shakespeare's works and the experiences of contemporary students.

One of the critical elements of Boal's Image Theatre is the use of embodied representation, which is particularly effective in the classroom when bringing to life the text, characters and scenarios from Shakespeare's plays. It helps students to develop a deeper understanding of the motivations and emotions of the characters and to see how these can be translated into their own experiences. In addition, by working together to create a tableau, students learn how to collaborate and build consensus, which are critical skills in both the classroom and the real world. Another approach Mr Jore used was 'Whoosh', an interactive storytelling technique that allows any scenario, no matter how intricate, to come to life, even if players have no prior knowledge. Students physically act out the tale in reaction to narrated chunks of the plot, resulting in a high level of involvement and ownership. The facilitator encourages a shared narrative, bringing individuals, groups, and occasionally the entire class into and out of the action. Participants engage in physical theatre, using their bodies and voices to portray the people, things, locations and events in the story. Reflecting on the progress of his learners through this work, Mr Jore told me:

> The learners' excitement and boost in confidence were due to them having the opportunity to read and speak in class and being held accountable for the collective learnings made by the class. Unlike when I teach as the teacher, here, the learner was engaged in the work and the ensemble technique and no one was left behind in this collaborative approach to learning.

An essential aspect of Boal's Image Theatre and 'Whoosh' is the emphasis on community and empowerment. Through creating images together, students learn to listen to each other, understand different perspectives and develop empathy. These ensemble drama approaches create a safe and supportive environment in which students can express themselves freely and challenge their own preconceptions, using the lens of Shakespeare to look at the world around them. This type of learning is especially important in South Africa, where the legacy of apartheid continues to have a profound impact on society and education by teaching literature. Specifically, Shakespeare through methods underpinned by the principles of ubuntu educators can encourage students to question the status quo and envision a more just and equitable world.

Epilogue

Throughout this book, we have explored a wide range of concepts and proposals to argue for our three key principles that theatre-based practice should: (1) invite in prior knowledge, ideas and values to bear on a shared experience of understanding a literary text; (2) combine intellectual, social and emotional learning through embodying the text; and (3) develop criticality in questioning a cultural inheritance and how that canon can in turn raise questions about today's world.

Our central proposition, derived from Dewey's progressive principles of learning through experience, is that Shakespeare should be treated not as an icon of literary heritage to be revered but as a living artist to be in conversation with. As the twenty-first century progresses, with all its complex local and global issues, calls grow ever louder from education experts, employers and young people themselves for schooling to move beyond acquisition of knowledge and traditional academic skills to additionally develop inquisitorial competencies of creativity, criticality and collaboration. It seems ever more vital that for Shakespeare to have any meaning for generations to come, study of him must be in dialogue with the specific and globalized concerns of young people and the shape of the world around them.

We have explored how working through theatre-based practice with Shakespeare is a broad-ranging and multi-disciplinary process. We have grounded this in an understanding of theatre practice as embodied, discursive and reflexive, drawing on models such as Turner's notion of dramatic performance as 'plural reflexivity' (Turner 1987); and explored how therefore, as Nicholson describes it, 'Participating in theatre can offer young people a chance to produce equitable spaces in which to work, in which they can be "me and not me", thereby meeting the alterity in themselves as others' (2011: 213). This concept of reflexive identity work was echoed by our interview contributors, such as Purple Door Artistic Director Karl Falconer's reflections on Shakespeare as offering a rich aesthetic 'mask' through which young people can both articulate and establish critical distance from their experiences and concerns. Drama and theatre practice involve far more than 'acting out' some scenes, trying some fun starter activities, or 'imagining yourself as a character'. As Peggy O'Brien states, it is about 'doing' (2006): exploring who we are and how we communicate in an embodied and collaborative forum. Getting the complex dramatic text of Shakespeare into the body as language in action not only eases the cognitive load of making sense of the words on the page, but creatively opens up the plurality of possible interpretations and perspectives available when young people are invited to bring their own thoughts, identities and experiences into play. As a critical practice, it requires careful attention to how Shakespeare uses language and how different social groups use Shakespeare, and it provokes discussion of Shakespeare's international places in history, in culture, as performance and literature.

By combining a more traditional monograph section with curated interview extracts from practitioners and invited chapters from teachers, we have aimed to demonstrate and articulate the diverse and discursive ecosystem of theatre-based Shakespeare education practice. Acknowledging Flaherty's exhortation to see global Shakespeare education and performance practice as localized but equal sites of cultural and scholarly knowledge creation (2013), we have argued that knowledge about Shakespeare can be actively produced and not just received in schools. School-age Shakespeare education has at times been a neglected area of Shakespeare studies, and we hope this book demonstrates the potential for mutual innovation and cross-fertilization.

Throughout this book, we have offered a sense of the range of inspiring theatre-based practice making an impact in schools around the world by teachers and practitioners driven by their passion for what the potential of working with Shakespeare can offer. Examples abound that 'For all its establishment power, Shakespeare education is being reimagined all the time – by everyone, everywhere' (Semler et al. 2023: 1). Creative practice in the classroom can readily become subordinate in overly metricized education systems to day-to-day pressures, yet, as a teacher in a cramped classroom in rural Brazil once told Tracy, 'We know this is how we want to teach, what we came into teaching to do, but we've forgotten because there are so many pressures telling us we have to teach in a certain way'. We hope that the examples we share, alongside our rationales for the value of this work, empower more Shakespeare educators to teach how they want to teach; encouraging more young people to interact critically, creatively and collaboratively with the richness that a democratic approach to the *inter*cultural inheritance that Shakespeare's texts can offer.

Teaching and learning Shakespeare through theatre-based practice is, as we have argued, radical, rich and immediate. It relies on our voices, our bodies, our physical and social sense of togetherness. In short it reminds us, as all the best encounters with complex, powerful and troubling artists such as Shakespeare should do, of our shared humanity. We do not claim the deeply humanistic quality of this pedagogy as an easy or trite positionality but rather one that pushes the work of education towards profound and profoundly challenging questions of how we live with ourselves, each other and the fast-approaching future.

REFERENCES

Adams, J. and A. Owens (2017), *Creativity and Democracy in Education: Practices and Politics of Learning through the Arts*, London: Routledge.

Adams Jr, C. N. (2013), 'TIE and Critical Pedagogy', 3rd edn, A. Jackson and C. Vine (eds), *Learning Through Theatre: The Changing Face of Theatre in Education*, 287–304, London: Routledge.

Adey, P. and J. Dillon, eds. (2012), *Bad Education. Debunking Myths in Education*, Maidenhead: Open University Press.

Alexander, R. (2008), *Essays on Pedagogy*, London: Routledge.

American Psychiatric Association (2013), *Diagnostic and Statistical Manual of Mental Disorders* (DSM-5®), Washington: American Psychiatric Publishing.

APPG (2021), 'Speak for Change: Final Report and Recommendations from the Oracy All-Party Parliamentary Group Inquiry'. Available online: https://oracy.inparliament.uk/ (accessed 22 January 2023).

AQA (2019), 'GCSE English Literature 8702/1 – Shakespeare and the 19th Century Novel Report on the Examination'. Available online: https://filestore.aqa.org.uk/sample-papers-and-mark-schemes/2019/june/AQA-87021-WRE-JUN19.PDF (accessed 18 June 2023).

Arnold, M. (1869), 'Culture and Anarchy an Essay on Social and Political Criticism'. Available online: http://www.gutenberg.org/cache/epub/4212/pg4212.html (accessed 3 February 2023).

Austen, J. ([1814] 2016), *Mansfield Park*, Richmond: Alma Classics.

Atherton, G., B. Lummis, S. Day and L. Cross, (2019),'What am I thinking? Perspective-taking from the perspective of adolescents with autism', *Autism* vol 23(5): 1186-1200.

Bache, C. (2021), *Circle of Life Rediscovery*. Available online: https://circleofliferediscovery.com/blog/the-secret-garden-outdoor-nursery/ (accessed 2 September 2022).

Bainbridge, D. (2009), *Teenagers: A Natural History*, London: Portobello Books.

Bakhtin, M. M. (1981), *The Dialogic Imagination. Four Essays*, Austin: University of Texas Press.

Banks, F. (2014), *Creative Shakespeare: The Globe Education Guide to Practical Shakespeare*, London: Bloomsbury.

Bannet, E. T. (1997), 'Analogy as Translation: Wittgenstein, Derrida, and the Law of Language', *New Literary History*, 28: 655–72.

Barnes, T. L. (2020), *Shakespearean Charity and the Perils of Redemptive Performance*, Cambridge: Cambridge University Press.

Barry, P. (2002), *Beginning Theory. An Introduction to Literary and Cultural Theory*, Manchester: Manchester University Press.

Bate, J. (1997), *The Genius of Shakespeare*, London: Picador.

Belfiore, E. (2011), 'The "Transformative Power" of the Arts: History of an Idea', in J. Sefton-Green, P. Thomson, K. Jones and L. Bresle (eds), *The Routledge International Handbook of Creative Learning*, 27–35, Oxon: Routledge.

Belfiore, E. (2012), '"Defensive Instrumentalism" and the Legacy of New Labour's Cultural Policies', *Cultural Trends*, 21 (2): 103–11.

Bell, H. and A. Borsuk (2020), 'Teaching Shakespeare: Digital Processes', *Research in Drama Education: The Journal of Applied Theatre and Performance*, 25 (1): 1–7.

Bellos, D. (2011), *Is that a Fish in Your Ear? Translation and the Meaning of Everything*, London: Particular Books.

Bennett, T. (2017), 'Creating a Culture: How School Leaders Can Optimise Behaviour', Department for Education. Available online: https://assets.publishing.service.gov.uk/government/uploads/system/uploads/attachment_data/file/602487/Tom_Bennett_Independent_Review_of_Behaviour_in_Schools.pdf (accessed 20 November 2022).

Berry, C. (2001), *Text in Action. A Definitive Guide to Exploring Text in Rehearsal for Actors and Directors*, London: Virgin.

Berry, C. (2008), *From Word to Play. A Handbook for Directors*, London: Oberon.

Bissonnette, J. D. and J. Glazier (2016), 'A Counterstory of One's Own: Using Counterstorytelling to Engage Students with the British Canon', *Journal of Adolescent and Adult Literacy*, 59 (6): 685–94.

Blackledge, A. (2009), 'Imagining a Monocultural Community: Racialization of Cultural Practice in Educational Discourse', *Journal of Language, Identity & Education*, 5 (4): 540–51.

Blakemore, S. (2019), *Inventing Ourselves The Secret Life of the Teenage Brain*, London: Penguin.

Blakemore, S. and U. Frith (2005), *The Learning Brain: Lessons for Education*, Oxford: Blackwell.

Blank, P. (2014), 'Introducing "Interlinguistics": Shakespeare and Early/Modern English', in M. Saenger (ed), *Interlinguicity, Internationality and Shakespeare*, 138–58, Montreal: McGill-Queens University Press.

Boal, A. (1985), *Theatre of the Oppressed*, New York: Theatre Communications Group.

Bogdashina, O. (2005), *Theory of Mind and the Triad of Perspectives on Autism and Asperger Syndrome: A View from the Bridge*, London: Jessica Kingsley Publishers.

Boix-Mansilla, V. and A. Schleicher (2022), 'Big Picture Thinking: How to Educate the Whole Person for an Interconnected World', OECD. Available online: https://issuu.com/oecd.publishing/docs/big-picture-thinking-educating-global-competence (accessed 4 February 2022).

Bolton, G. (1998), *Acting in Classroom Drama: A Critical Analysis*, Stoke-on-Trent: Trentham.

Bottoms, J. (2013), 'Doing Shakespeare': How Shakespeare Became a School "Subject"', *Shakespeare Survey*, 66: 96–109.

Bourdieu, P. (1986), 'The Forms of Capital', in J. G. Richardson (ed), *Handbook of Theory and Research for the Sociology of Education*, 241–58, London: Greenwood Press.

Bourdieu, P. and L. Wacquant (1992), *An Invitation to Reflexive Sociology*, Cambridge: Polity Press.

Braaten, E. B. and B. L. B. Willoughby (2014), *Bright Kids Who Can't Keep Up: Help Your Child Overcome Slow Processing Speed and Succeed in a Fast-Paced World*, New York: Guilford Publications.
Brandreth, B. (2021), *Shakespearean Rhetoric*, London: Bloomsbury.
Boyd, M. (2008), [Speech] 'Theatre and New Communities', New York Public Library, 20 June.
Brook, P. (1968), *The Empty Space*, London: Penguin Books.
Brook, P. (1996), 'The Culture of Links', in P. Pavis (ed), *The Intercultural Performance Reader*, 63–6, London: Routledge.
Brook, P. (1998), *Threads of Time: A Memoir*, London: Methuen.
Brook, P. (2013), *The Quality of Mercy: Reflections on Shakespeare*, London: Nick Hern Books.
Brown, B. (2017), [Talk] 'Daring Classrooms'. Available online: https://brenebrown.com/videos/sxsw-edu-2017-daring-classrooms/ (accessed 18 November 2022).
Brown, M. (2021), 'National Portrait Gallery to Feature More Women in Its Collection', *The Guardian*, 17 March.
Bruner, J. S. (1966), *Toward a Theory of Instruction*, Cambridge, MA: Harvard University Press.
Bruner, J. S. (1986), *Actual Minds, Possible Worlds*, Cambridge, MA: Harvard University Press.
Bruner, J. S. (1990), *Acts of Meaning*, Cambridge, MA: Harvard University Press.
Bruner, J. S. (1996), *The Culture of Education*, Cambridge, MA: Harvard University Press.
Bull, A., N. Wilson and J. Gross (2017), 'Towards Cultural Democracy', King's College London. Available online: https://www.kcl.ac.uk/cultural/resources/reports/towards-cultural-democracy-2017-kcl.pdf (accessed 18 June 2023).
Bullock, K. (n.d.), 'International Baccalaureate Learner Profile: Literature Review'. Available online: https://www.ibo.org/globalassets/new-structure/research/pdfs/iblearnerprofileeng.pdf (accessed 15 October 2022).
Burrow, C. (2013), *Shakespeare & Classical Antiquity*, Oxford: Oxford University Press.
Caldwell-Cook, H. (1918), *The Play Way; An Essay in Educational Method* [Kindle], New York: Frederick A. Stokes.
Cantle, T. (2012), *Interculturalism: The New Era of Cohesion and Diversity*, Basingstoke: Palgrave Macmillan.
Carrington, S. J. and A. J. Bailey (2009), 'Are There Theory of Mind Regions in the Brain? A Review of the Neuroimaging Literature', *Human Brain Mapping*, 30: 2313–35.
Castoriadis, C. (1997), *The Castoriadis Reader*, ed. D. A. Curtis, Oxford: Blackwell.
CBI (2012), 'First Steps: A New Approach for Our Schools'. Available online: http://www.cbi.org.uk/insight-and-analysis/first-steps/ (accessed 4 February 2023).
CBI (2019), 'Education and Learning for the Modern World: CBI/Pearson Education and Skills Survey Report 2019'. Available online: https://www.cbi.org.uk/media/3841/12546_tess_2019.pdf (accessed 15 November 2022).
Cheng, A. Y. and J. Winston (2011), 'Shakespeare as a Second Language: Playfulness, Power and Pedagogy in the ESL Classroom', *Research in Drama Education: The Journal of Applied Theatre*, 16 (4): 37–41.

Cobb, S., L. Beardon, R. Eastgate, T. Glover, S. Kerr, H. Neale, S. Parsons, S. Benford, E. Hopkins, P. Mitchell, G. Reynard and J. Wilson (2002), 'Applied Virtual Environments to Support Learning of Social Interaction Skills in Users with Asperger's Syndrome', *Digital Creativity*, 13 (1): 11–22.

Coles, J. (2013), '"Every Child's Birthright"? Democratic Entitlement and the Role of Canonical Literature in the English National Curriculum', *The Curriculum Journal*, 24: 50–66.

Coles, J. and M. Pitfield (2022), *Reading Shakespeare through Drama*, Cambridge: Cambridge University Press.

Core Knowledge Foundation (2022). Available online: https://www.coreknowledge.org/ (accessed 28 December 2022).

Copland, S. and G. Olson, eds. (2018), *The Politics of Form*, London: Routledge.

Craft, A., B. Jeffrey and M. Liebling, eds. (2001), *Creativity in Education*, London: Continuum.

Cultural Learning Alliance (2017), 'Key Research Findings: The Case for Cultural Learning'. Available online: https://www.leanarts.org.uk/app/uploads/key_research_findings.pdf (accessed 18 June 2023).

Cultural Learning Alliance (2019), 'Further Drop in Arts GCSE and A Level Entries for 2019'. Available online: https://www.culturallearningalliance.org.uk/further-drop-in-arts-gcse-and-a-level-entries-for-2019/ (accessed 21 July 2021).

Curré, G. (2019), 'Shakespeare in South African Schools: To Be or Not To Be?' *eNCA*. Available online: https://www.enca.com/life/shakespeare-south-african-schools-be-or-not-be (accessed 2 January 2023).

Dadabhoy, A. and N. Mehdizadeh (2023), *Anti-Racist Shakespeare*, Cambridge: Cambridge University Press.

Damasio, A. (2006), *Descartes' Error: Emotion, Reason and the Human Brain*, London: Vintage.

Damasio, A. (2012), *Self Comes to Mind Constructing the Conscious Brain*, London: Vintage.

Dangazele, N. (2010), 'Investigating the Use of Image Theatre, as a Method of Facilitating Dialogue in South African Organizational Teams', MA diss., University of Witwatersrand.

Dangazele, N. and S. Mokuku (2013, March), 'Shakespeare Friend of Foe', *Focus Education Overcoming Innovation. The Journal of Helen Suzman Foundation*, 68: 25–8.

Davies, P. (2000), 'The Use of Drama in English Language Teaching', *TESL Canada Journal*, 8/1: 87–99.

Della Gatta, C. (2019), 'Confronting Bias and Identifying Facts: Teaching Resistance Through Shakespeare', in H. Eklund and W. B. Hyman (eds), *Teaching Social Justice Through Shakespeare: Why Renaissance Literature Matters Now*, 165–73, Edinburgh: Edinburgh University Press.

Dernikos, B. P. (2020), 'Tuning into "Fleshy" Frequencies: A Posthuman Mapping of Affect, Sound and de/Colonized Literacies with/in a Primary Classroom', *Journal of Early Childhood Literacy*, 20 (1): 134–57.

Desai, A. N. (2019), 'Topical Shakespeare and the Urgency of Ambiguity', in W. B. Hyman and H. Eklund (eds), *Teaching Social Justice Through Shakespeare: Why Renaissance Literature Matters Now*, 27–35, Edinburgh: Edinburgh University Press.

Dewey, J. (1916), *Education and Democracy*, New York: The Free Press.

Dewey, J. ([1934] 2004), *Art as Experience*, London: Perigree.
Dewey, J. ([1938] 1997], *Experience & Education*, New York: Touchstone.
DfE (2014), 'The National Curriculum in England Key Stages 3 and 4 Framework Document'. Available online: https://assets.publishing.service.gov.uk/government/uploads/system/uploads/attachment_data/file/840002/Secondary_national_curriculum_corrected_PDF.pdf (accessed 3 February 2023).
DCSF(2008),'Shakespeare for all ages and stages'. Available online: https://dera.ioe.ac.uk/id/eprint/2540/ (accessed 19 July 2023).
DfE (2014), 'National Curriculum in England: English Programmes of Study'. Available online: https://www.gov.uk/government/publications/national-curriculum-in-england-english-programmes-of-study/national-curriculum-in-england-english-programmes-of-study (accessed 10 June 2022).
DfE (2019), 'School Inspection Handbook', *Ofsted School Inspection Handbook*, London: Department for Education. Available online: https://www.gov.uk/government/publications/school-inspection-handbook-eif/school-inspection-handbook (accessed 18 June 2023).
DfE (2019a), 'Early Career Framework'. Available online: https://assets.publishing.service.gov.uk/government/uploads/system/uploads/attachment_data/file/978358/Early-Career_Framework_April_2021.pdf (accessed 18 November 2022).
DfE (2019b), 'ITT Core Content Framework'. Available online: https://assets.publishing.service.gov.uk/government/uploads/system/uploads/attachment_data/file/974307/ITT_core_content_framework_.pdf (accessed 18 November 2022).
DfE (2021), 'Policy Paper. Initial Teacher Training (ITT) Market Review: Overview'. Available online: https://www.gov.uk/government/publications/initial-teacher-training-itt-market-review/initial-teacher-training-itt-market-review-overview (accessed 24 November 2022).
DfE (2023), 'State of the Nation 2022: Children and Young People's Wellbeing'. Available online: https://www.gov.uk/government/publications/state-of-the-nation-2022-children-and-young-peoples-wellbeing (accessed 18 February 2023).
Dolan, F. E. (2009), 'Learning to Listen: Shakespeare and Contexts', in G. B. Shand (ed), *Teaching Shakespeare: Passing it On*, 181–95, Chichester: Blackwell.
Dunn, F. and M. Stinson (2011), 'Not Without the Art! The Importance of Teacher Artistry When Applying Drama Pedagogy for Additional Language Learning', *Research in Drama Education*, 16 (4): 617–33.
Dweck, C. (2006), *Mindset: The New Psychology of Success*, London: Random House.
Dyches, J. (2017), 'Shaking Off Shakespeare: A White Teacher, Urban Students, and the Mediating Powers of a Canonical Counter-Curriculum', *Urban Review*, 49 (2): 300–25.
Dyches, J. (2018), 'Particularizing the Tensions between Canonical and Bodily Discourses', *Journal of Literacy Research*, 50 (2): 239–61.
Dyches, J., A. S. Boyd and J. M. Schulz (2021), 'Critical Content Knowledges in the English Language Arts Classroom: Examining Practicing Teachers' Nuanced Perspectives', *Journal of Curriculum Studies*, 53 (3): 368–384.
Eaglestone, R. (2021), 'IMPACT 26: "Powerful Knowledge", "Cultural Literacy" and the Study of Literature in Schools', London: Wiley.
Earley, C. P. and S. Ang (2003), *Cultural Intelligence: Individual Interactions across Cultures*, Stanford: Stanford Business Books.

Eco, U. (1992), *Interpretation and Overinterpretation*, Cambridge: Cambridge University Press.
Edgar, D. (2009), *How Plays Work*, London: Nick Hern Books.
EEF (2023), 'Arts Participation', *Teaching and Learning Toolkit*. Available online: https://educationendowmentfoundation.org.uk/education-evidence/teaching-learning-toolkit/arts-participation (accessed 5 February 2023).
Eklund, H. and W. B. Hyman, eds. (2019), *Teaching Social Justice Through Shakespeare: Why Renaissance Literature Matters Now*, Edinburgh: Edinburgh University Press.
Elliot, V. (2016), '"Study What You Most Affect": Beginning Teachers' Preparedness to Teach Shakespeare', *CEA Critic*, 78 (2): 199–212.
Elliot, V., L. Nelson-Addy, R. Chantiluke and M. Courtney (2021), 'Lit in Colour. Diversity in Literature in English Schools', commissioned by Penguin and Runnymede Trust. Available online: https://www.penguin.co.uk/lit-in-colour (accessed 8 April 2022).
Emmerson, K. (2022), 'Blended Identities and Shakespearean Success: Can Utilising Teenagers' Social and Ethno-Cultural Identities in the Classroom Enhance an Appreciation of Shakespeare's Work?', MA diss., University of Birmingham, Birmingham.
Enciso, P., C. Cushman, B. Edmiston, R. Post and D. Berring (2011), '"Is That What You Really Want?": A Case Study of Intracultural Ensemble-Building within the Paradoxes of "Urbanicity"', *Research in Drama Education: The Journal of Applied Theatre and Performance*, 16 (2): 215–33.
Enser, M. (2019, September), 'Ofsted, Social Mobility and the Cultural Capital Mix-Up', *Times Education Supplement*.
Enterline, L. (2012), *Shakespeare's Schoolroom: Rhetoric, Discipline, Emotion*, Philadelphia: University of Pennsylvania Press.
Equity and Directors Guild of Great Britain (2004), 'Ensemble Theatre Conference', in *23rd November, The Pit, The Barbican, London*, 1–84, London: Equity and Directors Guild of Great Britain.
Etheridge Woodson, S. (2015), *Theatre For Youth Third Space: Performance, Democracy and Community Cultural Development*, Bristol: Intellect.
Evans, M. (1989), *Signifying Nothing: Truth's True Contexts in Shakespeare's Text*, London: Harvester Wheatsheaf.
Evrard, Y. (1997), 'Democratizing Culture or Cultural Democracy?', *The Journal of Arts Management, Law, and Society*, 27 (3): 165–75.
Fauconnier, G. and M. Turner (2002), *The Way We Think: Conceptual blending and the mind's hidden complexities*, New York: Basic Books.
Faulkner, R. (2020), 'Professional Learning and the Teaching of Shakespeare', MA diss., University of Birmingham, Birmingham.
Fernie, E. (2005), 'Shakespeare and the Prospect of Presentism', *Shakespeare Survey*, Cambridge: Cambridge University Press.
Finley-Johnson, H. (1912), *The Dramatic Method of Teaching*, London: Nisbet Press.
Finneran, M. and K. Freebody, eds. (2016), *Drama and Social Justice: Theory, Research and Practice in International Contexts*, London: Routledge.
Fitch, W. T. (2010), *The Evolution of Language*, Cambridge: Cambridge University Press.

Flaherty, K. (2013), 'Habitation and Naming: Teaching Local Shakespeares', in K. Flaherty and L. E. Semler (eds), *Teaching Shakespeare Beyond the Centre Australasian Perspectives*, 75–86, Basingstoke: Palgrave Macmillian.
Fleming, M. (2010), *Arts in Education and Creativity: A Literature Review*, Newcastle: Creativity, Culture and Education.
Folger Shakespeare Library (2023) 'About the Folger'. Available online: https://www.folger.edu/about (accessed 24 January 2023).
Forster, E. M. (1985), *Aspects of the Novel*, New York: Harvest.
Freebody, K. and M. Finneran (2021), *Critical Themes in Drama: Social, Cultural and Political Analysis*, Oxon: Routledge.
Freebody, K., M. Finneran, M. Balfour and M. Anderson, eds. (2018), *Applied Theatre: Understanding Change*, London: Springer.
Freire, P. (1970), *The Pedagogy of the Oppressed*, London: Continuum.
Gallagher, K. (2014), *Why Theatre Matters. Urban Youth, Engagement, and a Pedagogy of the Real*, Toronto: University of Toronto Press.
Gallagher, K. (2016), 'Can a Classroom Be a Family? Race, Space, and the Labour of Care in Urban Teaching', *Canadian Journal of Education*, 39 (2): 1–36.
Gallagher, K. and A. Wessels (2013), 'Between the Frames: Youth Spectatorship and Theatre as Curated, "Unruly" Pedagogical Space', *Research in Drama Education: The Journal of Applied Theatre and Performance*, 18 (1): 25–43.
Gallagher, K., D. J. Rodricks and K. Jacobson, eds. (2020), *Global Youth Citizenry and Radical Hope*, Singapore: Springer.
Gallagher, S. (2008), 'Understanding Others: Embodied Social Cognition', in P. Calvo and T. Gomila (eds), *Handbook of Cognitive Sciences: An Embodied Approach*, 437–52, London: Elsevier Science.
Gibson, R. (1993), '"A Black Day Will It Be to Somebody." Key Stage 3 Shakespeare', *Cambridge Journal of Education*, 23 (1): 77–88.
Gibson, R. (1996), '"O, What Learning Is!" Pedagogy and the Afterlife of Romeo and Juliet', *Shakespeare Survey*, 49: 141–52.
Gibson, R. (1998), *Teaching Shakespeare*, Cambridge: Cambridge University Press.
Gibson, R. (2016), *Teaching Shakespeare: A Handbook for Teachers*, 2nd edn, Cambridge: Cambridge University Press.
Goffman, E. (1990), *The Presentation of Self in Everyday Life*, London: Penguin.
Goldin-Meadow, S. (2005), *Hearing Gesture: How Our Hands Help Us Think*, London: Harvard University Press.
Gonsalves, A. and T. Irish (2021), *Shakespeare and Meisner: A Practical Guide for Actors, Directors, Students and Teachers*, London: Bloomsbury.
Gorlée, D. L. (2004), *On Translating Signs: Exploring Text and Semio-Translation*, Amsterdam: Rodopi.
Grady, S. (2003), 'Accidental Marxists?: The Challenge of Critical and Feminist Pedagogies for the Practice of Applied Drama', *Youth Theatre Journal*, 17 (1): 65–81.
Gray, D. (1988), 'What Does Every American Need to Know?', *The Phi Delta Kappan*, 69 (5): 386–8.
Gregory, S. (2005), 'Making Shakespeare Our Contemporary: Teaching Romeo and Juliet at Key Stage Three', in M. Blocksidge (ed), *Shakespeare in Education*, 20–39, New York: Continuum.

Greenblatt, S. (1994) 'Invisible bullets: Renaissance authority and its subversion' in J Dollimore and A. Sinfield (eds), *Political Shakespeare. Essays in Cultural Materialism*, 2nd edition, Manchester: Manchester University Press.

Hall, E. T. ([1959] 1990), *The Silent Language*, New York: Anchor Books.

Hammersley, M. (1997), 'Educational Research and Teaching: A Response to David Hargreaves' TTA Lecture', *British Educational Research Journal*, 23 (2): 141–61.

Harari, Y. N. (2018), *21 Lessons for the 21st Century*, London: Vintage.

Hargreaves, D. H. (1997), 'In Defence of Research for Evidence-based Teaching: A Rejoinder to Martyn Hammersley', *British Educational Research Journal*, 23 (4): 405–19.

Hartley, A. J., K. Dunn and C. Berry (2021), 'Pedagogy: Decolonizing Shakespeare on Stage', in D. Ruiter (ed), *The Arden Research Handbook of Shakespeare and Contemporary Performance*, London: Bloomsbury Arden Shakespeare.

Hattie, J. (2009), *Visible Learning: A Synthesis of Over 800 Meta-analyses Relating to Achievement*, London: Routledge.

Hattie, J. (2012), *Visible Learning for Teachers: Maximising Impact on Learning*, London: Routledge.

Henderson, D. E. and K. S. Vitale, eds. (2021), *Shakespeare and Digital Pedagogy: Case Studies and Strategies*, London: Bloomsbury.

Hickey-Moody, A. (2013), *Youth, Arts and Education: Reassembling Subjectivity through Affect*, London: Routledge.

Hilský, M. (2009), *William Shakespeare Sonety*, Brno: Atlantis.

Hirsch, E. D. (1983), 'Cultural Literacy', *American Scholar*, 52 (2): 159–69.

Hirsch Jr, E. D., J. F. Kett and J. S. Trefil (1987), *Cultural Literacy: What Every American Needs to Know*, London: Vintage.

Hodgson, J. and A. Harris (2022), 'The Genealogy of "Cultural Literacy"', *Changing English*, 29 (4): 382–95.

Hofstadter, D. (2001), 'Epilogue: Analogy as the Core of Cognition', in D. Gentner, K. J. Holyoak and B. N. Kokinov (eds), *The Analogical Mind: Perspectives from Cognitive Science*, 499–539, London: MIT.

hooks, b. (2003), *Teaching Community: A Pedagogy of Hope*, Oxon: Routledge.

hooks, b. (2010), *Teaching Critical Thinking. Practical Wisdom*, Abingdon: Routledge.

Hughes, J. and H. Nicholson, eds. (2016), *Critical Perspectives on Applied Theatre*, Cambridge: Cambridge University Press.

Hunter, K. (2015), *Shakespeare's Heartbeat*, Abingdon: Routledge.

Hurrell, W. (2018), 'Naomie Harris and Inter-Mission Youth Theatre', *Vimeo*, 12 April. Available online: https://vimeo.com/264475327/recommended (accessed 15 June 2022).

IBO. Available online: https://ibo.org/about-the-ib/facts-and-figures/ (accessed 5 December 2022).

International Baccalaureate (2021), 'Language and Literature Curriculum Subject Brief'. Available online: https://www.ibo.org/contentassets/5895a05412144fe890312bad52b17044/curriculum.brief-languagea.literature-eng.pdf (accessed 12 October 2022).

Intermission (2023), 'About Us'. Available online: https://www.intermissionyouththeatre.co.uk/our-story (accessed 24 January 2023).

Irish, T. (2009), Personal notes from an exploration of 'Why Shakespeare in education today?' by the RSC in Stratford-upon-Avon.

Irish, T. (2011), 'Would You Risk it for Shakespeare? A Case Study of Using Active Approaches in the English Classroom', *English in Education*, 45: 6–19.
Irish, T. (2012), 'Shakespeare: A Worldwide Classroom'. Stratford-upon-Avon: RSC. Available online: http://www.academia.edu/23423997/Shakespeare_a_worldwide_classroom (accessed 3 January 2023).
Irish, T. (2015), 'Performing Shakespeare in the Olympic Year: Interviews with Three Practitioners', in P. Prescott and E. Sullivan (eds), *Shakespeare on the Global Stage*, London: Bloomsbury.
Irish, T. (2016), 'Shakespeare in English Education'. Available online: https://www.academia.edu/35609194/A_history_of_Shakespeare_in_English_education (accessed 14 February 2023).
Irish, T. and A. Gonsalves (2023), 'Teaching Shakespeare in Oman: Exploring Shared Humanity and Cultural Difference through Shakespeare's Texts', in L. E. Semler, C. Hansen and J. Manuel (eds), *Reimagining Shakespeare Education. Teaching and Learning through Collaboration*, Cambridge: Cambridge University Press.
Irish, T. and A. Rokison-Woodall (2023), 'Signing Shakespeare', in R. Shaughnessy and R. Mackenzie (eds), *Shakespeare and Social Engagement*, Oxford: Berghahn.
Jennings, S. (2021), 'Neuro-Dramatic Play Ltd'. Available online: https://www.ndpltd.org/ (accessed 12 February 2023).
Johnson, M. (2007), *The Meaning of the Body: Aesthetics of Human Understanding*, London: University of Chicago Press.
Jore, M. (2021), 'Investigating Learners' Difficulties In Analysing Drama In English First Additional Language: A Case Of Grade 12 Learners', MA diss., University of Limpopo.
Julian, E. and K. Solga (2021), 'Ethics: The Challenge of Practising (and Not Just Representing) Diversity at the Stratford Festival of Canada', in P. Kirwan and K. Prince (eds), *The Arden Research Handbook of Shakespeare and Contemporary Performance*, 192–210, London: The Arden Shakespeare.
Kahneman, D. (2012), *Thinking, Fast and Slow*, London: Penguin.
Keats, J. ([1818] 2005), *Selected Letters of John Keats*, Cambridge, MA: Harvard University Press.
Keenan, S. and D. Shellard, eds. (2016), *Shakespeare's Cultural Capital: His Economic Impact from the Sixteenth to the Twenty-First Century*, Basingstoke: Palgrave Macmillan.
Kemp, S. (2019), 'Shakespeare in Transition: Pedagogies of Transgender Justice', in H. Eklund and W. B. Hyman (eds), *Teaching Social Justice Through Shakespeare: Why Renaissance Literature Matters Now*, Edinburgh: University of Edinburgh Press.
Kerswill, P (n.d.), 'What is Multicultural London English (MLE?)', University of York Department of Language and Linguistic Science. Available online: https://www.york.ac.uk/language/research/projects/mle/what-is-mle/ (accessed 11 July 2022).
Kitchen, J. (2015), 'The Ensemble Domesticated: Mapping Issues of Autonomy and Power in Performing Arts Projects in Schools', *Power and Education*, 7 (1): 90–105.
Kitchen, J. (2021), 'Theatre and Drama Education and Populism: The Ensemble "Family" as a Space for Dialogic Empathy and Civic Care', *British Educational Research Journal*, 47 (2): 372–88.

Kitchen, J. (2022), 'Shakespeare Youth Performance Festivals as Spaces for Postcolonial Restorying', in S. Busby, K. Freebody and C. Rajendran (eds), *Routledge Companion to Theatre and Young People*, London: Routledge.

Kitchen, J. (2023), *Critical Pedagogy in Active Approaches to Teaching Shakespeare*, Cambridge: University of Cambridge Press.

Kmiec, E. A. (2020), 'The Effectiveness of the Royal Shakespeare Company's Pedagogy in a Neurodiverse Classroom: An Action Research Dissertation'. MA diss., University of Birmingham, Birmingham.

Knight, S. (2013), *Forest School and Outdoor Learning in the Early Years*, London: Sage.

Kuttner, P. J. (2015), 'Educating for Cultural Citizenship: Reframing the Goals of Arts Education', *Curriculum Inquiry*, 45 (1): 69–92.

Lakoff, G. and M. Johnson (1980), *Metaphors We Live By*, London: Chicago University Press.

Lamb, C. and M. Lamb ([1807] 1993), *Tales from Shakespeare*, London: J.M. Dent.

Lambert, C. and A. Parker (2006), 'Imagination, Hope and the Positive Face of Feminism: Pro/Feminist Pedagogy in "Post" Feminist Times?', *Studies in Higher Education*, 31 (4): 469–82.

Langer, S. K. (1953), *Feeling and Form: A Theory of Art Developed from Philosophy in a New Key*, New York: Charles Schribner's Sons.

Lauer, M. (2008), 'The Performing Arts in Second Language Acquisition: A Report on the Experience of Dramatizing a Novel', *Scenario*, 2/1: 18–40.

Lave, J. and E. Wenger (1991), *Situated Learning: Legitimate Peripheral Participation*, Cambridge: Cambridge University Press.

Lees, D. (2021), 'Citizen of the World, or Citizen of Nowhere? Shakespeare Lives in China in 2016', in E. G. C. King and M. Smialkowska (eds), *Memorialising Shakespeare: Commemoration and Collective Identity, 1916–2016*, 199–224, Cham: Springer.

Lees, D. (2022), 'Encouraging Deep Learning through an Interactive, Intercultural Approach to Shakespeare', in J. Shaules and T. McConachy (eds), *Transformation, Embodiment, and Wellbeing in Foreign Language Pedagogy: Enacting Deep Learning*, 129–52, London: Bloomsbury.

Leith, S. (2012), *You Talkin' to Me? Rhetoric from Aristotle to Obama*, London: Profile Books.

Li Lan, Y. (2013), 'Intercultural Rhythm in Yohangza's Dream', in P. Prescott and E. Sullivan (eds), *Shakespeare Beyond English. A Global Experiment*, Cambridge: Cambridge University Press.

Long, K. and M. T. Christel (2019), *Bring on the Bard: Active Drama Approaches for Shakespeare's Diverse Student Readers*, Urbana: National Council of Teachers of English.

Louv, R. (2021), 'Learning Outdoors', *Children and Nature Network*. Available online: https://www.childrenandnature.org/resources/learning-outdoors-keeping-students-and-teachers-safer-improving-education-and-bringing-healing-during-the-pandemic/ (accessed 12 September 2022).

Lucas, B. and G. Claxton (2015), *Educating Ruby: What Children Really Need to Learn*, Carmarthen: Crown House.

Lucas, B. and E. Spencer (2017), *Teaching Creative Thinking: Developing Learners Who Generate Ideas and Can Think Critically*, Carmarthen: Crown House.

Lyne, R. (2011), *Shakespeare, Rhetoric and Cognition*, Cambridge: Cambridge University Press.
Mamet, D. (1998), *True and False: Heresy and Common Sense for the Actor*, London: Bloomsbury.
Mance, H. (2016), 'Should Shakespeare be Taught in Africa's Schools?' *Financial Times*, August 18. Available online: https://www.ft.com/content/6a5737f8-5d63-11e6-a72a-bd4bf1198c63.
Mann, S. (2011), 'A Critical Review of Qualitative Interviews in Applied Linguistics', *Applied Linguistics*, 32 (1): 6–24.
Mansell, W. (2019), 'Ofsted Plan to Inspect "Cultural Capital" in Schools Attacked as Elitist', *The Guardian*, 3 September.
Mar, R. A. and K. Oatley (2008), 'The Function of Fiction Is the Abstraction and Simulation of Social Experience', *Perspectives on Psychological Science*, 3 (3): 173–92.
Massai, S., ed. (2005), *World-Wide Shakespeares*, Abingdon: Routledge.
Matthias, B. (2007), 'Improvisational Theatre and the Beginning Foreign Language Curriculum', *Scenario*, 1/1: 56–69.
McAllum, A. and B. Bleiman (2022), 'Response to Ofsted Curriculum Research Review: English', English and Media Centre, blog online, 5 June. Available online: https://www.englishandmedia.co.uk/blog/review-of-ofsted-curriculum-research-review-english (accessed 25 November 2022).
McBer, H. (2000), 'Research into Teacher Effectiveness', *DfEE*. Available online: https://dera.ioe.ac.uk/4566/1/RR216.pdf (accessed 4 February 2023).
McConachie, B. A. and F. E. Hart, eds. (2006), *Performance and Cognition: Theatre Studies and the Cognitive Turn*, London: Routledge.
McDonald, R. (2001), *Shakespeare and the Arts of Language*, Oxford: Oxford University Press.
McDonald, R. (2009), 'Planned Obsolescence or Working at the Words', in G. B. Shand (ed), *Teaching Shakespeare: Passing it On*, 25–42, Chichester: Blackwell.
McDuffie, A. (2013), 'Verbal Comprehension', in F. R. Volkmar (ed), *Encyclopedia of Autism Spectrum Disorders*, 3241, New York: Springer.
McEvoy, S. (2005), 'Shakespeare at 16–19', in Martin Blocksidge (ed), *Shakespeare in Education*, 97–119, New York: Continuum.
McGilchrist, I. (2009), *The Master and his Emissary: The Divided Brain and the Western World*, London: Yale University Press.
McGrath, J. (2001), 'Theatre and Democracy', *European Studies*, 17: 133–9.
McGregor, A. (2021), 'To Teach or Not to Teach: Is Shakespeare Still Relevant to Today's Students?', *School Library Journal*. Available online: https://www.slj.com/story/to-teach-or-not-to-teach-is-shakespeare-still-relevant-to-todays-students-libraries-classic-literature-canon (accessed 15 November 2022).
McLuskie, K. (2009), 'Dancing and Thinking: Teaching "Shakespeare" in the Twenty- First Century', in G. B. Shand (ed), *Teaching Shakespeare: Passing It On*, 132–41, Chitchester: Wiley-Blackwell.
McLuskie, K. and K. Rumbold (2014), *Cultural Value in Twenty-first-century England: The Case of Shakespeare*, Manchester: Manchester University Press.
Miazga, M. (2014), 'Getting into the Mind of Shakespeare in an IB Class', *Teaching Shakespeare! A Folger Education Blog*. Available online: https://teachingshakespeareblog.folger.edu/2014/04/17/getting-into-the-mind-of-shakespeare-in-an-ib-class/ (accessed 28 October 2022).

Micklem, D. (2019), 'Conference 19 Blog: People-Centred Design'. Available online: http://www.theatrestrust.org.uk/latest/news/1055-peoplecentred-design (accessed 29 November 2019).

Mithen, S. (2005), *The Singing Neanderthals: The Origins of Music, Language, Mind and Body*, London: Weidenfeld and Nicholson.

Molenaar-Klumper, M. (2002), *Non-Verbal Learning Disabilities: Characteristics, Diagnosis, and Treatment within an Educational Setting*, London: Jessica Kingsley Publishers.

Monk, N., C. Chillington Rutter, J. Neelands and J. Heron (2011), *Open Space Learning: A Study in Transdisciplinary Pedagogy*, London: Bloomsbury.

Morgan, N. and J. Saxton (1994), *Asking Better Questions. Models, Techniques and Classroom Activities for Engaging Students in Learning*, Ontario: Pembroke.

Morozov, E. (2023), 'The Problem with Artificial Intelligence? It's Neither Artificial nor Intelligent', *The Guardian*, 30 March. Available online: https://www.theguardian.com/commentisfree/2023/mar/30/artificial-intelligence-chatgpt-human-mind (accessed 1 April 2023).

Mueller, R. M. (1986), 'Teaching Writing through Literature: Toward the Acquisition of a Knowledge Base', National Council of Teachers of English. Available online: https://files.eric.ed.gov/fulltext/ED273963.pdf (accessed 10 October 2022).

Murphy, A. (2008), *Shakespeare for the People: Working-Class Readers, 1800–1900*, Cambridge: Cambridge University Press.

Murphy, E. (2004), 'Preface', *The International Schools Journal Compendium. Culture and The International School: Living, Learning and Communicating across Cultures*, 2: 10–14.

Neary, M. (2019), 'Student as Producer and the Democratisation of Science –', *MPact: The University of Lincoln Journal of Higher Education Research*, 1 (4).

Neary, M. and J. Winn (2009), 'The Student as Producer: Reinventing the Student Experience in Higher Education', in H. Stevenson (ed), *The Future of Higher Education: Policy, Pedagogy and the Student Experience*, 192–210, London: Bloomsbury.

Neary, M., G. Saunders, A. Hagyard and D. Derricott (2014), 'Student as Producer: Research-Engaged Teaching, an Institutional Strategy Section', York.

Neelands, J. (2002), '11/09 – The Space in Our Hearts'. Available online: http://mantleoftheexpert.co.nz/wp-content/uploads/2011/06/Neelands-space-in-our-hearts.pdf (accessed 1 September 2022).

Neelands, J. (2009a), 'The Art of Togetherness; Reflections on Some Essential Artistic and Pedagogic Qualities of Drama Curricula', *NJ*, 33 (1): 9–18.

Neelands, J. (2009b), 'Acting Together: Ensemble as a Democratic Process in Art and Life', *Research in Drama Education: The Journal of Applied Theatre and Performance*, 14 (2): 173–89.

Neelands, J. and B. Choe (2010), 'The English Model of Creativity: Cultural Politics of an Idea', *International Journal of Cultural Policy*, 15 (3): 287–304.

Neelands, J. and J. O'Hanlon (2011), 'There Is Some Soul of Good: An Action-Centred Approach to Teaching Shakespeare in Schools', *Shakespeare Survey*, 64: 240–50.

Neelands, J., E. Belfiore, C. Firth, N. Hart, L. Perrin, S. Brock, D. Holdaway, J. Woddis and J. Knell (2015), 'Enriching Britain: Culture, Creativity and Growth', Coventry.

Nicholson, H. (2011), *Theatre, Education and Performance*, Basingstoke: Palgrave MacMillan.
Ngozi Adichie, C. (2009), [TED talk] 'The Danger of a Single Story'. Available online: https://www.ted.com/talks/chimamanda_ngozi_adichie_the_danger_of_a_single_story (accessed 4 February 2023).
Ngozi Adichie, C. (2022), [BBC Radio 4] 'Freedom of Speech', BBC Reith Lectures. Available online: https://www.bbc.co.uk/iplayer/episode/p0dhrlhm/the-reith-lectures-2022-the-four-freedoms-1-chimamanda-ngozi-adichie-freedom-of-speech (accessed 4 February 2023).
Noddings, N. (2013), *Caring: A Relational Approach to Ethics and Moral Education*, 2nd edn, Los Angeles: University of California Press.
Nussbaum, M. C. (2010), *Not For Profit: Why Democracy needs the Humanities*, Woodstock: Princeton University Press.
O'Brien, P., ed. (1993), *Shakespeare Set Free*, New York: Washington Square Press.
O'Brien, P., J. Addison Roberts, M. Toyaydo and N. Goodwin, eds. (2006), *Shakespeare Set Free: Teaching a Midsummer Night's Dream, Romeo and Juliet and Macbeth an Innovative, Performance-Based Approach to Teaching Shakespeare*, 2nd edn, New York: Washington Square Press.
O'Connor, P. (2014), 'Drama as Critical Pedagogy: Re-Imagining Terrorism', in J. Dunn and M. Anderson (eds), *How Drama Activates Learning : Contemporary Research and Practice*, London: Bloomsbury.
OECD (2022), 'PISA 2022 Creative Thinking'. Available online: https://www.oecd.org/pisa/innovation/creative-thinking/ (accessed 16 November 2022).
OECD (2023), 'Is Education Losing the Race with Technology?: AI's Progress in Maths and Reading, Educational Research and Innovation', Paris: OECD Publishing, https://doi.org/10.1787/73105f99-en.
OED Online (2022), 'bark | barque, n.2', OED Online. Available online: https://www.oed.com/view/Entry/15568?rskey=aGQ3PS&result=2&isAdvanced=false (accessed 30 May 2022).
Ofsted (2022a), 'Research Review Series: English'. Available online: https://www.gov.uk/government/publications/curriculum-research-review-series-english/curriculum-research-review-series-english (accessed 1 November 2022).
Ofsted (2022b), 'Education Inspection Framework'. Available online: https://www.gov.uk/government/publications/education-inspection-framework (accessed 11 November 2022).
Olive, S. (2011), 'The Royal Shakespeare Company as "Cultural Chemist"', *Shakespeare Survey*, 64: 251–259.
Olive, S. (2015), *Shakespeare Valued: Education Policy and Pedagogy 1989–2009*, Bristol: Intellect.
Orwell, G. (1949), *1984*, Harmondsworth: Penguin.
Osterman, K. F. (2000), 'Students' Need for Belonging in the School Community', *Review of Educational Research*, 70 (3): 323–67.
Palmer, S. (2007), *Toxic Childhood: How the Modern World is Damaging Our Children and What We Can Do About It*, London: Orion.
Pigkou-Repousi, M. (2020), 'The Politics of Care in Indifferent Times: Youth Narratives, Caring Practices, and Transformed Discourses in Greek Education Amid Economic and Refugee Crises', in K. Gallagher, D. J. Rodricks and K. Jacobson (eds), *Global Youth Citizenry and Radical Hope: Enacting*

Community-Engaged Research through Performative Methodologies, 111–34, Singapore: Springer.

Pinker, S. (2018), *Enlightenment Now. The Case for Reason, Science, Humanism and Progress*, London: Allen Lane.

Porter, E. (1996), 'Women and Friendships: Pedagogies Of Care and Relationality', in C. Luke (ed), *Feminisms and Pedagogies of Everyday Life*, 57–80, New York: State University of New York Press.

Poston, C. (2003), 'Teaching across the Boundaries: Discover in Literature and Research-Writing Classrooms', in M. M. Tokarczyk and I. Papoulis (eds), *Teaching Composition/Teaching Literature*, 68–78, New York: Peter Lang.

Povey, H., L. Burton, C. Angier and M. Boylan (1999), 'Learners as Authors in the Mathematics Classroom', in L. Burton (ed), *Learning Mathematics, from Hierarchies to Networks*, 232–45, London: Falmer Press.

Purple Door (2023), 'About us'. Available online: https://www.thedoorisopen.co.uk/about-us/ (accessed 24 January 2023).

Rancière, J. (2009), *The Emancipated Spectator*, London: Verso.

Resende, A. (2019), 'Engrafting Him New: Educating for Citizenship via Shakespeare in a Rural Area in Brazil', in V. M. de Carvalho (ed), *Eating Shakespeare*, 249–71, London: Bloomsbury.

Rizzollati, G., L. Fadiga, V. Gallese and L. Fogassi (1996), 'Premotor Cortex and the Recognition of Motor Actions', *Cognitive Brain Research*, 3: 131–41.

Robinson, K. (2013), [Talk] 'How to Change Education from the Ground Up', RSA Event. Available online: https://www.thersa.org/events/2013/07/how-to-change-education---from-the-ground-up (accessed 4 February 2023).

Robinson, K., L. Minkin and E. Bolton (1999), 'National Advisory Committee on Creative and Cultural Education All Our Futures: Creativity, Culture and Education', *DfEE Report*, 16 (May): 1–243.

Rocklin, E. L. (2005), *Performance Approaches to Teaching Shakespeare*, Urbana: National Council of Teachers of English.

Rodricks, D. J. (2015), 'Drama Education as "Restorative" for the Third Space', *Research in Drama Education: The Journal of Applied Theatre and Performance*, 20 (3): 340–43.

Rogers, J. (2022), *British Black and Asian Shakespeareans: Integrating Shakespeare, 1966–2018*, London: Bloomsbury.

Rokison, A. (2014), *Shakespearean Verse Speaking: Text and Theatre Practice*, Cambridge: Cambridge University Press.

Roslin, H. (2018), *Factfulness*, London: Hodder and Stoughton.

RSC (n.d.), 'Rehearsal Room Approaches: Top Tips'. Available online: https://www.rsc.org.uk/learn/schools-and-teachers/teacher-resources/rehearsal-room-approaches-to-shakespeare/introducing-rehearsal-room-approaches (accessed 5 August 2022).

RSC (2010), *The RSC Shakespeare Toolkit for Teachers. An Active Approach To Bringing Shakespeare's Plays Alive In The Classroom*, London: Methuen Drama.

RSC (2016), 'The Learning and Performance Network Final Evaluation Report', Stratford-upon-Avon: RSC.

RSC (2023), 'About Us'. Available online: https://www.rsc.org.uk/about-us/ (accessed 24 January 2023).

Ruiter, D. (2020), 'This Is Real Life: Shakespeare and Social Justice as a Field of Play', D. Ruiter (ed), *The Arden Research Handbook of Shakespeare and Social Justice*, 1–22, London: Bloomsbury.

Ruiter, D., ed. (2020), *The Arden Research Handbook of Shakespeare and Contemporary Performance*, London: The Arden Shakespeare.
Rumbold, K. (2008), 'The Arts Council England's "Arts Debate"', *Cultural Trends*, 17 (3): 189–95.
Rumbold, K. (2011), '"Brand Shakespeare?"', *Shakespeare Survey*, 64: 25–37.
Rumbold, K. and K. McLuskie (2014), *Cultural Value in Twenty-First-Century England: The Case of Shakespeare*, Manchester: Manchester University Press.
Rutherford, A. (2018), *The Book of Humans: A Brief History of Culture, Sex, War and the Evolution of Us*, London: Weidenfeld and Nicolson.
Sawyer, W. (2004), 'The Interaction of Conscious and Ideal Selves in Drama Teachers' Motivation to Teach', *Research in Drama Education*, 9 (1): 27–40.
Sayet, M. (2023). Available online: https://www.madelinesayet.com (accessed 12 February 2023).
Schleicher, A. (2016), 'Teaching Excellence through Professional Learning and Policy Reform: Lessons from around the World', International Summit on the Teaching Profession, OECD Publishing, Paris. Available online: https://doi.org/10.1787/9789264252059-en (accessed 18 June 2023).
Schön, D. (1983), *The Reflective Practitioner: How Professionals Think in Action*, London: Temple Smith.
Schupak, E. B. (2018), 'Shakespeare and Performance Pedagogy: Overcoming the Challenges', *Changing English: Studies in Culture and Education*, 25 (2): 163–79.
Segal, L. (2017), *Radical Happiness: Moments of Collective Joy*, Brooklyn: Verso.
Seidel, S., S. Tishman, E. Winner, L. Hetland and P. Palmer (2009), 'The Qualities of Quality. Understanding Excellence in Arts Education', Cambridge, MA. Available online: https://pz.harvard.edu/sites/default/files/Understanding-Excellence-in-Arts-Education.pdf (accessed 20 June 2023).
Semler, L. E. (2016), 'Prosperous Teaching and the Thing of Darkness: Raising a *Tempest* in the Classroom', *Cogent Arts & Humanities*, 3 (1): 1235862, https://doi.org/10.1080/23311983.2016.1235862
Semler, L. E., C. Hansen and J. Manuel (2023), 'Introduction. Projecting Shakespeare', in L. E. Semler, C. Hansen and J. Manuel (eds), *Reimagining Shakespeare Education. Teaching and Learning through Collaboration*, Cambridge: Cambridge University Press.
Sen, A. (2006), *Violence and Identity: The Illusion of Destiny*, London: Penguin.
Shafer, G. (2013), 'The Problem of Literature in Composition Classes', *Language Arts Journal of Michigan*, 28 (2): 34–40.
Shakespeare4All (2023). Available online: https://www.s4a.org.hk/ (accessed 11 February 2023).
Shakespeare's Globe (2023), 'About Us'. Available online: https://www.shakespearesglobe.com/discover/about-us/ (accessed 24 January 2023).
Shakespeare North (2023), 'About Us'. Available online: https://shakespearenorthplayhouse.co.uk/about-us/ (accessed 24 January 2023).
Shakespeare Schools Foundation (2020), 'Impact Report 2019/2020', London.
Shakespeare Schools Foundation (2023) 'About Us'. Available online: https://www.shakespeareschools.org/ (accessed 14 February 2023).
ShakeXperience (2023). Available online: http://shakexperience.com/ (accessed 15 February 2023).

Shapiro, L. and S. A. Stolz (2019), 'Embodied Cognition and its Significance for Education', *Theory and Research in Education*, 17 (1): 19–39.

Sheets-Johnstone, M. (1999), *The Primacy of Movement*, ProQuest ebrary, Philadelphia, NL: John Benjamins Publishing Company.

Shellard, D. and S. Keenan, eds. (2016), *Shakespeare's Cultural Capital His Economic Impact from the Sixteenth to the Twenty-First Century*, London: Palgrave Macmillian.

Shuman, C. (2000), *Pedagogical Economies. The Examination and the Victorian Literary Man*, Stanford: Stanford University Press.

Snyder-Young, D. (2013), *Theatre of Good Intentions: Challenges and Hopes for Theatre and Social Change*, Basingstoke: Palgrave Macmillian.

Solga, K. (2021), 'Womxn Direct Shakespeare in the 21st Century', *QUORUM*, London. Available online: https://quorumqmul.wordpress.com/2021/10/26/womxn-direct-shakespeare-in-the-21st-century-by-kim-solga/ (accessed 18 April 2023).

Somers, J. W. (2008), 'Interactive Theatre: Drama as Social Intervention', *Music and Arts in Action*, 1 (1): 61–86.

Stern, T. (2005), 'Teaching Shakespeare in Higher Education', in Martin Blocksidge (ed), *Shakespeare in Education*, 120–40, New York: Continuum.

Stiller, J., D. Nettle and R. Dunbar (2003), 'The Small World of Shakespeare's Plays', *Human Nature*, 14: 397–408.

Storr, W. (2019), *The Science of Storytelling*, London: William Collins.

Stornaiuolo, A. and E. E. Thomas (2018), 'Restorying as Political Action: Authoring Resistance through Youth Media Arts', *Learning, Media and Technology*, 43 (4): 345–58.

Stredder, J. (2004), *The North Face of Shakespeare: Activities for Teaching the Plays*, Stratford-upon-Avon: Wincot Press.

Stredder, J. (2009), *The North Face of Shakespeare: Activities for Teaching the Plays*, Cambridge: Cambridge University Press.

Taylor, G. (1989), *Reinventing Shakespeare. A Cultural History from the Restoration to the Present*, New York: Weidenfeld and Nicholson.

Thomas, S. (2017), 'Souks, Saris and Shakespeare: Engaging Young, Diverse Audiences at Shakespeare's Globe and the National Theatre', in D. Jarrett-Macauley (ed), *Shakespeare, Race and Performance: The Diverse Bard*, 163–74, Oxon: Routledge.

Thomas, E. E. and A. Stornaiuolo (2016), 'Restorying the Self: Bending Toward Textual Justice', *Harvard Educational Review*, 86 (3): 313–39.

Thompson, A. (2011), *Passing Strange: Shakespeare, Race, and Contemporary America*, Oxford: Oxford University Press.

Thompson, A. and L. Turchi (2016), *Teaching Shakespeare with Purpose: A Student Centred Approach*, London: Bloomsbury.

Thompson, A. and L. Turchi (2020a), 'Shakespeare Teachers' Conversation: Teaching Anti-Racism through Shakespeare', *The English Association*. Available online: https://www.youtube.com/watch?v=514eXyZ5kBo&feature=youtu.be (accessed 8 August 2020).

Thompson, A. and L. Turchi (2020b), 'Active Shakespeare: A Social Justice Framework', in D. Ruiter (ed), *The Arden Research Handbook of Shakespeare and Social Justice*, 47–59, London: Bloomsbury.

Thompson, J. (2022), *Care Aesthetics For Artful Care and Careful Art*, London: Routledge.

Thomson, P. (2002), 'The Comic Actor and Shakespeare', in S. Wells and S. Stanton (eds), *The Cambridge Companion to Shakespeare on Stage*, Cambridge: Cambridge University Press.

Thomson, P., R. Coles, M. Hallewell and J. Keane (2015), 'A Critical Review of the Creative Partnerships Archive: How Was Cultural Value Understood, Researched and Evidenced?', London: Creativity, Culture, Education.

Thomson, P. and C. Hall (2015), '"Everyone Can Imagine Their Own Gellert": The Democratic Artist and "Inclusion" in Primary and Nursery Classrooms', *Education 3-13*, 43 (4): 420–32.

Thomson, P., C. Hall, K. Jones and J. Sefton-Green (2012), 'The Signature Pedagogies Project: Final Report', London: Creativity, Culture and Education.

Thurman, C. (2016), *Shakespeare's South African Afterlives*, Johannesburg: Wits University Press.

Thomson, P., C. Hall, D. Thomas, K. Jones and A. Franks (2010), 'A Study of the Learning Performance Network an Education Programme of the Royal Shakespeare Company', London.

Times Educational Supplement (2019), 'Social Mobility with Lee Elliot Major', *TES Podcast: Podagogy*. Available online: https://player.captivate.fm/episode/a92e025c-ea8e-4755-b853-6c182e42b33b (accessed 19 July 2021).

Tippens, D. (1984), 'Crossing the Curriculum with Shakespeare', *Shakespeare Quarterly*, 35 (5): 653–6.

Torres, C. A. and M. Tarozzi (2020), 'Multiculturalism in the World System: Towards a Social Justice Model of Inter/Multicultural Education', *Globalisation, Societies and Education ISSN*, 18 (1): 7–18.

Trimble, M. (2007), *The Soul in the Brain*, Baltimore: John Hopkins University Press.

Trimble, M. (2012), *Why Humans like to Cry: Tragedy, Evolution and the Brain*, Oxford: Oxford University Press.

University of California, San Francisco (2019), 'How the Brain Detects the Rhythms of Speech', *ScienceDaily*. Available online: https://www.sciencedaily.com/releases/2019/11/191120144948.htm (accessed 2 December 2022).

Turner, V. (1987), *The Anthropology of Performance*, New York: PAJ Publications.

University of Liverpool (2006), 'Reading Shakespeare Has Dramatic Effect On Human Brain', *ScienceDaily*. Available online: https://www.sciencedaily.com/releases/2006/12/061218122613.htm (accessed 2 December 2022).

University of Warwick (2021), 'CAPITAL Centre – Archive'. Available online: https://warwick.ac.uk/fac/cross_fac/capital/about/ (accessed 1 November 2022).

Varaidzo (2019), 'Seriously . . . The 21st Century Curriculum', London: BBC Radio 4.

Varela, F. J., E. Thompson and E. Rosch (1991), *The Embodied Mind: Cognitive Science and Human Experience*, London: MIT Press.

Vygotsksy, L. ([1934] 2012), *Thought and Language*, Cambridge, MA: MIT Press.

Vygotsky, L. (1978), *Mind in Society: The Development of Higher Psychological Processes*, Cambridge, MA: Harvard University Press.

Walker, G. (2000), 'One Way Streets of Our Culture', *The International Schools Journal Compendium. Culture and The International School: Living, Learning and Communicating across Cultures*, 2: 82–9.

Walmsley, B., A. Gilmore, D. O. Brien, A. Torreggiani and A. Nightingale (2022), 'Culture in Crisis: Impacts of Covid-19 on the UK Cultural Sector and Where We Go from Here', Lee.

Westby, C. and L. Robinson (2014), 'A Developmental Perspective for Promoting Theory of Mind', *Topics in Language Disorders*, 34: 362–82.

Williams, M. (2022), *The Science of Hate: How Prejudice Becomes Hate and What We Can Do To Stop It*, London: Faber and Faber.

Williams, N. (2018), 'Writing the Collaborative Process: Measure (Still) for Measure, Shakespeare, and Rape Culture', *PARtake: The Journal of Performance as Research*, 2 (1): 1–20.

Willis, D. B. (1992), 'A Search for Transnational Culture: An Ethnography of Students in an International School in Japan Part II', *The International Schools Journal Compendium. Culture and The International School: Living, Learning and Communicating across Cultures*, 2: 31–44.

Wilson, E. O. (2017), *The Origins of Creativity*, London: Penguin.

Wilson, J. R. (2021), 'Aphorisms on Writing about Shakespeare'. Available online: https://wilson.fas.harvard.edu/aphorisms/shakespeare (accessed 19 June 2021).

Wilson, R. (1997), 'NATO's Pharmacy: Shakespeare by Prescription', in J. J. Joughin (ed), *Shakespeare and National Culture*, 58–82, Manchester: Manchester University Press.

Wimmer, H. and J. Perner (1983), 'Beliefs about Beliefs: Representation and Constraining Function of Wrong Beliefs in Young Children's Understanding of Deception', *Cognition*, 13: 103–28.

Winston, J. (2015), *Transforming the Teaching of Shakespeare with the Royal Shakespeare Company*, London: Bloomsbury.

Winston, J. and M. Tandy (2012), *Beginning Shakespeare*, 5–11, London: Routledge.

Winston, J. and S. Strand (2013), 'Tapestry and the Aesthetics of Theatre in Education as Dialogic Encounter and Civil Exchange', *Research in Drama Education: The Journal of Applied Theatre and Performance*, 18 (1): 62–78.

Wittgenstein, L. (1967), *Philosophical Investigations*, 3rd edn, trans. G. E. M. Anscombe, Oxford: Blackwell.

Wittgenstein, L. (1958), *The Blue and Brown Books: Preliminary Studies for the 'Philosophical Investigations'*, Oxford: Blackwell.

Yandell, J. and M. Brady (2016), 'English and the Politics of Knowledge', *English in Education*, 50 (1): 44–59.

Yandell, J., J. Coles and T. Bryer (2020), 'Shakespeare for All? Some Reflections on the Globe Theatre's Playing Shakespeare with Deutsche Bank', *Changing English*, 27 (2): 208–28.

Yosso, T. J. (2005), 'Whose Culture Has Capital? A Critical Race Theory Discussion of Community Cultural Wealth', *Race Ethnicity and Education*, 8 (1): 69–91.

Young, S. (2021), 'How Have Post-Colonial Approaches Enriched Shakespeare's Works', in A. Thompson (ed), *The Cambridge Companion to Shakespeare and Race*, 254–67, Cambridge: Cambridge University Press.

INDEX

active approaches   4–6, 115, 130, 138, 166
  challenges to   7, 135–6, 165–8
  definition   5–6, 15
Adey and Dillon   22
Adichie, Chimamanda Ngozi   54, 57
agency   114, 116, 124
Alexander, Robin   78, 83, 84
ambiguity, *see under* nuance
Ancient Greece   29–31
Anderson, Jan   130–1
Anti-Racist Shakespeare (Ambereen Dadabhoy and Nedda Mehdizadeh)   10, 21, 42–3
antithesis   66–9
Arden Performance Editions   64
Arnold, Matthew   8–9, 41, 50
Artificial Intelligence (AI)   1–2, 51, 73
arts careers   108–9, 122
Arts Council   89, 92, 96, 99
Asking Better Questions (Norah Morgan and Juliana Saxton)   84
authenticity   15–18, 30
author/ity   18, 20–1, 44, 81, 86, 117, 119

Banks, Fiona   16, 18, 30, 139
bardolatry   109, *see also* Shakespeare, on a pedestal
Bate, Jonathan   15, 50
Berry, Cicely   61, 65, 68, 76, 78, 79
Bixter, Evonne   95, 102, 105, 108, 110, 114, 120, 122, 125, *see also* Shakespeare North Playhouse
Black Lives Matter   101–2, 147
Blakemore, Sarah-Jayne   22, 24–5, 55, 75
Boal, Augusto   62, 173–4

Boix-Mansilla and Schleicher   35, 37
Bourdieu, Pierre   39, 42–4, 52, 56
Boyd, Michael   29, 57, 59, 67
Bradley, A. C.   61
Brandreth, Benet   82, 83
Brazil   89, 176
Brook, Peter   33, 36, 63, 86
Bruner, Jerome   8, 34, 52, 54–5, 61, 70, 75
Burrow, Colin   85

Caldwell-Cook, Henry   51
Channel Islands   130
character study   58–61, 83, 166, 174
Chelsea, Chloe   131–2
China   133
classroom as rehearsal room   15–17, 20, 35, 121
close reading   4, 6, 52, 80–2, 85, 162, *see also* literary/textual analysis
code-switching   148–52
cognition, *see also* neurodiversity
  associative thinking   27–8, 64–5, 68, 82
  cognitive load   60–1, 63, 64, 131, 176
  embodied   22–8, 61, 77
  findings not facts   22
  memory   77, 155, 165, 168, 169
  metacognition   34–5, 52, 75, 165, 167–8
  mirror neurons   26
  social brain   22, 24–6, 28, 54, 60, 72, 75, 79, 83
  systems 1 and 2 (Daniel Kahneman)   23–4, 57, 75
  theory of mind (ToM)   22, 24–6, 62, 68, 156

Coles, Jane   7, 61
colonialism   62–3, 110, 114, 171–2, *see also* decolonizing
community colleges   159
community of practice   31, 34, 48, 89, 92
Confederation of British Industries (CBI)   73
confidence building   107–8, 117, 145, 168
Coram Shakespeare Schools Foundation (CSSF)   5, 91, 123, 125, *see also* Ellis, Francesca
Covid-19, impact of   72, 110, 141, 168
creativity   5, 18, 35, 45, 74, 105, 139
Creativity and Performance in Teaching and Learning (CAPITAL) Centre   28–9
cultural capital   10, 39, 42–5, 50, 52–3, 115, 164
  misreadings of in education policy   43, 50
cultural democracy   38, 39, 44–8, 93
  implications for Shakespeare education   45–6
cultural heritage   3, 49, 74, 86, 97, 135, 136, 151, *see also* literary heritage
Cultural Learning Alliance (CLA)   38, 43
cultural literacy   8–9, 39–43, 45, 48, 50, 52, 73, 148
  implications for Shakespeare education   41–2
  popularity within twenty first-century education policy   39, 42
cultural value   7–10, 38–52, 54, 60, 74, 90, 105, 109
  debates of   38
  ecological models of   45, 47
Cultural Value in Twenty-first-century England: The Case of Shakespeare (Kate McLuskie and Kate Rumbold)   38, 60, 68
Cuthbertson, Lucy   91, 93, 96–8, 101, 105, 106, 108, 110, 115, *see also* Shakespeare's Globe

Damasio, Antonio   23
Davies, Gina   134
decolonizing   10, 57, 101, 109, 111, 115, 136, 170–4
democracy   31–2, 40, 84
Dewey, John   3–4, 8, 11, 16, 20, 33, 51, 175
digital approaches   6, 92, 168
Dolan, Frances   33, 49
Drama and Social Justice (Finneran, Michael and Kelly Freebody)   21, 30, 32
Drama in Education   5, 21, 30–3
  critical social turn of   31–2
Dunbar, Robin   26

eco-Shakespeare   109, 110, 131
Edgar, David   59, 63
Education Endowment Foundation (EEF)   74–5
education policy   7–8, 135–6, 164, 166
  'All our Futures' report   38
  Centres of Excellence in Teaching and Learning (CETLs)   28
  'closing the gap' discourses of   43
  Common core (USA)   159
  Creative Partnerships   38, 89
  Department for Education (UK)   39, 148
  Department of Basic Education (SA)   170–1
  as high stakes and limiting   7, 169
  knowledge-rich curriculum   164–9
  National Curriculum (England)   7–8, 51, 76
  under New Labour (UK)   5, 28
  Science, Technology, Engineering and Maths (STEM)   74
Ellis, Francesca   91, 96, 97, 100, 103, 108, 115, 117, 120, 123, 125, *see also* Coram Shakespeare Schools Foundation (CSSF)
embodied cognition   22–8, 77
  definition   23
employers   70, 73–4, 84, 164, 175
English as an additional language (EAL)   2, 89, 132–3, 143, 149, 171, 173
English Association   51

English literature
  as dealing in possibilities 52, 55, 62, 70
  diversity 53, 57
  establishment as a subject 50–1
  psychological realism 55, 62
  stories 54–8
  as thought experiments 58, 75
ensemble 20, 28–32, 34, 37, 75, 131, 145, 157, 172, 174
  as a bridging metaphor 30–2
Enterline, Lynn 85
Equal Education (SA) 171
Evaristo, Bernadine 53

failure 107
Falconer, Karl 92, 95, 101, 102, 105, 107, 112, 116, 117, 175, *see also* Purple Door Theatre Company
Faulkner, Rosalind 135
Fernie, Ewan 59
Finlay-Johnson, Harriet 51
Flaherty, Kate 48, 176
Folger Library 5, 19, 95, 100, 111, 116, 117, 144, *see also* O'Brien, Peggy
  The Folger Method 106
Freire, Paulo 23

Gallagher, Shaun 26
Gibson, Rex 3–4, 6, 18–19, 66, 76, 165

habitus (Bourdieu and Wacquant) 56, 59
Hattie, John 34–5, 37, 83
Heathcote, Dorothy 30–1
Hilský, Martin 132
hip-hop 101–2
Hirsch, E. D. 8, 39–42
hooks, bell 32, 35
Hornbrook, David 31–2
Hunter, Kelly 133

Identity 6, 20–1, 31, 53–5, 111, 118, 120, 121, 123, 170, 175
incrustation 42, 44, 46, 49, 109
India 136

Initial Teacher Training (ITT) 109, 164–9
  Core Content Framework (CCF) 164–6, 169
  Early Career Framework (ECF) 164, 169
intercultural democracy 46–9, 63, 75, 109, 136, 176
  multiculturalism 46–7, 143
Intermission Youth Theatre 94, 97, 113, 116, 118, 149, *see also* Raymond, Darren
International Baccalaureate (IB) 110, 132, 143–7
international Schools 131–2, 143–7

Jennings, Sue 133
Johnson, Mark 23, 27, 82
Jore, Marvelous 136, 172–4

Karim-Cooper, Farah 101–2
knife crime 98, 117

Lane, Sam 133
Language
  acquisition 24, 78–80, 84–5, 103, 124, 130, 144
  articulacy 64, 78, 82
  as communication 37, 69, 71–4, 77–8, 83, 84, 113, 114, 155, 176
  evolution of 71–2, 98
  neologizing 78–9, 155
  oracy 83–5, 124, 165
  poetry 27, 64–9, 76–8
  rhetoric 81–3, 163
  signing 71, 77, 134
  story-telling 54–8, 113, 122, 141
  translation 85, 132–3, 148–52, 173
Lees, Duncan 47
Leith, Sam 81, 83
literacy 72, 130, 154–5
literary/textual analysis 60–1, 64, 74, 76, 135, 144–5, *see also* close reading
literary heritage 4, 5, 49–52, 58, 77, 85, 101, 111, 116, 171, 175, *see also* cultural heritage

Lucas, Bill and Ellen Spencer 33, 34, 37
Lyne, Raphael 83

McDonald, Russ 64, 67, 78
McEvoy, Sean 161
McGilchrist, Ian 23, 26
Mamet, David 61
Manton, Emma 91, 93, 95, 101, 104, 119–21
Mar, Raymond and Keith Oatley 55, 60
Marxism 42
Maslow's hierarchy of needs 24
mental health 34, 72, 84
metaphors
    conceptual 26–8, 64
    embodied 27–8, 58, 62
    literary 80, 149
Metaphors we live by (George Lakoff and Mark Johnson) 27, 78
#MeToo 101, 110, 147
moral playground 56–8
Multicultural London English (MLE) 148–52
multidisciplinary 74–6, 105, 162
    cross-curricular 147
musicality 59, 65, 82, 132

National Curriculum, *see under* education policy
Nayak, Chris 101, 103, 105, 106, 109, 119, 125
Neelands, Jonothan 16, 29–31, 43–4, 140, 144, 147
negative capability (John Keats) 66
neurodiversity 25, 134, 138, 153–8
    ADHD 134, 154–5
    ASD 134, 154–5
    circumscribed interests (CI) 155–6
    NLD 154, 157
Neuro-Dramatic Play 133
neuroscience, *see under* cognition
Nicholson, Helen 21, 32, 74, 175
1984 (George Orwell) 77
nuance 56–7, 61–4, 66–9, 72, 84, 130, 133, 136
Nussbaum, Martha 31, 45, 70
Nwokah, Cassandra 101, 109, 111, 114, 117, 118, 120, 121

O'Brien, Peggy 4, 5, 16, 20, 81, 92, 94, 95, 97, 100, 101, 105, 106, 111, 116, 117, 123, 125, 175, *see also* Folger Library
Ofsted (UK) 39, 165, 168
    'English research review' 164
    inspection framework 164
O'Hanlon, Jacqui 16, 29, 74, 93–5, 99, 103, 105, 107, 110, 115, 120, 124, 140, *see also* Royal Shakespeare Company (RSC)
Olive, Sarah 7, 38
The Organisation for Economic Co-operation and Development (OECD) 1, 73, 105
    Programme for International Student Assessment (PISA) 35
    Teaching Excellence 33
original practices 97
outdoor learning 130, 131
ownership 34, 52, 64, 81, 94, 97, 113, 115, 118, 122, 149, 173–4

pairing texts 81, 100–1, 116, 161
pedagogy
    care-led 31–2, 143
    constructivist 17–19, 34, 44, 165–6, 168
    critical 21
    direct instruction 165, 168
    enquiry-led 36, 49, 52, 109, 112
    feminist 31–2
    forest school 138
    progressive 18–19, 44
    transmissive 23, 33, 168
Personal, Social and Health Education (PSHE) 108, 122
play 8, 54, 57, 63, 79–82, 108, 116, 113, 118, 122, 146, *see also* Neuro-Dramatic Play
    rhetoric as language play 81–3
plural reflexivity 20, 44, 124, 175
power dynamics 61, 63, 81, 170
presentism 59, 161–2
primary schools 2, 100, 121, 130–1, 138–42, 145

Programme for International Student Assessment (PISA), *see under* The Organisation for Economic Co-operation and Development (OECD)
pro-social 24, 29–30, 46, 55, 75, *see also* social justice
Purple Door Theatre Company 92, 96, 175, *see also* Falconer, Karl

race 9, 47, 59, 63, 101–2, 110–12
 whiteness 120
Rancière, Jacques 61, 68
Raymond, Darren 94, 96–8, 113, 116, 118, 123, *see also* Intermission Youth Theatre
Reading Shakespeare through Drama (Jane Coles and Maggie Pitfield) 9–10, 42–3, 46
relevance 8, 10, 94, 96, 102, 114, 117, 119–20, 125, 144, 161, 171–2, *see also* salience
 resonance 10, 16, 19, 48, 68, 109, 118
re-storying 57–8, 64, 122, 132, 145–6
risk-taking 34, 75, 135, 173
Robinson, Ken 5, 33, 38
Rocklin, Edward 17, 19–20
Rogers, Jami 149, 152
Rokison, Abigail 64
Royal Shakespeare Company (RSC) 5, 29, 95, 115, 124–5, 154
 Associate Schools 99, 130
 Histories Cycle (2005-8) 60, 68
 Learning Performance Network 45–6
 literacy research 74, 103, 124–5
 Toolkit for Teachers 140

Saha, Anjana 136–7
salience 10, 36, 63, 97, 109, 130, *see also* relevance
Schleicher, Andreas 35, 70
Semler, Liam 32, 89
Sen, Amartya 45

Shakespeare
 as beautiful 68, 77, 104, 114–15
 difficult, reputation as 34, 116–20, 139
 exceptionalism 3, 46, 49–50, 53, 69
 as global cultural heritage 3, 132, 136, 176
 iconic status 3, 8, 38, 49–52, 66
 life and times of 84–5, 104, 121
 as living art 2, 4, 10, 11, 20, 35, 37, 42, 52, 89, 102, 136, 175
 in nineteenth century education 50
 on a pedestal 104, 111, 113–16
 removed from curriculum 160, 170, 171
 talking back to 85–6, 116
 in translation (*see under* language)
 in twentieth century education 50–1
'Shakespeare for all ages and stages' (DCSF) 5
Shakespeare North Playhouse 91, 94, 122, 125, *see also* Bixter, Evonne
Shakespeare's Globe 5, 16, 19, 91, 139, *see also* Banks, Fiona; Cuthbertson, Lucy
 Playing Shakespeare with Deutsche Bank 99
 shared light of 103–4
Shakespeare's works
 As You Like It 32, 65, 137
 Hamlet 20, 62, 80–1, 122, 165, 171
 The Histories 57, 60, 68, 81
  Henry V 139
  Henry VI Pt 3 67, 139
  Richard II 139
  Richard III 67, 162
 Julius Caesar 28, 79, 82, 98
 King Lear 27, 67, 79, 97, 170
 Macbeth 55, 59, 62, 67, 80, 102, 103, 117, 134, 137, 140, 144–5, 150–2, 167–9, 171
 The Merchant of Venice 56, 81, 112, 137
 A Midsummer Night's Dream 27, 55, 62, 100, 145
 Much Ado About Nothing 67, 81
 Othello 67, 76–7, 162, 170, 171

Romeo and Juliet 27, 56, 62, 67, 101, 119
Sonnets 86, 132, 137, 149
The Taming of the Shrew 56, 153
The Tempest 62–3, 140, 156–7
ShakeXperience 170
Signing Shakespeare 134
skills for the twenty-first century 1–2, 11, 73, 81, 175
social justice 19, 21, 30, 35, 56, 74, 81, 105, 109–13
  raising questions through Shakespeare 2, 58, 61–4, 109, 121, 162, 172, 174
  theatre as a model of 30–2
social learning 24–5, 37, 55, 71, 74
social media 25, 72
South Africa 136, 170–4
space 15–17, 30, 104, 111
  outdoors 138–42
  third space 32, 144–7
Special Educational Needs and/or Disabilities (SEN/D) 100, 103, 133–4, 139, 141, 153–8, *see also* neurodiversity
stereotypes 25, 54, 57, 149
Storr, Will 54, 68
Stredder, James 64, 66, 76, 165
student as producer 48–9

Tagore, Rabindranath 137
Tales from Shakespeare (Charles and Mary Lamb) 54, 56–7
Taylor, Gary 84
teaching
  comparison with directing 35–6, 107
  competencies for theatre-based Shakespeare 37
  effectiveness 32–7, 105
  issues of time and space 106, 108, 141, 176
  as a skilled and practical art 33–4
Teaching Shakespeare Through Social Justice (Hillary Eklund and Wendy Hyman) 9, 21
terminology 66–8, 81–2, 166

theatre
  organizations (*see* Coram Shakespeare Schools Foundation (CSSF); Shakespeare's Globe; Royal Shakespeare Company (RSC); Purple Door Theatre Company; Intermission Youth Theatre; Shakespeare North Playhouse; ShakeXperience)
  as a social event in real time 59–60, 113
theatre-based practice
  definitions 6, 35
  false binaries with 'desk based' teaching 7, 15, 123
  measuring impact 124–6
Thompson, Ayanna and Laura Turchi 2, 8–9, 76, 81, 109, 111, 163
'Towards Cultural Democracy' (King's College London) 45–7
Turner, Victor 20, 175

ubuntu 172
ungrateful, children as 79
universality 54, 56, 109–10, 137, *see also* relevance; salience

variables, children as 22, 124–5
Vygotsky, Lev 17, 77, 79

Warwick Commission 38, 74
Williams, Mathew 25, 57
Wilson, Richard 17, 48
Winston, Joe 5, 7, 8, 29, 44, 75, 165
Wittgenstein, Ludwig 77, 149–50
writing 71–2, 83, 130, 135
  with purpose 80, 160
  transferable composition skills 159–63

Young, Hannah 136

zone of proximal development (ZPD) 63, 69